Great Moments in Baseball

OTHER WORKS BY THE SAME AUTHORS

BY TOM SEAVER

The Perfect Game: Tom Seaver and the Mets (with Dick Schaap) 1970
Baseball Is My Life (with Steve Jacobson) 1973
Pitching With Tom Seaver (with Steve Jacobson) 1973
How I Would Pitch to Babe Ruth (with Norman Lewis Smith) 1974
Tom Seaver: Portrait of a Pitcher (with Malka Druker) 1978
Tom Seaver's All-Time Baseball Greats (with Marty Appel) 1984
The Art of Pitching (with Lee Lowenfish) 1984
Tom Seaver's Baseball Card Book (with Alice Siegel and Margo McLoone-Basta) 1985
Tom Seaver's 1989 Scouting Notebook
Tom Seaver's 1990 Scouting Notebook
Beanball: Murder at the World Series (with Herb Resnicow) 1990

BY MARTY APPEL

Baseball's Best: The Hall of Fame Gallery (with Burt Goldblatt) 1977
Thurman Munson: An Autobiography (with Thurman Munson) 1978
Batting Secrets of the Major Leaguers 1981
Tom Seaver's All-Time Baseball Greats (with Tom Seaver) 1984
Hardball: The Education of a Baseball Commissioner (as editorial assistant to Bowie Kuhn) 1987
Yesterday's Heroes 1988
The First Book of Baseball 1988
My Nine Innings (as editorial assistant to Lee MacPhail) 1989
Working the Plate (with Eric Gregg) 1990

Great Moments in Baseball

by Tom Seaver
with Marty Appel

A Birch Lane Press Book
Published by Carol Publishing Group

A Birch Lane Press Book
Published by Carol Publishing Group
Birch Lane Press is a registered trademark of Carol Communications, Inc.
Editorial Offices: 600 Madison Avenue, New York, N.Y. 10022
Sales & Distribution Offices: 120 Enterprise Avenue, Secaucus, N.J. 07094
In Canada: Canadian Manda Group, P.O. Box 920, Station U,
    Toronto, Ontario M8Z 5P9

Queries regarding rights and permission should be addressed to Carol Publishing Group, 600 Madison Avenue, New York, N.Y. 10022

Carol Publishing Group books are available at special discounts for bulk purchases, for sales promotions, fund raising, or educational purposes. Special editions can be created to specifications. For details, contact: Special Sales Department, Carol Publishing Group, 120 Enterprise Avenue, Secaucus, N.J. 07094

Manufactured in the United States of America
10 9 8 7 6 5 4 3 2 1

Library of Congress Cataloging-in-Publication Data

Seaver, Tom, 1944–
    Great moments in baseball / by Tom Seaver with Marty Appel.
    p. cm.
    "A Birch Lane Press book."
    Includes bibliographical references (p.) and index.
    ISBN 1–55972–095–6
    1. Baseball—United States—History. I. Appel, Martin.
II. Title.
GV863.A1S43 1992
796.357'0973—dc20   91–30596
                                                         CIP

To every youngster out there playing on the sandlots who will one day become part of the history of this wonderful game.

T.S.

For Brian and Deborah

M.A.

Contents

POSTWAR MATURITY

EXPANSION YEARS

THE AGE OF FREE AGENCY

Contents

ix

ACKNOWLEDGMENTS

Special thanks go to Bill Adler, Matt Merola, Hillel Black, Bill Guilfoile, Pat Kelly, Phyllis Berk, Brian Appel, and Tom Cherwin.

NOTE: Statistics used in this book are based on Macmillan's *Baseball Encyclopedia*, eighth edition, except where otherwise indicated.

Introduction

I N REVIEWING the text of this book, which one tends to do before writing the introduction (at least that's the way Seaver does it; I can't speak for Dickens or Faulkner or Hugo), I kept coming across a phrase that probably escaped even the thoughtful pens of Chaucer, Voltaire, and Ned in the Third Reader (whom Casey Stengel was forever quoting): ". . . only six outs from victory."

It would have made a good title, had all of these stories followed the same line. But it was remarkable to see how *many* memorable moments in baseball changed in the closing minutes. Perhaps that has been, and will always remain, part of the great charm of the game. As a former player, now a fan, I found it fascinating how often this was the case.

Most players do not go into baseball as "fans." They have spent, perhaps, too many hours on the field to study the backs of baseball cards or thumb through the record books. While most players can tell you who Babe Ruth and Ty Cobb were, you draw some blank stares when you get to Rogers Hornsby, Pie Traynor, or Jimmie Foxx. Forget about it if you're talking about Hal Newhouser, Bucky Harris, or Gene Bearden. Sadly, there are probably some young players who don't recognize the name Jackie Robinson, much less understand his significance in the history of the game.

That's really unfortunate, because the experience of playing major league baseball, exciting as it is for the competition, the fan attention, and, yes, the dollars, is incomplete without the knowledge of where it

1

all came from. We owe a debt to those who played before us, but more than that, a player is cheating himself if he doesn't develop an appreciation for the accomplishments of his ancestors of the diamond. That is the foundation for Americans, who attach themselves to teams or players, then pass on the tales to their children and grandchildren. If baseball began just yesterday—with José Canseco, Darryl Strawberry, and Roger Clemens—it would be a great sport. The rules see to that. But to have the characters who crossed the fields over the preceding hundred years ingrained in our minds is to appreciate more fully that part of our culture the game has truly become.

I must confess, I tended to enjoy the older stories more than the more modern ones, the ones I'd lived through. The thought of Christy Mathewson and Cy Young and Walter Johnson standing on the mound, facing the same circumstances I encountered, having the infield play at double-play depth or in close, walking a man to get to a weaker hitter, fascinated me. Although the old black-and-white photos make it seem out of reach, the idea that we played the same game in essentially the same manner made it feel to me as if we were all one.

It's Thursday afternoon, October 1, 1903. We're in Boston. Teddy Roosevelt is President and Lou Gehrig is three months old. Cy Young looks in from the mound and faces the first Pittsburgh batter, Ginger Beaumont, a left-handed hitter. Beaumont swings and lifts a fly ball to center. Chick Stahl strides to his left, pounds his little glove, and snares it for the out. The first batter of the first modern World Series has been retired. Routine play. It could have happened yesterday.

I'm in my forties. To a younger reader, the great events of the 1960s may seem prehistoric. My memory becomes your history. My father's memories are all black-and-white still photos to me. But I love them all.

These fifty-one stories cover more than fifty-one moments. Some carry a full season with them, others reveal the evolution of a record. That's part of what makes baseball great too—how one story tends to lead to another, further tying the game together.

Fred Clarke's coming up. Tough hitter; batted .351 in 1903. Is that Young taking his windup? Or is it Feller or Koufax or Gooden? It's still a tough sixty feet, six inches between pitcher and batter, after all these years.

Classic Moments
From Days of Yore

E VERY FEW YEARS, it seems, I pick up a copy of the *New York Times* and discover, right there on page one, that the planet on which we live is not 2.5 billion years old, but actually 4 billion. And then, a few years later, it turns out to be 4.5 billion years old.

Not long ago, the same newspaper informed me of the discovery of a reference to a game of BASS-BALL, played by nine men "for the sum of one dollar each per game." The revelation came from Delhi, New York, in 1825, about twenty-five years before Alexander Cartwright's volunteer firemen rowed the Hudson to play ball in Hoboken, New Jersey.

Although historians used to spend quite some time pondering the true evolution of baseball, it seems likely that somewhere along the way, some caveperson decided that it was fun to hit a flying rock with a stick. He may have begun by tossing it in the air and swinging with a "fungo stick," but he might have also convinced another caveperson to toss a rock toward him. If we could track that moment down, it would be the basis of chapter 1.

In lieu of that moment, we have skipped over the British games of cricket, rounders, and town ball, beyond the development of the "New York Game" and the "Massachusetts Game," beyond the question of whether Abner Doubleday did or did not ever even play baseball in

3

Cooperstown, and beyond the rather certain moment at which Cartwright codified the first rules of the game.

Cartwright created rules by which you had nine innings, three outs, three strikes, ninety feet, and all of the things we hold dear today, including eighteen time-outs for commercial breaks. Don't kid yourself—those breaks have kept the professional game alive and healthy for nearly half its life as a pay-for-play sport. (Do you suppose Cartwright first came up with the idea of commercial breaks and then needed something to do between them?)

We have begun then, not with the unbeaten Red Stockings, not with the nineteenth-century giants like Spalding, Anson, and Kelly, not with the championship series of the 1880s and '90s, but with a point in time that seems to feel comfortable to us today. That would be the very beginning of this century, when the American League was formed, creating eight teams in each league, representing major cities, and employing a style of play to which we can relate.

If there was a major distinction to the pre–Babe Ruth era, it was, of course, the use of a dead ball. The baseball was simply not constructed to sail over a fence if hit with great force in an upward arc. While that may have been frustrating to men of strength, as athletes tend to be, they learned to adjust by developing a hitting style that accepted the fact that few balls would ever clear the fences. One can imagine how a José Canseco or a Cecil Fielder would react today to a ball that simply didn't have the life in it to travel 375 feet. I suppose they would go through a period of frustration and then adjust to the circumstances, if they wished to keep earning a major league salary. Wagner adjusted. Cobb adjusted. Lajoie adjusted. Those who didn't went into more "respectable" work. (Ballplayers and actors did not always qualify for the best hotels in those days.)

These chapters detail the accomplishments of men who played in a rough-and-tumble era. They played for the love of the game, without ever thinking for a moment what the game would evolve into by the end of the century. It was fun, and it was a living, but it was not a path to wealth. They knew little of conditioning and nutrition, but they had long careers under difficult living conditions. The pitchers hurled incredible amounts of innings, which is baffling when you think of how today we baby our arms, count pitches, and give little thought to complete games.

Those were the days when pro baseball took its hold on America. They were the growing years, when the establishment of trust was critical, for the game had been tainted by betting in the nineteenth century. And these men went out there and earned the respect of an America that was coming of age.

1

The First World Series

Not too many years ago, Joe Namath boldly predicted that his New York Jets would defeat the National Football League's Baltimore Colts in the third Super Bowl. They did, in what was hailed as one of the great sports upsets of all time. The victory by the upstart American Football League over the established National immediately gave the newer league fan acceptance, and it hastened the merger that led to today's NFL.

Sixty-seven years earlier, baseball had gone through the same growing pains. The National League had been around since 1876; the American League had been born in 1901. In 1903 the two leagues met in the first modern World Series. The American League's Boston team won, an event we would tend to consider startling had not the American League been raiding the National's big stars since its birth. What made the 1903 matchup significant was not so much the parity and acceptance that it brought the two leagues, but the creation of a true great annual championship of America's national pastime.

Oh, there had been championship series in the past. In the days of the fledgling American Association, the National League had taken the opposing league's champion to measure each fall in a forerunner of the world series, with the New York Metropolitans ("Mets") winning in 1888 and 1889, a fact I just thought I'd toss in. After the American Association failed, there was the "Temple Cup" series, named for the

6

donor of the trophy, one William C. Temple. This series, which ran from 1894 to 1897, was dominated by the fabulous Baltimore Orioles of John McGraw, Willie Keeler, Wilbert Robinson, and Hughie Jennings. It was a playoff between the first- and second-place teams in the lone National League, but that series died when the fans learned that the players planned to divide the money equally no matter who won.

Thus, there was no postseason playoff at all between 1898 and 1902, coinciding with the first two years of the new American League. That was not surprising, as the leagues were bitterly at war, fighting over players. Among those raided was Cy Young, who had won 285 games in the National League but was now a member of the Boston Americans, or "Pilgrims," as some called them. (They did not become the Red Sox until 1907.)

The event that made a World Series possible was a peace agreement between the two leagues in January 1903 that brought to a close the raiding of talent. Why it took two years to accomplish could be viewed historically as a mystery, since it was to the advantage of both leagues to stop the bidding war and keep salaries low. As part of the peace settlement, the American League agreed not to put a team in Pittsburgh, but did gain approval for a team in New York, the team that would become the Yankees.

This good news gave Pittsburgh owner Barney Dreyfuss a benevolent spirit toward his fellow man. His club was composed largely of former Louisville players who had been folded into Pittsburgh when the National League was reduced from twelve teams to eight in 1900. Pittsburgh promptly won the first three National League pennants of the twentieth century, led by the bowlegged, barrel-chested shortstop Honus Wagner.

Had John McGraw's Giants triumphed in 1903, there might not have been a World Series, for he was still personally at war with the new league. This was demonstrated a year later when he did win but refused to meet the AL champions, the only gap in continuous World Series competition in the century.

In August of 1903 Dreyfuss issued a challenge to Boston owner Henry Killilea, who, promising victory, secured approval from Ban Johnson, the American League founder and president. The two owners, their teams well in front in their respective pennant races, met in early September to map plans. It was determined that the World Series would be a best-of-nine format, the first team to win five claiming the championship. It was also decided that no player placed on the roster after August 31 would be eligible to compete, a rule still in effect today. The only way that rule could be improved upon, I believe, would be to have no additional players brought up at all in September, putting their mark on a pennant race that ought to be decided by those who have been there to do battle all season.

And so the first World Series was scheduled to begin on October 1 in Boston. The Americans became the favorites, because the Pittsburgh pitching staff was largely out of commission. Ed Doheny, who was 16–8, had to be placed in an asylum for the insane after developing severe paranoia and attacking a faith healer and his nurse with a poker. Sam Leever, 25–7, though not disabled, had injured his shoulder when he foolishly entered a trapshooting tournament. This basically left Deacon Phillippe as the team's pitching "staff." He was 25–9 in 33 starts during the season, and would now be called upon to start five of the Series games. Leever started the other two, and Brickyard Kennedy one.

It did not help Pittsburgh's cause that Honus Wagner was hobbling on an injured right leg. How sad to have a great player at less than peak ability at such a moment. Wagner would hit only .222 in the eight games, with a double and five singles, and he made six errors at shortstop. In the last four games, he went 1-for-14.

While all these negatives made Pittsburgh look like big losers in retrospect, the team started off smashingly well, getting to Cy Young for four runs in the very first inning, with Phillippe beating him 7–3. Young, thirty-six, was not sharp at all, but that could not have been attributed to age, as he still had 133 victories left in that magnificent, tireless right arm. This awesome athlete, after whom the award for top pitcher of the year is now named, must have been sensational to watch. Sadly, no film exists of his pitching style, which somehow helped him avoid a sore arm and natural aging and allowed him to pitch a multitude of innings.

To Pittsburgh's Jimmy Sebring went the honor of hitting the first World Series home run, a seventh-inning shot to center field.

Boston left fielder Patsy Dougherty hit an unheard-of two home runs in the second game to lead the "Pilgrims" to a 3–0 victory behind Bill Dinneen, evening the series, but in Game Three, Phillippe again beat Young, this time 4–2. Now, the action moved to Pittsburgh.

Two rain delays permitted Phillippe to go again in the fourth game,

Huntington Avenue Base Ball Grounds in Boston during the first modern World Series in 1903. The crowd appears to be virtually all male, well attired, and respectful of avoiding the well manicured infield. (National Baseball Library, Cooperstown, N.Y.)

and he won his third outing, by a score of 5–4. The three victories in one World Series would remain a standard that has been seldom matched to this day, and Phillippe accomplished his feat in only four games. The Series, however, still had a long way to go.

The crowds jammed the two small wooden ballparks—whose seating capacities were each about nine thousand—overflowing into the outfield and causing a number of ground-rule doubles and triples throughout the Series. We think of this as primitive baseball, but, in fact, today's World Series usually feature a few extra rows of box seats added along the foul lines to accommodate VIPs and additional fans. I remember that during the 1973 World Series at Shea Stadium, the temporary wall in front of one of those boxes collapsed and play had to be halted while it was rebuilt.

Cy Young was back on the mound in Game Five, the game in which thirty-five-year-old Brickyard Kennedy got his only start. After a scoreless duel for five innings, Boston scored six times in the sixth and four times in the seventh to pull within one game in the Series, which Pittsburgh now led 3–2.

Dinneen got Boston even in the sixth game with a 6–3 win, setting up a seventh-game battle between Young and Phillippe, their third meeting.

This was the pivotal game. Young had not pitched well; Phillippe had been the star of the Series. The winning team would take a 4–3 lead and need only one more win for the championship.

If there was a big hit in this game, it belonged to Boston's manager-third baseman, Jimmy Collins, who tripled in the first inning to set up a two-run rally. Boston never fell behind, winning 7–3. Collins, the premier third baseman in baseball at the turn of the century, was still considered the greatest third baseman in history half a century later, according to a poll taken by *The Sporting News*. His reputation was eventually exceeded in the 1950s by that of Pie Traynor; today, fans think the honor goes to either Brooks Robinson or Mike Schmidt. Collins is virtually forgotten, although his plaque hangs in baseball's Hall of Fame in Cooperstown.

For the eighth game, it was on the train and back to Boston, with the Pilgrims up four games to three. A rainout gave Phillippe an extra day of rest, allowing him not only to make his fifth start but also to pitch his fifth complete game. Unfortunately for the Deacon, he gave up two runs in the fourth and one in the sixth, and Bill Dinneen stopped

Pittsburgh on four hits to make Boston the World Champions, five games to three.

Records of the day reveal that the celebrating was mostly confined to the Huntington Avenue Grounds, with players and fans mixing together during the festivities. Pittsburgh players actually came out ahead financially when Dreyfuss threw his earnings into the player pool and Killilea kept his. The first World Series had been a success, especially for the American League, which not only held bragging rights but clearly was now just as much a "major league" as the National League was.

Freddy Parent, the Boston shortstop who led all players with eight runs scored in the series, lived to age ninety-four, and died shortly after the Oakland-Cincinnati World Series of 1972. The man saw his little World Series grow into quite an event.

As for Cy Young, one can only look back and ask "How could he do it?" How could Cy Young, winner of a record 511 games (and loser of the most games as well, 315), do it? He started an average of 37 games a year for twenty-two years, about 334 innings a year. Strictly from the standpoint of physical demands, the game has obviously changed considerably, and the kind of strain put on a pitching arm must clearly have been very different in those days. The greater variety of pitches thrown today certainly has taken its toll on the ability of pitchers to work the number of innings men like Young could work in the game's infancy.

2

Wild Pitch to Nowhere

Although the New York Yankees would wait eighteen years before their first pennant, they almost won it in 1904, their second season in the American League, when they played under the nickname the "Highlanders." The circumstances of their setback, and the events that made 1904 the only season without a World Series, focus on two men: Jack Chesbro, the winningest single-season pitcher in modern history, and John McGraw, whose win-at-all-costs image suffered a severe blow that year.

But it all starts with Ban Johnson, the founder and president of the American League, who practically spoon-fed the New York franchise with good players and a strong manager, Clark Griffith, in an effort to put a competitive team in New York. This would mean not only a strong group of players within the American League but also a team that could compete with the National League in the same city where a feisty Giant team was playing ball in the Polo Grounds, just a mile south on Broadway from the new Hilltop Park of the American League.

Loaded with good players like Wee Willie Keeler, Norm "The Tabasco Kid" Elberfeld, and Wid Conroy, the Highlanders were made even tougher in midyear when Patsy Dougherty, one of Boston's star outfielders, was traded to New York. This aroused suspicion that the pennant race was being "rigged," or at least tightened between these two new rivals. There could be no doubt that Ban Johnson would enjoy nothing more than pinning back the ears of McGraw. There was no love lost there.

McGraw had been a charter American Leaguer, tapped by Johnson to manage the Baltimore Orioles in 1901. As fate would have it, this franchise was shifted to New York in 1903, but by then, McGraw was gone. Unable to cope with Johnson's strict enforcement of rules and respect for rules and umpires, the fiery McGraw had found a home in the National League, as manager of the Giants. He was now an avowed enemy of Johnson and all that the American League stood for. He even worked side by side with the Giants' owner, John Brush, to fight the establishment of a New York American League team, using all political means to prevent sites for a ballpark from being approved, until at last they conceded a site north of the last subway stop.

As the 1904 season progressed and the Highlanders stayed in the race, it appeared that there might be an all-New York World Series. This possibility delighted the fans, including those who followed the game from Brooklyn, where yet a third New York franchise played.

The Giants were having an easy time of their race, employing such talent as Christy Mathewson, Joe McGinnity, and Roger Bresnahan. McGraw himself, only thirty-one, played five games in the infield. Mathewson and McGinnity won sixty-eight games between them, but the pitching story of the year was over at Hilltop Park, where Jack Chesbro was winning and winning for the Highlanders.

Surpassing Cy Young as the league's top winner, Chesbro was having the season of the century. The thirty-year-old spitballer, who had been 28–6 with Pittsburgh in 1902, jumped to New York in 1903 as the prize pitching acquisition of the new team. He led the High-landers with a 21–15 record in their first season, but now was proving almost indestructible. He made fifty-one starts in 1904, forty-eight of them complete games, covering 455 innings. In early October, he became the first of only two pitchers in this century to win forty games in a season. Unless the nature of baseball undergoes a major change, we are unlikely to see that level approached again. Few starting pitchers even see forty starts in a year anymore, as the nature of the schedule has almost forced teams to go with five-man rotations through most of the regular season.

Because of the bad blood between the leagues, Brush and McGraw felt disinclined to play a World Series. Brush struck the first blow on September 25, when he issued a statement saying that there was "no

Jack Chesbro, winner of 41, hurler of a wild pitch. (National Baseball Library, Cooperstown, N.Y.)

reason why the champion of the National" should play the American League champion. "There is nothing in the constitution or playing rules of the National League," he commented, "which requires its victorious club to submit its championship honors to a contest with a victorious club of a minor league."

The press immediately jumped all over Brush. But it wasn't long before McGraw joined in vocal support of his boss and refused a public challenge from Joseph Gordon, the Highlanders' president.

McGraw, a star infielder on the Orioles in the 1890s, still remembered winning the pennant, then losing the Temple Cup in two consecutive years. He also recalled that Boston had beaten Pittsburgh in 1903, diminishing National League stature. He had been virtually expelled from the American League for what he considered a superior style of play. Now the obnoxious presence of a New York team in this "minor league" might have a shot at whipping his mighty Giants. It was too much of a chance to take, even for a battler like McGraw.

The fans showed little sympathy for the Giants' position; ten thousand of them signed a petition calling for a World Series. After the Giants clinched the National League pennant early (they ended up thirteen games ahead of the second-place team), they played lackadaisically, to the boos of their supporters, hardly giving the fans their money's worth of baseball. Having already proclaimed there'd be no postseason play, they seemingly quit. Once they even left the field and forfeited a game after a dispute with an umpire.

The players weren't happy to lose out on postseason money, however meager it might appear today. They were placated somewhat by a Broadway benefit in honor of the Giants, from which each player received about $1,000. (When the 1969 Mets went on "The Ed Sullivan Show" to sing "You've Got to Have Heart," we each received a small stipend but we earned $18,000 a piece for winning.)

Meanwhile, a pennant for the Highlanders was shaping up as no sure thing. They were locked in a tight battle with the defending champion Boston Pilgrims, and a season-ending, five-game series between the two teams was scheduled to begin on Friday, October 7. At that point, Boston had a half-game lead.

Chesbro, having told Griffith that he could pitch every game if needed, worked the first game at Hilltop Park, stopping Boston 3–2, running his record to 41–11, and putting New York in first by a half game.

The next day was a playing date, but Hilltop Park had been given away to Columbia University for a football game against Williams College. So the teams scurried up to Boston for a doubleheader, where Boston won twice to move back into first, one and a half games up. With Sunday by law an off-day, the teams returned to New York for a Monday doubleheader. One Boston win would clinch it.

A crowd of 28,584 journeyed up to Hilltop Park for the pennant-deciding doubleheader. It would be Chesbro in Game One, looking for his forty-second win, against Bill Dinneen, 22–14, the World Series hero of the year before.

The game was scoreless in the third when Chesbro came to bat. Time was called; the fans wanted to present him with a fur coat in honor of his great season. He accepted the coat and slammed a triple to right. But there he was stranded when Willie Keeler, of all people, failed to "hit 'em where they ain't" and struck out.

In the fifth, the Highlanders scored the game's first run when ex-Pilgrim Dougherty singled home Red Kleinow, New York's catcher. A bases-loaded walk to Kid Elberfeld forced in a second run. In the top of the seventh, Boston tied the game 2–2, and there things stood as they went to the ninth.

Boston's Lou Criger got an infield hit, and Dinneen sacrificed him to second. Kip Selbach hit back to the mound for the second out, Criger moving to third. Up stepped shortstop Freddy Parent.

Chesbro, his forty-one wins under his belt, got two quick strikes on Parent, then threw a "waste pitch." It was a spitball, as were most of Chesbro's deliveries. But this one sailed high over the head of Kleinow and all the way back to the seats for a wild pitch. Criger scored, and Boston led 3–2. After this most brilliant of seasons, Chesbro had thrown a wild pitch that would cost New York a pennant!

The Highlanders put two men on in the last of the ninth, but Dougherty, who had been dispatched to New York to tighten the pennant race, struck out to end the game. Boston had defended its championship.

The wild pitch—the most talked-about moment in New York baseball until the Fred Merkle boner in 1908—put a sad, sad finish on Chesbro's season. He never forgot it, and never stopped second-guessing the pitch. Why did a waste pitch have to be a spitball? Was it smart to throw a waste pitch at all? No doubt Chesbro replayed the moment thousands of times before his death in 1931.

Boston attempted to talk the Giants into a World Series, but

McGraw wouldn't reconsider even with the Highlanders out of the way, with the Giants continuing to stand on "principle." So the Pilgrims rightfully announced that, having met no challenge to their 1903 World Championship, they would continue to be called World Champions until proven otherwise.

If nothing else, the embarrassment suffered by the National League through McGraw's actions undoubtedly reinforced the belief that a World Series should be played in 1905, no matter who won. When it turned out to be the Giants, and they played Philadelphia and won, a World Series was assured forever after. Thus, 1904, which provided one of the great finishes in American League history, put to rest at last the war between the two leagues and also made the World Series a goal every young baseball player dreams of reaching.

3

Over the Top With Wild Bill

This is the story of the day Wild Bill Donovan tossed a twenty-hitter to lead the Detroit Tigers to their first American League pennant. It was a game that Ty Cobb would call the greatest one he ever played in, yet it was only a tie game, and one that was never even replayed. But it defined one of the first great pennant races of this century.

This classic matchup between the Tigers and the Athletics took place on September 30, 1907, and marked the culmination of a tight American league pennant race that had been waged all summer among Detroit, Philadelphia, Chicago, and Cleveland. Philadelphia had won the pennant in 1905, Chicago in 1906, but Detroit and Cleveland had never won it. Fan interest was growing each year in American League baseball, and the 1907 season proved to be a dandy.

Wild Bill Donovan was a five-foot-eleven right-hander, born in Lawrence, Massachusetts, and raised in Philadelphia. His father was a Civil War veteran who had marched through Georgia with General Sherman. Wild Bill broke into the big leagues in 1898 with Washington, then of the National League. He played for Brooklyn from 1899 to 1902, leading the league with twenty-five wins in 1901, and then was awarded to the Tigers in 1903 as part of a peace settlement between the two leagues to halt the jumping of players back and forth. Outfielder Sam Crawford was awarded to the Tigers from Cincinnati at the same time.

Wild Bill Donovan (National Baseball Library, Cooperstown, N.Y.)

Bill loved the nightlife, although he was not a drinker, and he was one of the most popular players in the game, especially with other players. While his enjoyment of evenings on the town could have brought him his nickname, he did walk 152 batters in 1901, so we can assume the moniker may have come from his lack of control on the mound.

The Tigers arrived in Philadelphia on September 27, trailing Connie Mack's first-place Athletics by three percentage points and a half game. They had a three-game series scheduled—Friday, Saturday, and Monday. (Sunday ball was not yet allowed. It would be a long time before baseball owners overcame objections on religious grounds and were able to play on what proved to be the best day of the week to draw fans. Players often scheduled Sunday exhibitions against local clubs out of the big cities for a little extra cash, but at the start of the century, Sunday ball was permitted only in Chicago, St. Louis, and Cincinnati. Not until 1933 did all the other cities fall into line.)

In the crucial Friday game, Donovan pitched against Eddie Plank, one of Mack's outstanding starters, and beat him 5–4 to put Detroit into first place by a half game. The victory gave Donovan a sensational 25–4 record for the season, the top winning percentage in the league.

Saturday it rained on Columbia Park, necessitating a doubleheader on Monday. Columbia Park, on Columbia Avenue and Thirtieth Street, was home to the A's from 1901 to 1908. It was in the Brewery-town section of Philadelphia, and the wooden structure smelled of beer. There were no dugouts—the players sat on outdoor benches—and the place held about eighteen thousand fans.

With the whole weekend to get excited about the doubleheader, some twenty-five thousand fans clawed their way into the park on Monday, with an extra five thousand or so standing on rooftops and looking through windows of adjoining buildings. Fans were packed several rows deep in the outfield, where ropes and mounted policemen restrained them.

In addition to Plank, Mack had Rube Waddell, Chief Bender, Jack Coombs, and Jimmy Dygert to rotate as pitchers. He selected Dygert, 21–8 and a spitballer, to pitch the first game. Hughie Jennings, the peppery manager of the Tigers, went with Donovan again on two days' rest.

It did not appear to be a smart move. In the last of the first, the Athletics touched up Donovan for three runs and four hits. Under ordinary circumstances, Jennings might have removed Donovan, but Philadelphia was his hometown. His father and a lot of other relatives were in the stands, and Jennings, in a moment of sentimentality, stayed with his thirty-year-old veteran.

The Tigers got one in the second and chased Dygert, as Mack wasted no time bringing in Waddell, the eccentric left-hander, from the bullpen. Rube, the league's strikeout king, whose presence at any game was always in doubt until he arrived, struck out the last two hitters in the second to halt the rally.

The A's came back with two in the third and another two in the fifth for a 7–1 lead, but still Jennings stayed with his ace with first place on the line.

The Tigers thought of themselves as a spirited bunch of players, and they battled back. In the seventh, Sam Crawford hit a two-run double as the Tigers scored four times to cut the lead to 7–5. The A's scored in their seventh and the Tigers got one in their half of the eighth.

Heading into the top of the ninth, Philadelphia led 8–6. Crawford opened with a single and Cobb came to bat. Ty was the cleanup hítter in the lineup, just twenty years old and on the way to his first of twelve batting titles. So good was Cobb with the bat that his .350 that year would be seventeen points below his lifetime average. The Georgia Peach picked out a good offering from Waddell and socked one over the right-field fence for his fifth home run of the season. He clapped his hands as he circled the bases, the score tied 8–8, and Waddell departed in favor of Plank.

In the eleventh, it looked as though Cobb would be the hero of the day when he poked one among the fans in the outfield for a double to put the Tigers on top. But Donovan yielded a run in the last of the eleventh and on they went, tied 9–9.

In the fourteenth there was a big dispute with the umpires over fan interference when a policeman stepped in front of Crawford in center field as he chased a drive by Harry Davis. The ump ruled that Davis was out.

The seventeenth inning ended with the score still tied at 9–9. Darkness was falling, and there being no lights the umpires called the game. The tie kept the Tigers in first place by a half game, and with the second game also canceled, the teams went on to finish their schedules elsewhere.

Donovan had pitched all seventeen innings. He had allowed twenty hits but only three walks. He struck out eleven as the A's left thirteen men on base. The Tigers left seventeen in getting fifteen hits and four walks.

The Tigers went to Washington and took four straight. The A's went to Cleveland, where Dygert hurled three shutouts to keep Philadelphia in contention. On October 4, rookie Walter Johnson beat Plank 2–1, and the next day the Tigers stopped the St. Louis Browns 10–2 to clinch it, without having to make up the tie game and the unplayed one. The Tigers' winning margin ended up one and a half games. Although the Cubs took them in four straight in the World Series, it had been an outstanding season for baseball in Detroit.

If 1907 was the year that launched Cobb onto greatness, it was also Donovan's finest hour, but it is amazing how little is remembered of him. The gutsy pitcher, whose career record was 186–139, remained a Tiger starter into the 1912 season.

After his playing days, Donovan went to the International League, where he managed Providence and won the 1914 pennant. In 1915, ownership of the New York Yankees passed to Colonel Jacob Ruppert and Captain Til Huston, who, after consulting with local sportswriters, hired Donovan as their manager.

Bill managed the Yankees for three years in the Polo Grounds as the team was moving toward respectability. He was fired after the 1917 campaign and replaced by Miller Huggins, who would become the beneficiary of Babe Ruth's arrival and the birth of the Yankee dynasty.

After managing his hometown Phillies in 1921, Wild Bill became manager of New Haven in the Eastern League, a team run by George Weiss, later the general manager of the Yankees and the Mets. On December 9, 1923, Weiss and Donovan were taking a train to the winter meetings in Chicago when it crashed, killing Donovan. He was only forty-seven.

Those wonderful early pennant races, symbolized by crowds lining the outfield behind mounted police and ropes, and by the courageous efforts of guys like Wild Bill Donovan, were the stuff of romance and made baseball great in the first part of this century. Ball parks may not have had the amenities they do today, nor players the benefits of Nautilus machines and arthroscopic surgery for what ailed them, but something about games like those 9–9 ties called by darkness took hold of the public heart and mind and transformed baseball from a pleasant diversion into our national pastime.

4

Forever the Bonehead

When you visualize turn-of-the-century baseball, the diamond has the same geometry as the game we play today. The baggy uniforms, small gloves, rickety wooden bleachers, and other little touches made it seem primitive, but the game's the same, more or less.

And, oh, can baseball choose to be cruel when it wants to be! Ask Bill Buckner, who can tell you a little about fate. He made an error in the 1986 World Series, and an otherwise outstanding career was forever destined for blooper replays.

I don't know if Buckner ever heard of Fred Merkle, but if not, Bill, this chapter is for you. It's the sad tale of a nineteen-year-old first baseman who would go on to a fine career. But he made a forgivable error—they called it a "bonehead play" back in 1908—and for the rest of his life, he carried its weight on his back.

Merkle was a popular, generous, likable person. His teammates always admired him. But as late as the 1960s, when author Lawrence Ritter interviewed teammate Al Bridwell for the classic book *The Glory of Their Times*, Bridwell would say, "Oh, the Bonehead, he was a helluva guy." Imagine that! More than half a century later.

World history has given us Catherine the Great and William the Conqueror and Richard the Lion-Hearted, but baseball gave us Fred the Bonehead.

It happened in 1908 during the great pennant race between the New

Fred Merkle (The Sporting News)

York Giants and the Chicago Cubs. The Giants, managed by John McGraw, featured Christy Mathewson, a thirty-seven-game winner, and an eighteen-year-old hurler named Rube Marquard, the only teen-ager on the squad besides Merkle. The Cubs had a stronger team on paper, with Mordecai "Three Finger" Brown, 29–9, heading the pitching staff, and the famous infield of Tinker to Evers to Chance, who would be immortalized in poetry two years later. Chance, the first baseman, was also the manager.

On September 23, the Giants were in first place, six percentage points ahead of the Cubs, and the two were to meet at the Polo Grounds in New York. The Giants were the favored team in New York in those days, and the talk up and down Broadway was the day's pitching matchup between the great Matty and the Cubs' Jack Pfiester. Pfiester was only a 12–10 pitcher that season, but since his nickname was "Jack the Giant Killer," he seemed the right man to take on the battle for first place. About eighteen thousand fans showed up, a big crowd for that era.

In the Giants' lineup that afternoon was Fred Merkle, playing first base, batting seventh. Why was this nineteen-year-old kid playing such a big game? Because Fred Tenney, the regular first baseman, was suffering from a lumbago attack, and was bandaged from the waist down. It was the only game he would miss all season.

Merkle's entire experience in the major leagues consisted of twenty-two hits in eighty-four at-bats over two seasons. As a kid out of Toledo, he was content to sit by McGraw's side and learn about major league baseball from the master. Now, he was about to play in the biggest game of the season.

It was every bit the pitching duel it was supposed to be. Joe Tinker hit a rare inside-the-park home run in the fifth off Mathewson, his club-leading sixth homer of the year. (The Cubs had nineteen for the season, the Giants twenty.) In the last of the sixth, Mike Donlin singled over Johnny Evers's head at second to bring home the tying run.

The pace of the game quickened. (It took only ninety minutes to play the entire contest.) One can imagine the intensity of New York's rooters as the late innings arrived, but the Giants couldn't knock out the Cubs' Pfiester. Pfiester didn't strike out anyone, but walked only two. Mathewson had nine strikeouts, no walks. The Cubs turned three double plays, none of them Tinker to Evers to Chance.

Then came the historic and chaotic bottom of the ninth. Pay close attention.

With one out, the Giants' Art Devlin singled to center. He was forced at second by Moose McCormick. Two out.

Now Merkle was up. He came through with a clutch hit, a clean single to right that sent McCormick to third with the potential winning run. Merkle must have felt like smiling as he chalked up his eleventh hit of the year, but no doubt showed the proper polite restraint.

The next hitter was shortstop Al Bridwell, the number 8 hitter in the lineup, a .285 singles hitter that season. Bridwell swung at Pfiester's first pitch, a waist-high fastball, and lined it past Evers into right-center for a base hit. McCormick came storming home from third with the Giants' winning run, and the fans poured onto the field to celebrate.

Merkle, who had headed for second at the crack of the bat, saw what transpired and turned toward the Giants' center-field clubhouse before he reached second. He would have had three thoughts at that moment: (1) We've won the game; (2) Let me get the hell out of here before the fans trample me; and (3) I don't have to touch second because it's just not done when the game ends like this.

Merkle would have been right on all three counts. Umpires had never called anyone out for running off the field after the winning run scored.

Ironically, nineteen days earlier, when the Cubs had played the Pirates in Pittsburgh, the same umpire, Hank O'Day, was on the field, and the same situation had occurred. Second baseman Johnny Evers had gotten the ball and stepped on second, insisting that the runner was out. O'Day said no, it's never been that way. But Evers talked him into agreeing that the next time it happened, it would be ruled an out. The play was discussed in the newspapers; Merkle probably—but not certainly—was aware of it. Today, players always talk about odd play in other games. One would guess that similar conversations took place then.

At the Polo Grounds, Evers frantically screamed for center fielder Art "Solly" Hofman to throw him the ball. The throw, however, never reached Evers. It was lost in the mob of Giant fans on the field. Joe McGinnity, coaching third for the Giants, retrieved it and fired into the stands. Somehow Evers got hold of another ball, stepped on second, and appealed for a ruling.

Base umpire Bob Emslie looked around hopelessly. O'Day, his

partner, knew déjà vu when he saw it. "Out!" he yelled, amidst the fans and the scattering players.

He had ruled that the run did not count, that the inning was over, and that, given the fans on the field and the impending darkness, the game was a 1–1 tie. If the teams wound up tied for first, they'd make up the game at the end of the season.

Umpire O'Day filed a quick report with National League president Harry Pulliam. McGraw, hearing of the report, contacted Merkle and made him return to the Polo Grounds that very night and step on second so that he could swear he did in fact touch second base on September 23. Merkle, who must have been both frightened and confused, did as he was told.

There never was a hearing or any testimony from Merkle, however. Pulliam accepted O'Day's ruling, and an appeal to the league's board of directors got nowhere. Neither team was happy with the tie. The Giants felt they had a win; the Cubs wanted a win by forfeit. (Pulliam, it may be noted, was a suicide victim ten months later.)

Sure enough, the season ended in a tie, and the teams met again in the Polo Grounds on October 8. Again it was Mathewson against Pfiester, but this time the Cubs won it, 4–2, and took the 1908 National League pennant away from a screaming John McGraw.

Was Merkle's baserunning really such a "bonehead" play? There is no doubt he should have touched second. But baseball is very much a game of precedent, and although the rule had been changed weeks before, Merkle's training had told him to take off for the clubhouse. As far as anyone could determine, McGraw never scolded his young infielder.

In fact, Merkle became a favorite of McGraw's. By 1910 he had become the team's regular first baseman, and he held that job through 1916, playing in three World Series. He then went to Brooklyn for two years and, of all places, to the Cubs, where he spent three years and played in his fifth World Series in 1918. In all, he spent parts of sixteen seasons in the big leagues, compiling a .273 career average. He finally retired from baseball in 1927 and moved to Florida, distancing himself from the game and coming to terms with his legacy.

He wasn't the first and he won't be the last player to be remembered for a single moment in his career. Even worse is the stigma attached to a player early in his career because he "can't play" or "can't hit left-handers" or "can't go to his right." When the tag is applied in the minor leagues, it can stick to a professional player like glue. If it is repeated often enough, it becomes the "truth" and virtually impossible to shake. Many players acquire a tag unjustly. They end up having lengthy careers but are always the reserve infielder or outfielder, seldom playing regularly and often filling the role of pinch hitter.

If there was a hero of the day, it was the quick-thinking Johnny Evers, whose greatest fame in baseball would come as part of the game's first famous double-play combination. Joe Tinker, the shortstop, Evers at second, and Frank Chance at first—Tinker to Evers to Chance—were immortalized in a poem in 1910 in the *New York Evening Mail* by Franklin P. Adams, who wrote:

> These are the saddest of possible words—
>   Tinker to Evers to Chance
> Trio of Bear Cubs and fleeter than birds—
>   Tinker to Evers to Chance
> Thoughtlessly pricking our gonfalon bubble,
> Making a Giant hit into a double,
> Words that are weighty with nothing but trouble—
>   Tinker to Evers to Chance

Pretty much on the basis of that poem, the three were elected to the Hall of Fame as a unit in 1946. Without the legend associated with that classic baseball poem, it is questionable whether all three would have made it. Their double-play prowess was, if truth be told, somewhat enhanced by the poem. Statisticians have failed to prove that they were measurably better than many other double-play combinations over the years.

As for Merkle, he did not accept a Giant invitation to an Old Timers Game until 1950, at which time he was cheered warmly by the fans and made to feel at peace with his place in history.

He died in 1956. But a decade later, Bridwell was still calling him the Bonehead.

It can be a cruel game.

5

Winner Gets a Horseless Carriage!

When you're a kid and learning all the great names in baseball history, the one you look at without pronouncing is Napoleon Lajoie. The difficult French name would properly be pronounced "La-jwah," but fans called him "Laj-away." Fans even had their way with his first name, which became Nap or Larry. In any case, it hardly rolled off the tongue like Babe Ruth or Ty Cobb.

But Lajoie was right in there during baseball's first decades, and when the greats gathered in Cooperstown in 1939 for the dedication of the Hall of Fame, Nap was among them, the sixth player elected. His role in the formation of the American League, his place in Cleveland Indian history, and his batting average of .422 in 1901 are an integral part of the game's past.

And then there was the 1910 batting race, one of the most closely watched, hotly contested races of all time, and certainly one of the game's uglier episodes.

Lajoie was the son of French Canadians, born in 1875 in Woonsocket, Rhode Island. He was playing semipro ball at twenty when he turned pro to play in the New England League. It took him just three months—during which he batted .429—to find himself in the National League, with the Philadelphia Phillies. There he resided for five seasons, averaging .349, until the American League was formed in 1901.

Lajoie became the biggest star to jump to the new league, signing a four-year, $24,000 contract with the crosstown Philadelphia Athletics of Connie Mack. He immediately became the biggest star of the new league, adding instant credibility to its operation. The Phillies sought an injunction against his playing, and while the court battle ran on, Lajoie batted .422 in the American League's first season, a mark never since bettered in the junior circuit. To accomplish this high average while the courts were weighing his very right to play for the A's was a remarkable achievement.

In 1902, the injunction was granted, but it limited his right to play only in Philadelphia. Thus, Connie Mack was forced to abandon his great star, and sent him to Cleveland.

So popular was Lajoie as Cleveland's great second baseman that by the time he was named player-manager in 1905, the team was known simply as the Cleveland Naps. And by 1909, when he had tired of managing and asked the club owners to let him resume playing full-time, the fans still continued to call the team the Naps.

He won batting titles in 1903 and 1904, en route to a .339 career mark. He was a beloved figure in professional baseball, and if fans had trouble pronouncing his name, it hardly mattered: Every kid wanted to be "Larry Laj-away" when he grew up.

Lajoie was thirty when the Detroit Tigers purchased the young Georgian outfielder who would replace him as the league's top hitter. Ty Cobb was only nineteen, the son of a politician and schoolmaster and a fierce competitor. He did not make friends easily—not on opposing teams, not on his own team. His contemporaries respected his talent as one of the greatest natural athletes to come along, but most wondered why he always seemed at war with the world, in view of the fact that his success derived from a recreational occupation. No one withheld accolades for "the Georgia Peach," but few showered him with adoration, then or now.

Cobb won the 1907 batting title in his second full season, hitting .350. Lajoie was then in his third year as Cleveland manager, and barely cleared .300. The changing of the guard was taking place. Cobb won again in 1908 and 1909, but in the latter season, Lajoie shed his managing responsibilities and found his average rejuvenated from .289 to .324.

In 1910, the Chalmers Automobile Company decided to offer a new car to each of the two major league batting champions. It was a huge

Nap Lajoie and Ty Cobb pose in a new Chalmers auto after they were each awarded one in 1910. (The Sporting News)

promotion for Chalmers. In those days, very few people owned cars or thought they would ever be able to afford one. The enormity of the prize can hardly be appreciated today. In fact, with the 1910 pennant races runaways for both the Cubs and the Athletics, fan attention was riveted to the "Great Automobile Races."

It should be noted at this point that early baseball included primitive record keeping. Newspapers were filled with misprints, communication was anything but instant, and days could pass before people knew how the races were going. One team's averages might be "through August 30," another's "through September 3." One newspaper might say .377, another .375. It was a time not only before computers, but even before baseball statistics had come to be appreciated. In 1910, nobody particularly cared whether a misprint or a lost base hit might bother people at an Elias Sports Bureau in 1992.

As the September days passed, no one was sure of the leader in the American League race, but one thing was certain—everyone wanted Lajoie, at thirty-five, to beat Cobb, the twenty-three-year-old three-time defending champion. Lajoie, the grand old master, hadn't won a title in six years and was thought to be in decline. That alone would have made for a great story. But his popularity, contrasted with Cobb's surly reputation, made the race for the car a clear "good guy vs. bad guy" chase.

The season was to end on October 9. On October 2, one set of published figures showed Lajoie leading .374 to .368, another .370 to .366. A few days later, Cobb saw a newspaper report that showed *him* leading by eight points. Convinced that the lead could not be overtaken, and complaining of an eye infection, Cobb sat out the final two games of the season.

Cleveland was to conclude its season in St. Louis in a doubleheader with the Browns. Lajoie was in his customary cleanup slot in the batting order, right behind a rookie center fielder named Shoeless Joe Jackson, who had just been called up from the minors. The St. Louis manager was Jack O'Connor, whose club was in last place with more than a hundred losses.

On his first at-bat of the afternoon, Lajoie hit a triple over the center fielder's head: 1-for-1.

His second time up, he found the Browns' third baseman, Red Corriden, playing unusually deep at third base. Lajoie bunted and easily beat it out for a base hit: 2-for-2.

His third time up, Corriden was still playing deep. Another bunt, another single: 3-for-3. Something was amiss.

The doubleheader ran on. Six more times Lajoie came to bat, always with Corriden playing deep. Five of the six times he bunted down third. Sometimes no throw was made. He was credited with four more singles and a sacrifice. In his sixth time up, he grounded to Bobby Wallace, the thirty-six-year-old shortstop and future Hall of Famer, who threw wildly to first. On another day it might have been scored an error. On this day, the official scorer called it a hit, deciding that even a good throw would not have nailed him.

When it was all over, Lajoie had gone 8-for-8. The *New York Times* reported that he had won the batting title, .3868 to .3834.

Ugly stories followed about the events of the day. One report said that the official scorer had been handed a note offering him a new suit of clothes for a "good day" of scoring.

Never had Lajoie been involved in "scandal," even in baseball's rough-and-tumble days. He was adamant that there was no scar on his performance, claiming he deserved *nine* hits and should not have been given a sacrifice on one of the bunts.

Cobb took the high road. Not having seen the games, he simply said that he was sorry "that either Lajoie or I did not win the prize without anything occurring that could cause unfavorable comment."

Chalmers rose above the fray and gave a new car to both Cobb and Lajoie, plus one to Sherry Magee, the National League batting champ. No doubt the Chalmers promotion budget for 1910 was well in the red.

American League president Ban Johnson called in O'Connor, third baseman Corriden, and a Brown coach, Harry Howell, for an investigation. Both O'Connor and Howell were fired by the Browns, and Corriden was sent to the minors. (He managed the White Sox forty years later, in 1950.) They all maintained that Lajoie was such a hard hitter, and had belted that triple so deep to center, their strategy had to be to play back.

Three days before Thanksgiving, the league office finally issued the "official averages" for 1910. Cobb was given credit for .385, Lajoie for .384. It was Cobb's fourth batting title in a row in what would become a streak of nine straight and twelve overall, both major league records.

Lajoie continued to have big seasons, hitting .365 and .368 in 1911 and 1912. In 1915 he returned to Philadelphia to play his final two seasons with the A's before retiring at age forty-one. He died in 1959, two years before Cobb.

The controversy did not end there, however. In 1981, researchers at *The Sporting News* found a discrepancy in the handwritten daily stat sheets from 1910. They showed what appeared to be a duplicate entry of a 2-for-3 performance by Cobb in September. Subtraction of the duplicate line would lower Cobb's mark to .383 and make Lajoie the champ, seventy-one years later.

Commissioner Bowie Kuhn and American League president Lee MacPhail said no. They felt it would be unfair to rewrite history without completely rechecking all stats from that period, an impossible task. They also felt that the "official" averages, approved by Ban Johnson with all evidence fresh before him, should be considered more worthy than hindsight history. Official baseball records thus continue to show Cobb the champion, with his streak of nine straight titles intact.

The controversy over the 1910 batting race only highlights the continuing debate regarding official scorers. Should they be paid out of a fund supplied by Major League Baseball, on a rotation basis, the same way umpires are rotated, thus eliminating the hometown call?

Could the pool of scorers come from retired players and retired writers, such as Red Foley, who spent many years with the *Daily News* in New York and is a totally competent official scorer?

Objection would probably come from the Baseball Writers Association of America, whose active members earn added income as scorers during the baseball season and who provide free "advertising" with their daily coverage of games. That confrontation is one Major League Baseball would like to avoid.

About the only thing we are sure of regarding the 1910 batting race is that we have heard the last from the Chalmers Automobile Company, which got a lot of promotional value from the season, but failed to survive in its own race to provide a popular car for the masses.

6

Classic Early Pitching Duels

One thing that I miss about baseball today is the classic pitching duels there used to be when I was growing up. You would get Koufax against Marichal on occasion, and Ford against Gibson or Ford against Koufax in the World Series, and there was a particularly memorable Spahn-vs.-Marichal game in 1963, but you don't see much of this dying art form anymore.

There are several reasons. One is that teams today tend to use five starters, not four, and the chances of getting the right two guys against each other have decreased. Another is that attendance figures are now so high that pitching duels are no longer needed to build the gate. Owners do not "ask" managers to hold back the ace so they can hype the big matchup.

Another reason is that managers don't want to "waste" their ace. They would rather play the percentages and go for the victory than use the ace with only a fifty-fifty chance of winning.

And, of course, in World Series competition, you do not necessarily have your ace rested for Game One after the League Championship Series. So even Koufax-Ford or Gibson-Ford is an endangered species.

There were great matchups not long before I was born, like Dizzy Dean against Carl Hubbell, but the early part of this century was probably the "golden age" for such contests.

Perhaps the longest-running, most-followed rivalry was between Christy Mathewson of the Giants and Mordecai "Three Finger" Brown of the Cubs. After Matty beat Brown with a no-hitter in 1905, Brown took nine straight from Mathewson, a remarkable achievement considering that Christy was probably the game's best pitcher at the time. One of the nine was the deciding game of the 1908 season, necessitated by the "Merkle Boner" (see chapter 4). They were 12–12 against each other lifetime by 1916, when they faced each other in what was to be the final season for both. Mathewson won their last confrontation for a 13–12 edge.

In that crazy 1908 season, one other American League duel stands out in addition to the Mathewson-Brown pairing on the last day of the season. The contest took place in Cleveland, where Addie Joss faced Chicago's Ed Walsh on October 2 with four days left in the season. Walsh, a spitballer, had forty wins that year, which remains one short of Chesbro's major league record. Three days earlier, he had pitched and won two complete games in a doubleheader, allowing only one run.

Joss, one of the best-liked players in the game, had a 1.16 earned run average in 1908 and was on his way to a 24–12 season, his fourth straight twenty-win campaign. Joss's lifetime ERA is 1.88, which gives you some idea of how good he was.

Cleveland, Chicago, and Detroit were locked in a pennant race as the days ran down, putting tremendous pressure on both hurlers. And they both came through beautifully. Walsh fired a four-hitter, allowed only one run, and struck out fifteen. Joss, however, treated the hometown crowd to a perfect game.

It would be nice to say that Cleveland went on to win the pennant, but the Tigers emerged as champions. Still, it was an epic event. Two years later, Joss no-hit the White Sox again.

Joss, it should be noted, was one of the game's early tragic figures. In spring training of 1911, he was stricken with tubercular meningitis and died at age thirty-one. Because he appeared only in parts of nine seasons, and the Hall of Fame requires ten, he had to wait until 1978 for the Veterans Committee to bend the rules to accommodate him.

By 1912 the two most talked-about pitchers in the American League were Walter Johnson of Washington and "Smokey Joe" Wood of Boston.

Johnson had joined the Senators in 1907. In this, his sixth year, he

Smokey Joe Wood greets Walter Johnson before the big matchup in Boston. (Boston Red Sox)

rolled off a record-setting sixteen-game winning streak in mid-season, en route to a 32–12 year with a 1.39 ERA and 303 strikeouts. He was only twenty-four, but it was said that no one threw the ball any harder than "The Big Train."

Wood, however, may have been a better pitcher that year. He was only twenty-two but already a five-year veteran, and he was the toast of Boston, where baseball is a religion.

The Senators were to meet the Red Sox in Boston on Friday, September 12, at Fenway Park, which had opened only twenty weeks earlier. This was to be the biggest matchup in Boston since John L. Sullivan defended his heavyweight championships.

Johnson's sixteen-game winning streak had ended on August 25, but Wood had a thirteen-game streak alive. His had begun just five days after Johnson's, on July 8. So on through the summer both men kept winning, and now the theory was that Johnson would have a chance to stop Wood himself and protect his record.

Without a second thought, Boston manager Jake Stahl moved Wood up a day in the rotation to accommodate the match. The newspapers loved it, running comparison charts that made the two aces look like heavyweight boxers, with biceps size, arm span, and all.

Talk about sellouts! On this particular day in Fenway Park, they kept selling tickets and worried later about where to put the fans. A half hour before the game, ushers had to clear a path in front of the first-base dugout so that Wood could take his warmups, but the fans surrounded him and his catcher. By game time the fans were roped off in the outfield, and occupied so much foul territory that there was essentially none left. The two teams had to vacate their dugouts, and benches were set up along the first- and third-base lines for the players.

Both teams were scoreless through five innings, which is just what the fans expected. But in the sixth, Tris Speaker, Wood's roommate, doubled down the third-base line. Duffy Lewis hit a fly to short right that fell near the foul line for another double, scoring Speaker. And that was all the scoring in the game. The Red Sox won, 1–0, for Wood's fourteenth consecutive victory. By the following week, he had run his streak to sixteen, tying Johnson for the American League record.

It is a record that still stands, although it has been equaled by Lefty Grove (1931) and Schoolboy Rowe (1934). For an event that has happened only four times, it is remarkable to think that two of those times were virtually concurrent. Wood's streak ended on September 15 on an infield error.

Smokey Joe Wood wound up his season with a 34–5 record, ten shutouts, a 1.91 ERA, and 258 strikeouts. He completed thirty-five of his thirty-eight starts. But he wasn't through yet, as he won three games in the 1912 World Series against the Giants to cap one of the greatest seasons a pitcher has ever had. His final win was in the eighth and deciding game of the Series, when he pitched three innings of relief to redeem himself and the Sox after being bombed in Game Seven. The next day, he shared the lead automobile with Mayor "Honey Fritz" Fitzgerald, President Kennedy's grandfather, in the victory parade through Boston.

The rest of this story should be about the many future matchups between Johnson and Wood. We know how well Johnson did, winning 416 games and striking out over 3,500 batters while throwing 110 shutouts. Wood, however, did not fare so well. In spring training of 1913, while he was on top of the world, he broke the thumb on his pitching hand while fielding a ground ball. He may have tried to come back too soon, and when he resumed pitching, he hurt his shoulder. He was never able to throw hard again.

Joe was just a spot starter after that, and although he was able to post a 15–5 record with a 1.49 ERA in 1915, it would be his last year on the mound, save for an occasional appearance. He retired from baseball in 1916, but the following year, his buddy Speaker, now playing for Cleveland, persuaded manager Lee Fohl to take a chance on Wood as an outfielder. Joe was still only twenty-seven, and a superb athlete.

Joe spent five years as a Cleveland outfielder, and while he was no star, he made quite a comeback and became a lifetime .283 hitter. In 1923, he left the major leagues to become baseball coach at Yale University, where he spent twenty years. He died in 1985 at the age of ninety-five.

Many felt Joe was qualified for Hall of Fame consideration, but he really only had the one sensational year. Still, to have reached the pinnacle at twenty-two must have been some compensation for him.

In recent years, you occasionally see the kind of pitching duel that harks back to olden times. On July 2, 1963, the Giants' Juan Marichal, twenty-five, and the Braves' Warren Spahn, forty-two, went at each other for sixteen innings before the Giants took home a 1–0 victory. (See chapter 36.)

Of more recent vintage, one recalls the pitching matchups between Oakland's Dave Stewart and Boston's Roger Clemens. The most memorable one, so far, was their meeting in the 1990 League Championship Series in Boston, when Clemens, in ol' Fenway Park, was ejected by the home-plate umpire for using profanity and Oakland won the pennant. This historic moment occurred seventy-eight years after Wood and Johnson jammed them in, but Fenway obviously had some magic moments left.

There was another matchup, on Sunday, April 30, 1989, I would have loved to see. Two power pitchers, one a veteran and the other in the prime of his career, took each other on. Nolan Ryan, in his first month back in the American League after nine years with Houston, faced Clemens before 40,429 in Arlington Stadium.

Boston took a 1–0 lead in the first inning, and there it stood. Two masters at work, putting up zeros. Finally, in the last of the eighth, Rafael Palmeiro hit a two-run homer, and Ryan had a 2–1 victory, with a save from Jeff Russell.

The all-time leader in strikeouts against the best pitcher in the game today: a matchup that would have been classic in any era and, despite the decreasing frequency of such pairings today, certainly "one for the ages."

7

Last to First in Ten Weeks

Long before there were the 1967 "Impossible Dream" Red Sox or the 1969 "Miracle Mets," there were the "Miracle Braves" of 1914, a team that not only reversed its fortunes of previous years but also handled a mid-course correction during the season to spin a turnaround of twenty-five and a half games and win a pennant in just ten weeks.

If it is possible to have a great team without "great" players, then that was clearly demonstrated by the Boston Braves of 1914, who had few stars and few players who are remembered today. What they did have was a fighting spirit passed on from an inspiring manager, George Stallings, plus three starting pitchers who caught fire in the second half and a shortstop-second base combo with the determination to win.

The Boston Braves, ancestors of the Milwaukee and Atlanta Braves, had little to brag about during the National League's early years: The last time they had finished at .500 was the 1903 season. So awful had they become that in 1909 they were 65½ games out of first; in 1910, 50½; in 1911, 54; and in 1912, 52. They lost over a hundred games in each of those seasons, finishing dead last each year. Between 1904 and 1912, covering nine years, they lost exactly nine hundred games.

Doing what all teams have done before and since, they fired their manager after the 1912 season and hired Stallings, whose last stop had been with the New York Highlanders in 1909–10. Stallings was an interesting character in that he was an urbane, educated man who had attended medical school but who could shout profanity and resort to rowdy behavior with the best of 'em.

Stallings had been recruited into baseball by no less a figure than Harry Wright, one of the Wright brothers (not the ones of flying fame), a founder of professional baseball with the Cincinnati Red Stockings in 1869. Wright was managing the Philadelphia Phillies in 1886 when Stallings caught his attention. Wright encouraged him to pursue a playing career.

Wright was not much of a scout on this call, for Stallings's big-league career consisted of twenty at-bats and two hits. But he did become a highly regarded minor-league manager, and now the Boston Braves job was his.

Stallings spent much of 1913 weeding out the 1912 players and found a measure of success, lifting them up to fifth place with a 69–82 record. It was more respectable than Braves fans had been accustomed to, but with the Red Sox the reigning world champions, few paid much attention to the other Boston team. The season attendance was listed as 208,000 for the tiny South End Grounds, up 87,000 from the year before but less than half what the Red Sox drew to Fenway Park.

The general housecleaning continued prior to the 1914 season and, in fact, throughout it as well. The big addition was second baseman Johnny Evers of the legendary Tinker-to-Evers-to-Chance infield of the Cubs. Evers, who had made his reputation for heady play in the Merkle Boner game of 1908, had managed the Cubs to a third-place finish in 1913. His greatest sin, it was said, was in losing the exhibition Chicago City Series to the White Sox.

It can be difficult for a player-manager to change teams and become just a player again, but Evers had an immediate respect for Stallings, never questioned his authority, and fit right in. For his part, Stallings recognized Evers as a team leader and allowed him to be a captain (without the title) on the field, chewing out teammates for dumb plays and generally firing up the troops. Evers, all 130 pounds of him, brought the lineups to the plate (Stallings never wore a uniform and didn't even pose for the team photo) and set a high standard for play on the field.

His shortstop partner was little Rabbit Maranville. The 155-pound Rabbit was a Springfield, Massachusetts, product who had come up at the end of the 1912 season and played as a regular in 1913. Maranville

The Miracle Boston Braves of 1914. Johnny Evers is in the front row, on the right; Rabbit Maranville is fourth from the right. Manager Stallings didn't do team photos. (National Baseball Library, Cooperstown, N.Y.)

was not a great hitter—.259 lifetime with twenty-eight homers in twenty-three seasons—but this future Hall of Famer could play the field, score the big run, and spark an infield.

A third player who proved his worth in 1914 was catcher Hank Gowdy, in his first season as a regular. Gowdy was an outstanding handler of pitchers, a soft-spoken gentleman in a rough-and-tumble environment who would later earn the respect of all baseball by becoming the first player to enlist for World War I.

In 1914 Evers hit .279, Maranville .246, and Gowdy .243. These are not normally numbers you expect from key players on pennant-winning clubs, but these three had qualities of leadership that set them apart. Stallings was doing that little extra something that was making it work.

Opening Day took place on April 14; the Braves' first win came on April 21. They didn't win two straight until May 21–22. By that time they were 4–18 and in last place, and the few fans who showed up probably figured the fifth-place finish in 1913 had been a fluke.

A little surge in June brought the team to 20–29, but by July 4—the date by which people predict pennant winners based on who's leading at the time—the Braves were dead last, 26–40, and fifteen games behind the class of the league, the New York Giants.

Three days later they lost an exhibition game to Buffalo of the International League, 10–2. This humiliation so angered Evers, he turned it into a positive experience by goading his teammates into overcoming their embarrassment. And they started to play better base-ball. On July 19 they rallied with a three-run ninth to move ahead of Pittsburgh, ten and a half games out of first. The next day they passed Brooklyn and found themselves in sixth place.

The following one Dick Rudolph shut out the Pirates and Boston jumped two notches, past Cincinnati and Philadelphia, into fourth place. They were still ten and a half out, but hey, this was the first division!

On August 1 they reached .500 for the first time since 1903. Even today, .500 is a major psychological hurdle. When a team is playing badly it needs short-term incentives. Getting to .500 is always a key step. At that point, you hope to catch fire and take off; at this juncture, the Braves were already on their way.

Rudolph, Bill James, and Lefty Tyler had emerged as strong starters. Each would work regularly in rotation for the rest of the year, giving way only on occasion to a fourth man. Oldest of the three at twenty-six, Rudolph would go 27–10 for the season, James 26–7, and Tyler 16–14. Totaled, that was sixty-nine victories; the rest of the staff won twenty-five. Further, the three pitched 939 innings, the rest of the staff 482. A bullpen? Rudolph, James, and Tyler started 107 games and completed 82 of them.

These stats make me wonder many times what it was like in the old days. At the turn of the century the game of baseball was played so differently, with spectators on the field and pitchers completing 80 percent of their games.

That was still the norm when the Braves faced the Giants for two series in their first-ever pennant race. On August 13 they began a tremendously important three-game series in New York at the Polo Grounds, trailing by six and a half games, but in second place at 51–46.

Facing Rube Marquard, Jeff Tesreau, and Christy Mathewson, the Braves swept the series. The final game was a 0–0 pitching duel between Tyler and Matty, decided in the tenth on a triple by Gowdy, and then by Tyler stopping the Giants with the bases loaded.

A wearying twenty-two-game road trip with little time off in August brought sixteen Brave victories and found the team in a dead heat for first at 67–52. With the Giants now coming to Boston, the Red Sox graciously permitted the games to be played in Fenway Park, which seated three times as many people as the South End Grounds.

A Labor Day doubleheader, featuring separate admissions for the two games, brought out 74,162 fans. Boston was now Braves-crazy!

In the ninth inning of the opener, the Braves were losing 4–3 to Mathewson when Johnny Evers delivered a two-run single to win the game. The fans went wild and many hid in bathrooms and closets so they could sneak into the second game, which New York went on to win, keeping the tension high. The next day, James won 8–3 to send the Giants on their way—in second place. The miracle now seemed within reach.

In the few remaining weeks, Rudolph, James, and Tyler kept the Braves on top. Two other pitchers contributed with surprise efforts. George Davis, making one of only six starts for the Braves, pitched a no-hitter against the Phillies on September 9. And then finally, twenty days later, the Braves clinched their first National League pennant as

Tom Hughes, who had pitched for Stallings with the Highlanders in 1909–10 (including a 1910 no-hitter, the first in "Yankee" history), made his first start and won his only decision of 1914.

It was over! The Braves had finished ten and a half games ahead of New York. Of their final eighty-seven games, they had won sixty-eight, for the most extraordinary midyear turnaround in baseball history.

And with momentum and destiny on their side, they went out and beat Connie Mack's Philadelphia A's in four straight in the World Series (also played in Fenway Park).

By 1917 they had fallen out of contention gain, even with Stallings at the helm, and were back to their losing ways. The Boston Braves never did build a proud history on that first stepping-stone. By the time they left for Milwaukee in 1953, they had won only one other pennant, in 1948, and could usually be found near the bottom of the standings.

But for ten thrilling weeks in 1914, they were, and will always be, the "Miracle Braves," providing hope to all July Fourth cellar dwellers to this day.

They also make me wonder how turn-of-the-century baseball would stack up today. Would you compare the level of play then to our Triple A, Double A, or sandlot? There are those who believe the comparison should be made the other way around—sometimes, rightfully so. But the Braves had a formula in 1914 that still works today: strong starting pitching, a solid catcher, sparkplug-type leaders at second and short, and a good manager. Whatever the relative comparisons, the ingredients have not changed.

Seventy-seven years after the Miracle of 1914, the Braves, now settled in Atlanta, reached back into their history for another miracle. After finishing dead last in 1990, they righted themselves to win the National League pennant in 1991, marking the first "last to first" maneuver over two seasons in league history. It came in the same year in which the Minnesota Twins pulled off the same stunt for the first time in American League history.

8

The Ultimate Relief Stint

Our image of Babe Ruth is one of a fun-loving, devil-may-care man-child, always with a smile or a "Hiya kid" and, of course, great with children. How many times have we seen that wonderful personality, larger than life, flashing that big grin?

But the Babe had a troubled youth. The first sentence of his autobiography reads, "I was a bad kid." Although he was not an orphan, he was raised in an orphanage, which doubled as a reform school for children whose parents couldn't cope with them. He had little contact with his father, except for visits to the old man's saloon. It was not an environment guaranteed to be trouble-free.

And so when we find a blemish on the Babe's character, it is almost refreshing to realize that he was, in fact, human. He was a product of his times and his past, and it would be wrong to assume that he was always smiling, always carefree. There was the time, for example, that he slugged an umpire.

The year was 1917. He was in his fourth season with the Red Sox, the ace of their pitching staff. His ability as a home-run hitter was still unknown, but in 1916 he had compiled a 23–12 record with a 1.75 ERA, and in the World Series had hurled a fourteen-inning victory over the Dodgers in Game Two at Fenway Park. He was one of the best pitchers in the American League and a darling of the Boston fans.

Had his career not taken him to the outfield and on to New York, it is likely he would still have been an all-time great.

Ruth began his professional career at nineteen with the Baltimore Orioles of the International League. A teammate and fellow pitcher was twenty-three-year-old Ernie Shore, a six-foot-four right-hander from North Carolina who had pitched a game for the Giants in 1912, then found himself with the Babe in Baltimore. Together they were sold in 1914 to the Red Sox, where they became roommates. Shore once told a story of complaining to management about Ruth borrowing his shaving brush without ever cleaning it afterward, but called Ruth "the best-hearted fellow who ever lived."

Shore was college-educated and later became a sheriff in North Carolina. He seemed an unlikely companion for Ruth, but they liked each other, and their careers were closely linked. Shore went to the Yankees in 1919, a year before Ruth, and was again the Babe's roommate in his first Yankee season.

He was a good pitcher, too, probably better than Ruth at the time they were both purchased from Baltimore. He was 10–4 with a 1.89 ERA in his rookie season, and then 18–8, 1.64 in 1915, a pennant-winning year. Ruth was also 18–8, but in the 1915 Series Shore started twice, including the first game, while Ruth made only a single pinch-hitting appearance. In 1916, Shore was 15–10 and 2–0 in the Series.

The 1917 season is remembered for a number of no-hitters: seven in all, one of the highest single-season totals ever. (In 1990 and 1991, big-league hurlers reached back to pre-lively-ball days with a slew of them.) The first came on April 14, the third day of the regular season. Eddie Cicotte, who would later become one of the Chicago "Black Sox," no-hit the Browns 11–0 in St. Louis. It was a good omen for the Sox; they would win the pennant that season.

Ten days later a Yankee pitcher named George Mogridge no-hit the Red Sox 2–1 in Boston before 3,219 rain-soaked fans. Watching the feat from the dugout were Babe Ruth and Ernie Shore.

On Wednesday, May 2, a remarkable feat took place at Weeghman Park in Chicago, known today as Wrigley Field. Fred Toney of the Reds and Jim "Hippo" Vaughn of the Cubs hooked up for a double no-hitter. The drama, played out before a sparse crowd of about three thousand, finally ended in the tenth inning when the Reds pushed across a run on two hits, the winning blow coming from Jim Thorpe, the legendary Olympic hero, who chopped one in front of the plate.

Ernie Shore (National Baseball Library, Cooperstown, N.Y.)

Vaughn fielded it himself and threw home, but the throw hit base runner Larry Kopf in the back, and the Reds had a 1–0 lead. Toney then pitched his tenth no-hit inning and won the game. (To this day, there has never been another double no-hitter.)

Three days later, May 5, Cicotte was on the mound again in St. Louis, his first appearance there since his no-hitter the previous month. This time however, it was the Browns' pitcher, Ernie Koob, who achieved greatness by hurling a no-hitter, with an assist from the official scorer. It happened this way:

The game's second batter, Buck Weaver, hit a smash to second baseman Ernie Johnson. Johnson knocked it down, but when he tried to throw to first, the ball slipped over his shoulder and landed at his feet. The official scorer called it a hit. But as the game went on and it appeared to be the only blemish in a no-hitter, the scorer, one J. B. Sheriden, consulted with the umpires and players and reversed himself. It is safe to assume he felt some intimidation from the hometown partisans, and the next day, a movement was begun to prevent the changing of scorers' decisions.

To this day decisions are sometimes changed, but by and large, scorers stand by their calls, even when they feel the heat of the fans as a no-hitter is unfolding. That big sigh of relief you hear when a no-hitter is broken by a solid hit, after a questionable earlier call, usually emanates from the press box.

Amazingly, the season's next no-hitter came the very next day, May 6, in the very same park, Sportsman's, in St. Louis. This time it was the second game of a doubleheader, and the pitcher was Bob Groom. There were some twenty thousand fans present to see him set down the White Sox 3–0. The overflow crowd resulted in some fans having to sit deep on the outfield running track and grass, but no balls were hit there and the no-hitter was free of controversial calls.

Groom actually pitched eleven no-hit innings that day, because he also hurled the final two of the first game in relief of Eddie Plank, without allowing a hit.

Then on Saturday, June 23, in Fenway Park, Babe Ruth took the mound for the Red Sox against the Washington Senators. The Sox were just one and a half games out of first, and this was the first game of a doubleheader. About half of the sixteen thousand fans present that day were in their seats as the first game began. Clarence "Brick" Owen, a florist in the offseason, was the home-plate umpire.

Leading off for the Senators was second baseman Ray Morgan, who walked. The called fourth ball—and probably a couple of others— caused Ruth to challenge Owen's abilities.

Newspaper accounts had Ruth telling Owen to keep his eyes open. Said Owen, "You get back there and pitch or I'll run you out of the ballpark."

Ruth answered, "If you run me out of the ballpark I'll take a punch at you on my way."

"You're out now!" shouted Owen, gesturing with his arm for all to see.

At that point Ruth went wild, charging the umpire. His catcher, Pinch Thomas, jumped between the two, but Ruth got off a punch, grazing Owen. Contact had been made.

Manager Jack Barry, also the second baseman, brought in Ernie Shore from the bullpen. It was one of only two relief appearances Shore would make that season. He took his warmups, and working from a stretch, checked Morgan at first and pitched to Eddie Foster. Morgan suddenly took off for second, but new Boston catcher Sam Agnew cut him down for the first out of the game. Foster was retired and then so was Clyde Milan, to end the inning.

And so Shore continued. And each inning, the Senators went down one-two-three. The Red Sox had a 4–0 lead as Shore faced his twenty-sixth batter, pinch hitter Mike Menosky, with two out in the ninth. Menosky popped to Barry, and the game was over.

Was it a perfect game? Shore had faced twenty-six batters, not twenty-seven. There had been a walk. Shore pitched in relief. Was it even a complete game?

Yes, on all accounts, at least until record book revisionists said no in 1991. The game was entered, footnotes and all, on the list of perfect games in record books. It was only the fifth in baseball history, the first in nine years, the third of the century, and one of only fifteen ever recorded.

Ruth was treated fairly lightly by AL president Ban Johnson, whose reputation for backing up his umpires was legendary. Ruth was fined $100 and suspended for ten days. When he came back on July 11, he pitched a one-hitter.

Shore went off to World War I duty the following year and won only seven games after his return. He lived until 1980, forever linked with Ruth, and forever the man who pitched a perfect game while retiring only twenty-six batters.

9

Work or Fight

By all accounts, 1918 was hardly a baseball season at all. Even the World Series would be marked briefly by a sit-down strike by the players, an event that seemed in keeping with the surrounding chaos. But somehow, the season and the Series were completed, and the continuity of the game was left intact.

They didn't call it World War I in 1918 because it was thought to be "the war to end all wars," and hence, no Roman number was needed. Instead, it was "The Great War," or just "The World War." Baseball felt little of its effect in 1917, despite falling attendance, but in 1918 the players themselves were called to military service. Although President Woodrow Wilson recommended that sports continue as usual, the provost marshal issued a "work or fight" order on May 23, 1918, requiring all men of draft age either to enter military service or to obtain war-related jobs. War Secretary Newton Baker gave baseball a "grace period" that would allow the season to run through Labor Day, but it did not prevent the players themselves from taking up arms and heading for Europe, or at least into war-related jobs.

Among the 227 players who found themselves wearing military uniforms were the great pitchers Grover Cleveland Alexander and Christy Mathewson. Mathewson became one of the game's great war tragedies. Hit with poison gas during a training exercise, Captain Mathewson would develop tuberculosis and eventually die from it in

1925 at the age of forty-seven. Matty's Giant teammate, Eddie Grant, was killed in action.

Other early call-ups were Boston Red Sox player-manager Jack Barry and Duffy Lewis, the team's left fielder. This created two problems for the Red Sox—who would manage, and who would play left. For the former, the Red Sox selected Ed Barrow, the authoritarian figure and minor-league executive who had managed the Tigers in 1903 and 1904. It was Barrow's job to solve the left-field problem, and he looked no farther than his pitching staff and a twenty-three-year-old left-hander named Babe Ruth, who had led Boston to the 1916 world championship with a 23–12 record. He was 24–13 in 1917 but showed such adeptness during his brief times at bat that, circumstances being what they were, the time seemed right to try him in the lineup every day that he wasn't pitching.

And so Barrow made the move, and the rest, as they say, is history. Ruth played in fifty-nine games in the outfield in 1918 and thirteen more at first base. He hit eleven home runs off dead-ball pitching to tie Tilly Walker of Philadelphia for the home-run title. He also belted twenty-six doubles and eleven triples, showing a power that seemed to belie the type of baseball then being played.

On the mound, Babe made nineteen starts and had a 13–7 record, and although he was no longer the number one pitcher on the staff (future Yankee teammates Joe Bush, Carl Mays, and Sam Jones all had more victories), he had clearly become a dual-purpose player. And as the years passed and people debated "who was the greatest player ever," Ruth would usually win the nod over the likes of Cobb or Wagner because he had shown his abilities on the mound as well as at the plate.

The Red Sox lost fourteen players to war duties as the season moved on, but Barrow kept the team atop the American League. When Labor Day arrived, the Sox had clinched the pennant in the 126-game season, finishing two and a half games ahead of Cleveland. Ruth was able to avoid service when he received a deferment as a married man, but he did join the Massachusetts Home Guard, a unit assembled to replace National Guardsmen who had been called to active duty.

In the National League, the Cubs had obtained Alexander from the Phillies prior to the season, only to lose him to the war after three starts. But they lost only eight players in total and had excellent pitching from Hippo Vaughn, Claude Hendrix, and Lefty Tyler, the old "Miracle Braves" star, who collectively won sixty-one games despite the shortened season. The team hit only twenty-one homers, but it did have Fred Merkle at first base, an irony considering how he had helped the Cubs win in 1908 while wearing a Giant uniform. Merkle, still only twenty-nine, hit a solid .295 for Chicago under Fred Mitchell, and the Cubs managed to lead the league in runs scored.

The shortened season didn't hurt Ty Cobb's streak of batting titles, as he won his eleventh with a .382 mark. Cobb had been deferred from military service by being a married man with three children. The White Sox, defending world champions of 1917, fell to sixth place after losing Joe Jackson to a shipbuilding job in Wilmington, Delaware. Jackson had been Ruth's "hero" and role model as a batter.

As it came to a close, the season was hardly on the minds of the general public. The war was costing the nation thousands of lives and baseball seemed insignificant. American League president Ban Johnson had even ordered play to stop after the May "work or fight" edict, but his powers had diminished, and the owners basically overruled him. It was seen as a blessing by many when Labor Day arrived and the industry could shut down.

To avoid paying the players their September salaries, the owners "released" them all with the proper ten days' notice; their gentleman's agreement also included not signing anyone else's players. Two players who sued, Jake Daubert of Brooklyn and Burt Shotton of Washington, were traded away.

Secretary of War Baker did permit the World Series to take place, although he stipulated that the first three games be played in Chicago and the next four in Boston to cut down on travel.

When Ruth took the mound in Game One before a small crowd of 19,274, he brought with him a streak of thirteen and a third consecutive World Series shutout innings, having hurled a 2–1, fourteen-inning victory over Brooklyn in Game Two of the 1916 series. Now, working with a new curveball, he stopped the Cubs 1–0 to run the streak to twenty-two and a third with a route-going performance. The winning run was produced on a walk and two singles in the fourth inning. It wasn't a thriller, but the Babe had a victory.

The Cubs won the second game 3–1 behind Tyler, with Ruth on the bench against the left-hander. In Game Three, with the crowd having grown to 27,054, Carl Mays put the Red Sox up 2–1 with a 2–1 victory.

The fourth game, on September 9 in Fenway Park, found a major insurrection afoot. Seeing small crowds and calculating their potential shares at under $1,000 a man, the players rebelled. They felt abused because regular-season ticket prices were in effect, and because the second-, third-, and fourth-place teams would be included in the money for the first time. Talking among themselves on the train ride from Chicago, they decided to strike in Boston. Thus, the gates opened and the fans filed in, but there were no players on the field.

For a full hour the fans sat, unaware of the politics below the stands. Mayor "Honey Fitz" Fitzgerald pleaded with the boys to take the field. Ban Johnson, part of the three-man National Commission that preceded the arrival of a baseball commissioner in 1920, reportedly was drunk and unable to conduct a serious dialogue with the players. Finally, persuaded to "do it for the fans," and assured there would be no penalties for their actions, the players took the field.

Ruth was back on the mound, but batting seventh in the lineup. (He had hit in the pitcher's traditional ninth spot in the opener.) On hand were 22,183 to see him continue his masterful pitching, as the Cubs went down for seven innings. Ruth's streak had reached twenty-nine and two-thirds innings by the eighth, when he finally yielded two runs. Shortstop Charlie Hollocher, the Cubs' leading hitter in the regular season, grounded home a runner from third, and Les Mann singled in the tying run.

In the last of the eighth, the Cubs' relief pitcher, "Shufflin' " Phil Douglas, made a wild throw to permit Wally Schang to score a go-ahead run, which proved to be the margin of victory. In the ninth, Ruth gave up a single to Merkle and walked Rollie Zeider, at which point Barrow moved the Babe to left field and brought in Bullet Joe Bush, who set the side down in order for a save.

The Cubs won the fifth game 3–0 behind Vaughn, but the Red Sox took the world championship on September 11 as Carl Mays beat Tyler in another close one, 2–1. Ruth went to left field in the eighth inning after George Whiteman injured his shoulder making a great somersault catch.

Ruth's magnificent streak of twenty-nine and two-thirds consecutive shutout innings in the World Series lasted until 1961, when Whitey Ford broke it and went on to post a streak of thirty-three and two thirds. Ironically, it came in the same year in which Roger Maris broke Ruth's single-season home-run record of sixty.

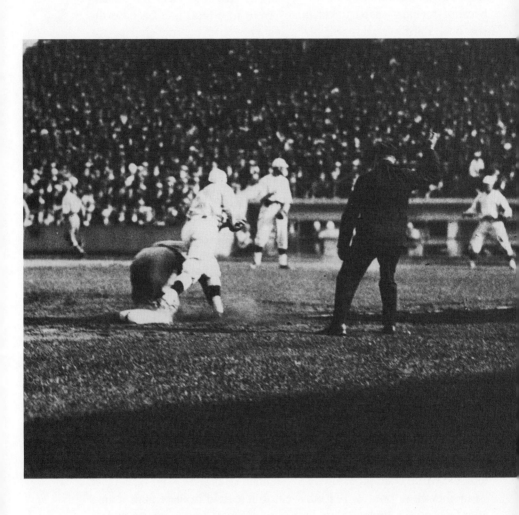

Action in the 1918 World Series, with Fred Merkle out at third. (National Baseball Library, Cooperstown, N.Y.)

Each of the winning Red Sox players received $1,102.51, and each Cub got $671.09, the smallest shares ever handed out. Fortunately, the war was over by the start of the 1919 season, and baseball was able to resume a normal course, even if the 1919 season was fated to end with the Black Sox scandal in the World Series.

Ruth's final year on the mound was 1919. He was 8–5 in fifteen starts, but played the outfield 111 times, belting a remarkable twenty-nine home runs. Second best in the league was a three-way tie among Tilly Walker, Home Run Baker, and George Sisler—with ten each. The dead-ball era was coming to an end, but Boston would trade Ruth to New York for the 1920 season, and to this day, it has never won another World Series.

There are those who say the team they root for is decided by their birthplace, a premise difficult to argue against. Well, pity the poor New Englander, who by birthright automatically becomes a Red Sox fan. Loyal and frustrated Bosox fans are and have been since the Babe left, and many now wonder if the drought will continue into the next century.

If they are to be led to the promised land and gain a World Series victory, one Roger Clemens is the pitcher who must show them the way.

10

The Death of
Ray Chapman

When the 1989 baseball season ended, most fans agreed that the numbing list of off-field events had made it the worst season in the game's history.

The Pete Rose gambling scandal unfolded; Wade Boggs was caught in a marital scandal; the Dodgers' Al Campanis defamed black people for lacking the "necessities" to hold management positions; and the clubs were fined over $10 million each for collusion on free-agent movement. What's more, the respected new commissioner, Bart Giamatti, suddenly died of a heart attack, and the World Series was halted for two weeks when an earthquake struck San Francisco.

It was a lousy season, all right. But the worst? How about 1920? That was the year the Black Sox scandal in the 1919 World Series threatened to ruin the game, and the year of the only on-field fatality in major league history. You hardly need a longer list.

Ray Chapman, twenty-nine, was the Cleveland Indians' shortstop. He was in his ninth season on the job, and was the most popular player on the team. Fans and opponents loved "Chappie" too. In a time when players were less self-conscious about such things, he could entertain his teammates endlessly with a beautiful tenor singing voice. With his career still unfolding, he might well have been Hall of Fame caliber.

Fast afoot, he stole 52 bases in 1917, an Indian record that stood for sixty-three years. In 1918, he led the league in runs scored and walks. He batted over .300 three times, and his quality of leadership was never more in evidence than in 1920, when the Indians were locked in a pennant race, hoping to win their first American League pennant.

While much of the attention in 1920 was focused on Babe Ruth's first season with the Yankees and his remarkable 54 home runs (breaking his record of 29), the Indians, second-place finishers in 1919, were playing the best ball of their history. Tris Speaker, the gifted center fielder, was player-manager and enjoying a .388 season. The team batting average of .303 included high-level performances by Larry Gardner at third, Elmer Smith and Charlie Jamieson in the outfield, and Steve O'Neill behind the plate. Jim Bagby was winning thirty-one games, while Stan Coveleski and Ray Caldwell were both twenty-game winners.

Chapman was hitting .303, leading the league in sacrifices and the team in stolen bases, and had scored 97 runs in 111 games.

On Monday, August 16, the Indians found themselves in New York to face the Yankees in what would be a battle for first place. They were only a half game behind. Three days earlier, in Cleveland, the Yankees had completed a four-game sweep that had turned the race into a close one. So important was this game that the Yankees decided to use Carl Mays, their best pitcher that season, out of rotation, one day earlier than he was supposed to have worked. A misty rain was falling on the Polo Grounds as the teams prepared for the afternoon's contest.

Mays, ten months younger than Chapman, was in his sixth season in the league. He had broken in with the Red Sox in 1915, and like so many of his teammates, including Ruth, had been traded to the Yankees. He arrived during the 1919 season, and was thus in his first full year in New York. Twice he had won twenty with Boston, using his odd, submarine, underhand delivery to fool batters. The delivery did not hurt his speed; he was a hard thrower.

Mays, largely on the basis of his personality, was also generally disliked, even by his teammates. But although he was not about to win any popularity contests, he *was* the team's top winner, and like the Indians, the Yankees were attempting to win their first pennant. Personalities aside, this was going to be a very important game.

Chapman was batting second in the lineup, between Jamieson and

Ray Chapman (National Baseball Library, Cooperstown, N.Y.)

Speaker. In the top of the first, Jamieson singled and Chapman bunted him to second, his thirty-fourth sacrifice of the season. But Mays got out of the jam.

The Indians took a 1–0 lead in the second on a homer by O'Neill. In the third, Jamieson again singled, but this time Chapman was unable to bunt successfully, popping out to Wally Pipp at first in what became a double play when Jamieson couldn't get back to first.

The rain stopped in the fourth as the Indians took a 3–0 lead. The inning ended with Chapman in the on-deck circle as Jamieson grounded out.

Leading off the fateful fifth inning, Chapman stood in, shifting his feet slightly as Mays prepared to pitch. He might have been thinking of a bunt. Mays might have caught the movement and decided at the last second to throw high and tight. Whatever the reasoning, Chapman held fast, almost frozen in place. He made no attempt to get out of the way as the pitch landed flat on his left temple with a crack heard by everyone in the Polo Grounds.

Ray stood in place for a brief moment and then fell to his knees. Umpire Tom Connolly quickly turned to the crowd and yelled for a doctor. Blood from Chapman's ear told him it might be serious. Speaker ran over from the on-deck circle as catcher Muddy Ruel tried to help Chapman up. After a few minutes, with the crowd hushed, Chapman got to his feet. The crowd cheered as he walked on his own power toward the clubhouse in deep center field. But by the time he reached second base, his knees again buckled, and two players assisted him the rest of the way.

Mays, who stayed on the mound, held the fateful ball. At first, he had thought it struck the bat and had attempted to make a play to first with it. Now he tried to show Connolly how badly scuffed it was. The baseball—the instrument of death—was taken out of play and lost to history, as it mixed in with others in a canvas ball bag, destined for batting practice. The game ended, the Indians winning 4–3.

Chapman was taken by ambulance to the hospital, conscious all the way but barely coherent. His pregnant wife rushed to New York by train from Cleveland. Surgery revealed that his skull had shattered and penetrated the brain. At 4:40 A.M. on August 17, he was pronounced dead. His teammates were stunned by the news. Players were always getting "beaned." They never died.

Mays chose neither to call Chapman's widow nor to visit the funeral home, explaining that either action would "haunt me as long as I live." That decision was not well received; threats were made on his life and a boycott was suggested if Mays wasn't thrown out of baseball. Mays blamed the umpire for not disposing of the scuffed ball earlier. "It was an accident for which I am absolutely blameless," he said.

The Indians brought up Joe Sewell from the minors to play short for the rest of that sorrowful season. Sewell not only played well, but went on to have a Hall of Fame career. The Indians hung on to win their first pennant—"for Chappie," of course—edging the White Sox by two games and the Yankees by three.

As for the White Sox, they were not only unhappy over losing a close pennant race, but were devastated in the final days of the season to learn that eight of their players had been indicted on charges of conspiring with gamblers to fix the 1919 World Series, which they had lost to the underdog Cincinnati Reds. The sting of that announcement, six weeks after Chapman's death, nearly dealt a death blow to baseball. It was one thing to have a freak accident kill a star player; it was quite another to have fans suspect that games weren't all on the up-and-up. If fans thought baseball was only about gambling, the sport would lose its credibility.

The appointment of commissioner Kenesaw Mountain Landis to "clean up the game" was probably the best move the owners could make at that moment in history. Landis tossed all eight players out of baseball for life, and while historians have questioned the severity of his decision, or its fairness toward Buck Weaver and Joe Jackson (who were possibly guilty only of knowing of the fix), the action put the game beyond reproach in the minds of fans and secured their everlasting loyalty.

The Indians went on to win the World Championship in 1920. Stan Coveleski won three games in the World Series, Bill Wambsganss turned an unassisted triple play at second base, and Elmer Smith hit the first World Series grand slam.

The unassisted triple play was especially noteworthy, in that it was performed by Chapman's old keystone partner and was only the second one in baseball history. Coming as it did in the World Series, it ranks with Don Larsen's perfect game as one of the great achievements in that unique spotlight. "Wamby," in the fifth inning of the fifth game, caught a line drive, stepped on second for a double play, and tagged the oncoming runner from first for a triple play.

The first unassisted triple play had been turned in by Cleveland's Neal Ball in 1909, Chapman's predecessor at shortstop. Five others followed Wambsganss's in the 1920s, and then it seemed as if baseball would never see another. But in 1968, Ron Hansen of Washington turned the feat against the Indians, and as this is written, he finds himself the only man between 1927 and the present to have been in the right place at the right time—at least as far as unassisted triple plays are concerned.

It would be nice to say that one legacy of Ray Chapman's death was that it brought about the use of helmets by batters. But that wasn't the case. Helmets didn't appear for more than thirty years. Still, Chapman remains the only player ever killed in the major leagues during a game.

Do pitchers ever give any thought to the lethal weapon disguised as a baseball they are holding and preparing to throw at over ninety miles an hour? Or how about the reverse? How far can a batter lean out over the plate and hit a ninety-mile-an-hour pitch, blasting it up the middle at over a hundred miles an hour, straight at a pitcher's head?

What is fair and what is not, and how far a pitcher should go not only to protect his portion of the strike zone but also to protect himself from being seriously injured by a line drive up the middle, are questions that will be argued for as long as the game is played.

The unwritten rules are certainly different today from what they were before the lords of the game instituted the no-retaliation rule. Namely, if I hit one of your hitters leaning out over the plate, I, as the opposing pitcher, can be penalized by being thrown out of the game simply for protecting myself or my teammates.

But there are also more subtle questions that relate to character, and you develop that character through the years, through the things you observe in the game. Memories are long when it comes to pitching-batting duels. If you have ever seen a pitcher struck in the head by a line drive, as I saw my teammate Jon Matlack felled, your perspective is changed forever. Baseball is not without its character-building moments.

The Age of the
Lively Ball

I**N THE NICE** even year of 1920, baseball underwent some important
changes that have changed the game to this day.

The principal change, the introduction of the lively ball, was coinci-
dental with the uncovering of the 1919 Black Sox Scandal, the coming
of Kenesaw Mountain Landis as commissioner, and the death of Ray
Chapman, but it was directly related to Babe Ruth. The four events,
coming within months of each other, raised the public's consciousness
about its "national game," and what emerged was a rejuvenated sport,
wholly accepted by the population.

A cork-center baseball, in fashion in the first two decades of this
century, was still causing frustration to muscular athletes, whose
natural instinct was to whack it over the fence. So, too, did the public
want to see power, and no one made that clearer than Babe Ruth, the
game's dominant personality. Ruth delighted the fans with his tremendous clouts, accomplishing remarking feats of distance with the still-
comatose ball. When baseball owners saw the interest in Ruth and the
crowds he was drawing, their pocketbooks did their talking for them.
Spalding and Reach, the baseball manufacturers, were quietly in-
structed to "juice up" the balls. The new, lively balls were phased in
during the 1920 and 1921 seasons, Ruth's first years in the nation's
glamour capital, New York. After 29 homers in 1919, he hit 54 home
runs in 1920—more than any *team* in the league—and he belted 59

more in 1921. The owners had seen enough—Ruth's style of long ball was in, Cobb's style of base hits was out. The "Golden Age of Sports" in America had been ushered in.

The 1919 Black Sox Scandal, in which eight members of the White Sox were accused of fixing the World Series, resulted in a perceived lack of confidence by the American people. Nineteenth-century baseball was riddled with gambling; the intent of the twentieth-century game, to this point, had been to carefully develop fan trust. That was potentially destroyed following the revelations that some of the Sox had met with gamblers, taken money, and played poorly against Cincinnati.

The sixteen owners, recognizing that their business was in danger, hired the cantankerous Landis, a federal judge whose white hair made him look older than his fifty-four years. His task was to restore public confidence in baseball, and he responded by throwing the eight suspects out of the sport for life. No matter how later events might shade their degrees of guilt, no matter that their cases had been thrown out of court due to insufficient evidence and missing written confessions, he never backed down from his decision.

His stern position on that single issue, coming in his first months of office, set the tone for a twenty-five-year reign. Little of substance actually tested the Judge's powers in those twenty-five years. He held the subtle status quo on segregation, witnessed no franchise moves or expansion, kept the game alive during World War II, and died in office, the game intact, firmly in place as the "national pastime." Still, its growth was slight in those years, most clubs barely breaking even, unknowingly awaiting the invention of television to fortify it with new revenues. Even night baseball was still a novelty.

Chapman's death forced the owners to ban spitballs and other trick pitches, and compelled umpires to keep new, unscuffed, white baseballs in play. The spitball was clearly a dangerous pitch, not given to precise control by even its most polished practitioners. It dipped and dropped and moved in bizzare patterns, leaving only gravity to bring it down. It was also unsanitary, and the game had been struggling for two decades to appear more wholesome to the general population. Part of this strategy was to permit Sunday baseball. Many cities had laws forbidding games on the Sabbath.

The ban on the spitter, combined with the debut of the lively ball, gave an edge to hitters. Fans seemed to welcome it. Hitters were able to take advantage of their muscles and give spectators the show they wanted. When men like Jimmie Foxx and Lou Gehrig displayed those strong physiques, people did not want to see a Wee Willie Keeler hit 'em where they ain't; they wanted to see a Babe Ruth hit 'em where they couldn't find 'em. And with these changes, they got their money's worth.

The elimination of pitches aided by foreign substances pretty much reduced the pitcher's arsenal to fastball, curveball, and change, except for those few who could throw the screwball or knuckleball.

There is an old adage that asks, "What is the best pitch in baseball and what is the second-best pitch in baseball?"

The answer to both is the fastball.

It is a pitch that can be gripped in several different ways to create different types of movement, such as a sinker, a cutter, or a running fastball. All are thrown hard.

The fastball is the pitch all of the other pitches benefit from, because hitters have to protect against it. As long as the game is played, it will be the game's dominant pitch.

The curve, invented in the nineteenth century by Candy Cummings, is the granddaddy of all breaking pitches. It has been known by many names through the years and remains one of the basic pitches. Years ago it was called the "drop," which pretty much explains what it does, but it can be thrown at several different speeds and from several different release points to create a different angle for the break.

Likewise the change, or change-up, or change of pace has been known by many names and thrown with many different grips, depending on what is effective for each individual pitcher. The change is the pitch used to throw off the hitter's timing.

For some pitchers it is very difficult to learn and control, but when used in conjunction with the power pitches, it is a great complement.

The slider came along in the late 1940s and early 1950s. It is now the third most important pitch in a pitcher's arsenal. It is thrown with much more velocity than the curve and a much shorter but faster break. It is a pitch that when thrown with improper mechanics can cause elbow or shoulder problems. The slider will remain as a basic pitch for pitchers, because it is relatively easier to learn than the curve.

The modern addition to a pitcher's tool kit is the splitter, or "split-finger fastball." It has become the vogue pitch of the eighties and nineties. When thrown correctly, it can be a power pitch, with great movement in the hitting zone.

The jury is still out on whether the high number of injuries to pitchers' arms nowadays is attributable to the splitter. The one mistake so many young pitchers make is "falling in love" with the splitter, and over a period of time it takes away from the fastball, the pitcher's number one pitch.

11

When Casey Ran the Bases

The first time Mickey Mantle ever played in Ebbets Field—it was during the 1952 World Series—his manager, Casey Stengel, walked him to the outfield and showed him how the ball might carom off the walls.

Mantle looked at him as if he were crazy. He viewed Stengel as a very old man who might be capable of making up a lineup but who would never in a million years know how to play balls bouncing off outfield walls.

Stengel later told people that he said to Mantle, "You think I was born this old?" And he proceeded to take a few minutes to explain to his young prodigy that he had, in fact, played those walls in that very park a few hundred years earlier. He had been a Dodger outfielder, right there in Ebbets Field, from 1912 to 1917, and had played in the 1916 World Series there.

No doubt it was hard for Mantle to imagine Stengel the ballplayer. When I first met Casey in 1967, I was a rookie with the Mets and he was a visitor to spring training in St. Petersburg, a little old man with a cane who loved to hold court with what he called "my writers." He had retired as Met manager in 1965 after breaking his hip, but for the rest of his life, he was a part of the Met scene in spring training, as well as at Old Timers Days, and he was always a delight to be around. Tug

McGraw, who came up in '65, had the honor when he retired in 1984 of being the last active player to have played for Casey.

My favorite story about Casey took place during that rookie year with the Mets in '67. I remember he was describing the vast number of prospects on the Mets and how they would soon become contenders with their talented youth. When he came to the catchers, he described Greg Goossen as "a young man, twenty years old, with a great arm, and a quick release to go with an accurate arm and great power at the plate, who in ten years has a good chance to be thirty."

I also remember sitting with Bud Harrelson and Casey at Al Lang Field in Florida one day, just yakking about baseball. I was sitting with the master, as it were, soaking up every observation he made. The famous "Stengelese" double-talk that everyone laughed about wasn't there at all. Except, that is, when a writer ambled over to chat for a few moments; then Casey slipped right into the double-talk. The writer thanked him and wandered off. Casey winked at us as though he'd just put on quite a show, and continued to talk in a normal manner, offering his wealth of baseball experience.

I've seen players talk to old-timers and not take them very seriously, probably thinking that they would have to be very much out of touch with today's game. Not so with Casey. You sort of hung on every word.

The funny thing about Mantle's reaction in 1952 to the sixty-two or sixty-four-year-old Stengel (no one was sure how old he really was) is that Casey was considered an "old man" as far back as the first World Series ever played in Yankee Stadium, in 1923.

This was so in part because, at thirty-three (or thirty-five), Casey was among the oldest Giants, along with Heinie Groh and Hank Gowdy, and in part because, well, he looked older than he was. He had this wrinkled face and these bowlegs. And, although he was not a coach, he was sort of a pal to John McGraw, the manager, looked older than McGraw (who was fifty), and was a platoon player, which was still unusual in those days. (Only Casey Stengel could be responsible for a story that has both John McGraw and Tug McGraw in it.)

Stengel later made platoon baseball, the tailoring of a lineup to respond to whether the opposing pitcher was a lefty or a righty, a part of the modern game. One can plainly see where he learned it. In 1922 and 1923, his only two full years under McGraw, he played in 150 games and batted .355, with 12 homers, 87 runs batted in, and 10 stolen bases. They were the most productive two years of his fourteen-year playing career, and he got into the World Series both times. It's easy to understand how he would react when future players complained about platooning.

The 1923 World Series offered the third consecutive matchup between the Yankees and the Giants, with the Giants seeking to become the first team to win three straight world championships. The year 1923 was different because the Yankees would play their home games not at the Polo Grounds, where they had been tenants since 1913, but in the new Yankee Stadium. It had been hastily constructed prior to the season just across the Harlem River from the Polo Grounds on an old Bronx lumberyard turned park.

The arrival of Babe Ruth in 1920 had made the Yankees a more popular attraction than the Giants in New York, and a growing jealousy was the inevitable result. The 1920 Yankees became the first team ever to draw a million fans, and their 1,289,422 total continued to be a record until 1946. This record did not sit well with Giant management, so at the start of the 1922 season, it informed the Yankee owners that it would be good for them to look for a place of their own for the following year. This suggestion actually suited the Yankee owners just fine, particularly Colonel Jacob Ruppert. They felt ready for their own place as an acknowledgment of their new stature.

McGraw still looked down on the American League. In 1904, you will recall, he had refused to participate in a World Series. By 1923, he wasn't putting up such roadblocks, but he did have his players dress in the Polo Grounds and take taxis to Yankee Stadium, rather than use the new visiting-clubhouse facilities.

The first game, on October 10, drew an attendance of 55,307 at Yankee Stadium, almost twenty thousand fewer than had attended the team's opener in April. Miller Huggins, the Yankee manager, had a former Giant right-hander on the mound, Waite Hoyt, so McGraw had Stengel, a left-handed hitter, in center field, batting sixth. The Yankee fans no doubt expected Ruth to hit the first World Series home run in the new stadium, just as he had hit the first one in the regular season.

The Yanks jumped off to a 3–0 lead after two innings, driving Giant starter Mule Watson out of the game. The big hit for the Yanks was a two-run single in the second by center fielder Whitey Witt, the team's leadoff hitter. But then the Giants knocked out Hoyt in the third as they scored four times, the big hit a two-run triple by Heinie Groh with his odd-shaped "bottle bat." Bullet Joe Bush, one of the many ex-Red Sox players who had been sold to New York, came in for the Yanks.

The game continued 4–3 Giants until the Yanks tied it in the seventh on a single by Bush and a triple to right by Joe Dugan. Ruth, the next batter, grounded to first, where George Kelly made a terrific play and fired home to nail Dugan and keep the score 4–4. Neither team scored in the eighth.

In the ninth the Giants had Ross Youngs, Irish Meusel, and Stengel due to hit against Bush. Youngs lined out to Witt in center for the first out. Meusel grounded to Dugan at third for the second out. Up came Stengel, who had flied deep to Ruth in right, walked, and singled, the single being the only hit off Bush since he'd come on in the third.

Bush delivered, and Casey smacked it on a line into left-center field. Witt from center and Bob Meusel (Irish's brother) from left raced for the ball, but it was soon beyond them, heading for a fence that was 460 feet away.

Pushing his old body as hard as he could, Casey proceeded around the bases. It looked as though he had almost run out of gas near third but, in fact, one of his shoes had come loose and was only half on his foot. Witt picked up the ball and fired it to Meusel. Now it was the relay home as Casey gave it everything he had. Wally Schang, the Yankee catcher, waited for the throw, which was just a moment late as Casey slid for the plate in a cloud of dust. He got up slowly, dusted himself off, smiled, and walked to the Giants' dugout, to the cheers and laughter of his teammates.

The man who would go on to earn Hall of Fame honors by leading his Yankees to ten pennants in twelve years as manager had hit the first World Series home run ever in Yankee Stadium. It was an inside-the-park homer and it gave the Giants a 5–4 win.

You know who hit the second World Series home run in Yankee Stadium history? And the first to clear the fence?

It was Game Three, two days later, a scoreless tie in the seventh inning. Sad Sam Jones was on the mound for the Yankees with one out in the seventh when Casey Stengel blasted one into the right-field bleachers. The Giants hung on to win that game 1–0, giving Stengel his second game-winning hit of the Series and the Giants a 2–1 lead in games. But the Yankees went on to win their first World Championship, no thanks to the .417 hitting and two game-winning homers by

Casey Stengel slides home with an inside the park home run, the first World Series homer in Yankee Stadium, 1923. Joe Bush is the pitcher, Wally Schang the catcher, and Bill Evans the umpire. (National Baseball Library, Cooperstown, N.Y.)

their future manager. Had they given sports cars to series MVPs back then, Casey might have driven off with a handsome roadster.

Those who only know of the wrinkled old face, so full of character, that belonged to Casey Stengel, Manager, will find his exploits as a player simply "amazin'," one of the favorite words of "the Ol' Perfessor."

12

A World Series for Walter Johnson

I have always found the accomplishments of Walter Johnson extraordinary, perhaps more so than those of any other pitcher in history.

In the first place, he had those incredible statistics, all on the plus side, while the Washington Senators, for whom he pitched during his entire career, were usually a second-division team. He won 416 games, 376 of them as a starter, and 110 of those shutouts, which was fortunate, given how little run support he usually had to work with. He had 3,508 strikeouts—for years the major league record—which is certainly one way to overcome weak defenses. He pitched over three hundred innings during nine seasons, which probably says something about his lack of bullpen support. And, oh yes, he allowed only ninety-seven home runs in twenty-one years.

Of greater fascination is the story told by old-timers that Johnson apparently did all of this with just a fastball. He had no great breaking pitches to speak of, and his off-speed pitch was used more to upset a batter's timing than to induce him to go after a breaking ball. They never measured the speed of Johnson's pitches—I think the first pitcher they ever did that with was Bob Feller—but he must have been in a class of his own. Photos seem to show him with very long arms. Perhaps they contained his magic potion.

Johnson's fastball was obviously fast beyond normal standards for his era. Indeed, when you speak of Walter Johnson, you mean fast-balls. In my second year in the big leagues, my pitching coach was Rube Walker, and he passed along to me one of those pieces of advice that stays with you forever. Rube believed the best pitch in baseball was the fastball, and he asked me, "Tom, what's the second most important pitch?" Before I could offer what would undoubtedly have been the wrong answer, he said, "The fastball. It's so important it's number one and number two."

Johnson's era began in 1907 when the American League was still young and he was a nineteen-year-old right-hander from Humboldt, Kansas, with a 5–9 record, but seventy strikeouts and only seventeen walks. It took him a couple of years to move to the head of the class, but in 1910 he was 25–17 with a 1.35 earned-run average and 313 strikeouts. From that point on, he was the best pitcher in the league, if not in the majors, with a 32–12 record in 1912, a 36–7 record in 1913, eleven seasons with ERAs under 2.00, and twelve seasons leading the league in strikeouts.

But his team never supported him with a stellar cast. By the end of the first two decades of American League baseball, Cleveland, St. Louis, New York, and Washington—half the league—had failed to win a pennant. Then Cleveland won in 1920 and New York in 1921. In all those years since Johnson had arrived in 1907, the Senators were second twice and third twice, but never really close. And throughout all those years, Johnson pitched on, never getting a taste of the World Series, the event that had now become the nation's premier sporting event. He hurled regularly on Opening Day before the President of the United States, but Teddy Roosevelt, William Howard Taft, Woodrow Wilson, and Warren Harding had come and gone, and still there was no World Series in Washington.

As the 1924 season beckoned, Calvin Coolidge became Johnson's fifth president, and Bucky Harris his new Washington manager. Johnson was thirty-six now and contemplating retirement, looking perhaps to purchase a minor-league team somewhere. But the Senators of 1923 had finished fourth, had handed the managing job to their kid second baseman (Harris was twenty-seven), and had high hopes for '24. Team owner Clark Griffith persuaded Johnson to go another season, although he was clearly not the pitcher he had once been: he went 17–12 in 1923, with "only" 130 strikeouts and "only" eighteen complete games.

Walter Johnson

Bucky Harris

Because his loyalty to Griffith and the fans of Washington was strong, Johnson accepted the request. Backed by the best Washington team in history, which included Joe Judge, Sam Rice, Roger Peckinpaugh, Goose Goslin, and Harris, Johnson responded by leading the league in wins (twenty-three), strikeouts, shutouts, and earned-run average. He won thirteen games in a row in the final two months, helping the Senators to cling to a two-game lead over the Yankees with two games left. On the next-to-last day of the season, Washington beat Boston and the Yankees lost to the A's. You don't have to dream too hard to imagine the tears that must have been in Walter Johnson's eyes as the team returned home to Washington's Union Station to be met by adoring fans. This was Walter's eighteenth season and his first pennant.

The victory parade swung down Pennsylvania Avenue past President Coolidge, who promised to be at the World Series. He kept his word and was there with his wife in Griffith Stadium on October 4 for Game One against the New York Giants, winners of their fourth straight pennant.

Johnson was the starting pitcher, of course, but he fell early victim to two home runs, hit into the temporary seats that had been added to the left-field bleachers. The homers, by George Kelly and Bill Terry, gave the Giants a 2–0 lead after five, but the Senators came back to tie the game 2–2 and send it into extra innings. Johnson pitched gamely, stopping the tough Giant lineup with seven straight zeros. But in the twelfth he finally yielded two runs, and lost the game 4–2.

Johnson hung his head in the clubhouse. He blamed himself for losing his first World Series outing and for letting down the fans, who had showered him with so much love.

With the Series tied at two games apiece, Johnson took the mound again in Game Five in New York's Polo Grounds. This time he allowed thirteen hits and struck out only three, as the Giants beat him 6–2. Freddy Lindstrom, the young Giant third baseman, touched him up for four singles.

For all he had accomplished to get to this point, Johnson was deeply disheartened. He was now 0–2 in his first World Series and ashamed of his work. It did not appear that he would pitch again, and thus he was faced with either playing no part in a Senator win or blaming himself for the loss of the championship.

To his closest friends he talked about retiring after the Series, since he already had an opportunity to purchase the Oakland team in the Pacific Coast League. It looked as though Walter Johnson would leave a loser.

Then Washington tied the Series 3–3 in Game Six, setting the stage for a decisive seventh game at Washington on October 10. Harris told all his pitchers to be ready, as is always the case in a seventh game. The Giants started Virgil Barnes, the Senators Curly Ogden, a right-hander. But Harris had a plan. After working to only two batters, Ogden was lifted for the left-handed George Mogridge, throwing off John McGraw's lefty lineup.

President and Mrs. Coolidge were among the 31,667 fans in the ballpark that afternoon, and whether their voices were among those saying ''We want Johnson, we want Johnson'' is lost to history. But the Giants took a 3–1 lead in the sixth when the Washington defense faltered, and they held it to the last of the eighth. Then Washington gamely battled back with two runs to tie the game, the big hit a two-run single by Harris himself off Barnes. (What pressure there must be on a player-manager in such a situation! What a feeling to deliver a big hit like that!)

Now, it was the ninth inning of the seventh game. Washington needed a new pitcher. Harris called for Walter. The fans roared. Yes, he'd lost two games in the Series, but he was ''The Big Train,'' the man who'd pitched his heart out for this ragtag team since 1907. Sentiment was on his side.

Walter was struggling. A one-out triple by Frankie Frisch put him in deep trouble, but he was able to strike out Kelly and get Irish Meusel to ground out. When Washington failed to score in the ninth, it meant extra innings for the World Championship.

Walter walked the leadoff man in the tenth, but initiated a double play to end the inning. The Senators failed to score off Hugh Mc-Quillan, and it was on to the eleventh.

A leadoff single by Heinie Groh led nowhere for the Giants, as Johnson struck out Frisch and Kelly. He was reaching back for something extra when he had to. He wasn't sharp—but he knew how to pitch. Washington failed to score in the bottom of the inning.

In the twelfth, another leadoff single got Johnson in the hole, but he retired the next three batters. That made four innings of relief on one day's rest for the aging superstar.

In the last of the twelfth, Muddy Ruel doubled down the third-base line with one out, after Hank Gowdy, the Giants' veteran catcher, stepped on his mask and dropped a foul pop. Johnson batted for himself and grounded to short, where Travis Jackson fumbled the hop. Ruel went to third.

Up came leadoff batter Earl McNeely. He connected for a sharp grounder to third, but the ball seemed to hit a pebble and bounced over Lindstrom's head into left field. Ruel came tearing home with the winning run, and the Senators were World Champions for the first—and only—time in their history! Winning pitching: Walter Johnson. Unfortunately, the pebble, the bad hop, and nineteen-year-old Freddie Lindstrom came to be better remembered than the valiant effort by Johnson for his first World Series victory.

Ironically, there was not a similar, extra-inning, seventh game drama until fifty-six years later, when the Senators' descendents, the Minnesota Twins, beat Atlanta 1–0 behind a complete game from Jack Morris.

Johnson did, in fact, play the following year, and Washington repeated its pennant, although this time it lost to Pittsburgh in seven games. Johnson started three times and won twice, but he lost the deciding game, 9–7, allowing fifteen hits. It must have seemed anticlimactic after the previous Series.

So The Big Train finally tasted glory late in his pitching life, and is still the greatest player in the history of the Senators. He retired after the 1927 season, managed Washington from 1929 to 1932 (it won its last pennant a year later under Joe Cronin), and managed Cleveland from 1933 to 1935. He died in Washington in 1946.

His strikeout record lasted until Nolan Ryan and Steven Carlton both passed him in 1983. I myself passed him in 1985, although of course it wasn't a record anymore. Still, to have my name linked to his was quite an honor. That same year I broke his record of fourteen Opening Day starting assignments. (His fourteenth, at age thirty-nine, was a 1–0 shutout in fifteen innings.)

I was luckier than Johnson. I waited only three years for my first World Series. Some have never gotten there at all, men like Ernie Banks, Ralph Kiner, Phil Niekro, or Don Mattingly, who is still active and so still has a shot. But I can understand how Johnson must have felt to be standing on that mound in his eighteenth year, accomplishing all that he had but still lacking that final victory, that World Series triumph.

13

Alex Fans Lazzeri

The career of Grover Cleveland Alexander included more victories (373) than anyone's but Cy Young, Walter Johnson, and Christy Mathewson. Yet it was forever epitomized by a single batter late in his career, and by the belief that he struck the man out while hung over from an alcoholic binge the night before.

The strikeout of Tony Lazzeri was perhaps the most famous play of the 1920s. It is also emblematic of a time when alcohol was a much greater part of the game, treatment almost unheard of, and heroics built on a reputation based on its use.

Sportswriters were almost like members of a team in the days when they traveled with the club for a full season, day after day on the long train rides, keeping any dirt buried and protecting their friends, the players. Thus, fans seldom knew who the big drinkers were or whether, in fact, alcohol ever affected their games. (Drugs were still unknown in the game.) This practice of silence pretty much went on even into my time. The world was shocked when it learned that Mickey Mantle and Whitey Ford liked to tear up the town, and alcoholics like Sam McDowell, Don Newcombe, and Ryne Duren didn't reveal their problem until their playing days were ended.

Now that drugs have entered the world of baseball, and especially since the Pittsburgh drug trials of 1985, the public is more aware of the underside of life on the road. And baseball itself has awakened to the needs of young athletes who develop problems; the entrance of a player into medical rehabilitation, while hardly a badge of honor, no longer earns him a scarlet letter either.

The tragic figures, those with brilliant on-the-field accomplishments but ever-so-human frailties off the field, have always been present in games of sport, and always will be. Sports remains a microcosm of our society, with its changing personal and social problems. The one difference is that now players' lives are portrayed on the sports pages every day. But players are no different from the "common working man," and rehabilitation programs for athletes are really similar to programs established by the private sector.

In Alexander's time, however, alcohol was something to be chuckled about by the baseball fraternity, even if it was destroying a player's body, as it was Grover's. As long as he kept winning—and he did—he could order up anything he wanted during those lonely nights on the road.

The facts were these: The 1926 World Series was the first ever for the St. Louis Cardinals, one of the charter teams in the league. They had waited a long time for this moment. It was the fourth for the New York Yankees, but their first as "Murderers' Row," that lethal lineup with Babe Ruth, Lou Gehrig, Earle Combs, Bob Meusel, Tony Lazzeri, Mark Koenig, and Joe Dugan. It was Gehrig's first series.

Alexander's career dated back to 1911 when, as a twenty-four-year-old rookie, he had won twenty-eight games for the Phillies. In 1915, when he pitched the Phillies into the World Series, he had a 31–10 record, a 1.22 earned-run average, and twelve shutouts. A year later he had sixteen shutouts and thirty-three wins, and with the completion of his seventh season in 1917, he had won 190 games, sixty-one of them shutouts.

World War I changed things forever. Alexander was sent to France for combat duty in 1918, lost his hearing in one ear from the shelling, and became an alcoholic. Upon his return, as a member of the Cubs, his affliction was viewed as typical of the boys in combat, nothing to be concerned about. Some joked that he pitched much better when he'd been drinking.

He won twenty-seven games in 1920 and twenty-two in 1923, but in 1926 his manager, Joe McCarthy, gave up on his binges and had him placed on waivers, two weeks after "Alexander Day" in Chicago. The

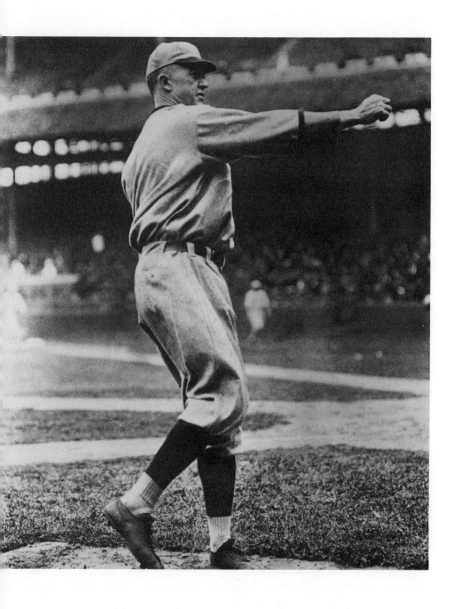

Grover Cleveland Alexander

Cardinals claimed him in June, and he rewarded them by winning nine games to help them clinch their first pennant, under player-manager Rogers Hornsby.

The Series opened in New York, and after losing the opener, Hornsby went with Alexander in Game Two. "Ol' Pete," by now thirty-nine years old, beat the Yankees 6–2 on a four-hitter, striking out ten, walking one.

Jess Haines won the third game in St. Louis to put the Cardinals ahead 2–1, but the Yankees won the next two to lead the Series 3–2. In Game Five, Babe Ruth hit three home runs. Back in Yankee Stadium for Game Six, their backs to the wall, the Cardinals started Alexander against Bob Shawkey. Again, Ol' Pete was brilliant. He stopped New York on eight hits, striking out six, walking only two, and winning 10–2 to set up a seventh game.

So it's now Saturday night in New York City in the "Roarin' Twenties," you've just beaten the Yanks for the second time in the World Series, there's no way you're pitching tomorrow, and you're known to enjoy a drink or two. What's a fellow to do?

According to Alexander, "I don't want to spoil anyone's story, but I was cold sober that night. There were plenty of other nights, before and since, that I wasn't, but that night I was as sober as a judge should be." He maintained that he spent the night in his hotel room.

Sunday, October 10, was cold and overcast with a threat of rain that kept the crowd in huge Yankee Stadium down to thirty-eight thousand. Haines started for the Cardinals, while Miller Huggins went with Waite Hoyt. Alexander headed down to the bullpen, where, apparently, he fell asleep.

The Cardinals led 3–2 after six innings. Herb Pennock relieved Hoyt in the seventh for New York, and Haines continued on the mound for St. Louis, his knuckleball working well.

In the last of the seventh, Combs, representing the tying run, led off with a base hit. Koenig sacrificed him to second and Ruth was walked intentionally, his tenth walk of the series. As he'd already hit four home runs in twenty at-bats, it was good strategy, even with Meusel and Gehrig coming up. Meusel hit into a force play and Gehrig walked to fill the bases with two out.

At this point Hornsby left his position at second and went to speak to Haines on the mound. A blister had popped on Haines's pitching hand, and he couldn't continue. Hornsby had Herman "Hi" Bell and Art Reinhart warming up in the bullpen, and he had to make a move. The Series was on the line.

There were no telephones to the bullpens then, and no bullpen coaches either. It was just the relief pitchers and a spare catcher or two down there. Hornsby cupped his hands together and called for Alex, who had thrown not a single warm-up pitch in the bullpen. But Rogers had told him he might need him, and he was now playing his trump card.

Hornsby later wrote in his autobiography, *My War With Baseball*, "There was a little delay before anybody came out of the bullpen. I yelled 'Alexander' and when he didn't come out real quick, people thought he was asleep or something. Then he came out, walking real slouchy-like. Alexander could have been drunk for all I cared, but he certainly wasn't. Hell, I'd rather have him pitch a crucial game for me drunk than anyone I've ever known sober.

" 'Well, the bases are full,' I told him. 'Lazzeri's up and there ain't no place to put him.' "

" 'Yeah,' Alex drawled, 'well, guess I'll have to take care of him then.' "

The catcher was Bob O'Farrell. He later told Lawrence Ritter, in *The Glory of Their Times*, "Alex didn't really intend to take a drink [Saturday] night. But some of his 'friends' got hold of him and thought they were doing him a favor by buying him a drink. Well, you weren't doing Alex any favor by buying him a drink, because he just couldn't stop.

"So in the seventh inning of the seventh game, Alex is tight asleep in the bullpen, sleeping off the night before, when trouble comes."

The "trouble"—in addition to the fact that the bases were loaded—was Lazzeri, a twenty-one-year-old rookie from San Francisco. Tony had batted .275 that season, but was hitting only .200 in the Series. Still, he had driven in 114 runs during the regular season, second to Ruth in the league. (Of course, it helped to have Ruth, Gehrig, and Meusel batting ahead of him in the lineup.)

Alex took the mound and tossed three warm-up pitches to O'Farrell. The writers in the press box and the players in the dugouts and on the field were all thinking that he was hung over. In those prehelmet days, this couldn't have been a comforting thought for Lazzeri.

Lazzeri held up on a slow curve that was low for ball one. He took a fastball for a strike. Then he lined the next pitch down the line, but foul. It was 1-and-2.

The next pitch—one of the most famous in Series history—was a curve, low and outside. Lazzeri swung and missed. Strike three. Three runners left on base. Alex slouched off toward the dugout and Lazzeri stood for a moment in disbelief.

As many fans came to remember it, that was the end of the game. But there were still six outs to go, and they were not without historic content either.

In the eighth, with the Cardinals still up 3–2, Alex got the side one-two-three, the last out being pitcher Pennock, a .212 hitter that season. In the ninth, Alex eliminated the first two batters, then walked Ruth on a full count. That brought up Meusel, representing the winning run, with Gehrig on deck.

Suddenly, Ruth started to steal second, hoping to startle the Cardinals and put the tying run in scoring position. But it was a dumb play—probably the dumbest of his career, according to Ed Barrow, his general manager. O'Farrell fired a perfect peg to Hornsby at second, who made the tag to end the game and give the underdog Cardinals the World Championship. Hornsby called the simple tag "my biggest thrill in baseball."

All America talked of the Alexander-Lazzeri duel for years. Tony went on to have a great twelve seasons with the Yankees, before he died as a result of a fall down a staircase at age forty-one, seven years after his retirement. He had been suffering from epilepsy.

Ol' Pete played until 1930, when he was forty-three, winning twenty-one for the Cards in 1927 and pitching twice in the 1928 Series against the Yankees. He faced Lazzeri three times in that Series, getting him to ground out twice in the second game, and then coming in to face him in relief in the fourth and final game in St. Louis. This time, Tony doubled to left and later scored as the Yanks touched up Alex for three runs and swept the Series.

Alexander himself developed epilepsy, in addition to alcoholism and cancer, the latter illness costing him an ear. He ended up touring with the House of David barnstorming team and working in a Times Square sideshow, where for a nickel people could listen to him tell the story of the day he fanned Lazzeri.

He was twice divorced from the same woman, and was living alone in a rented room on $160 a month—partly his war pension, partly charity from the National League—when he died in 1950 at the age of sixty-three. Ronald Reagan portrayed him in the film *The Winning Team* in 1952.

14

Murderers' Row

Baseball's most legendary character, Babe Ruth, changed the game forever during its most romantic year, 1927, the same year Charles Lindbergh flew the Atlantic on the wings of the *Spirit of St. Louis.*

But 1927 was more than just a year in baseball. It was a year in which a legendary ball club was assembled, a club that has become the standard for measuring the best a team can be.

"Who were those guys out there today, the 1927 Yankees?" That's an expression you still hear in baseball circles after a particularly one-sided game. (The other team about which you hear that type of historic reference is the 1962 Mets, who lost 120 games.)

Winners of 110 games—a league record that stood until the Indians won one more in 1954—the Yankees of '27 still inspire awe. They were the ultimate team of baseball's so-called "Golden Age," an era when the Babe, Jack Dempsey, Red Grange, Bill Tilden, and others were genuine American heroes, weaving their respective sports into the nation's collective consciousness. No longer did you have to be a "fan" to know about sports. Now, all you needed was to be an American.

The 1927 Yankees, nicknamed "Murderers' Row," were the mature product of Miller Huggins's command. He had won pennants with the Yankees in 1921, 1922, 1923, and 1926. He had brought the team into the new Yankee Stadium in 1923 but had completely reshuffled it by the 1926 season. Now before him stood assembled one of the greatest teams in baseball's relatively brief history, one that would be recalled for its greatness long into the future.

That the Yankees won 110 games, lost only forty-four, and finished nineteen games ahead of the Athletics seemed remarkable, for in '26, they had won by only three games over Cleveland, six over Philadelphia, eight over Washington, and nine and a half over Chicago. Any one of these teams certainly appeared capable of making a race of it in '27, especially after the Yankees' embarrassing defeat to St. Louis in the 1926 Series, when Grover Cleveland Alexander struck out Tony Lazzeri, and Ruth was called out stealing to end the final game.

One remarkable thing about the '27 Yanks was that they went through the entire season with twenty-five players. There were no disabling injuries, no options, no call-ups—not even in September. Huggins decided on his club in St. Petersburg and had no reason to make even a single roster move all season. The expression today would be "If it ain't broken, don't fix it." Huggins knew it wasn't broken.

He took six new players north with him, two of whom were key pitchers. Wilcy Moore was a thirty-year-old rookie who had recorded a 30–4 record in the Sally League in 1926. Years before relief pitching was considered significant, Moore would give the Yankees thirteen saves plus thirteen relief victories. His overall record for fifty games would be 19–7, with a 2.28 ERA. His was the first great relief season, and while it did not immediately change baseball, it did pave the way for the relief role to become the proud one it is today.

George Pipgras, who later became an umpire, had pitched seventeen games for the Yankees in 1923 and 1924, after coming over from the Red Sox with Herb Pennock in another fiasco trade for Boston. He had been back in the minors for two years when Huggins pronounced him ready for 1927. He would go 10–3 in twenty-one starts.

The four other new faces played minor roles in 1927: pitcher Joe Giard, who had been on the champion Cardinals in 1926; rookie Julie Wera, a third baseman who batted only forty-two times; catcher Johnny Grabowski, who came over from the White Sox; and outfielder Cedric Durst, who came over from the Browns, and who in 1930 was traded to Boston for Red Ruffing, another steal for the Yankees.

With 110 victories that year, one looks to the pitching staff for thirty-game winners, or at least a handful of twenty-game winners. Try no thirty-game winners and only one pitcher who won twenty. Huggins, without a pitching coach, wove his staff artfully throughout the season, no pitcher making more than thirty-two starts. That man, Waite Hoyt, was 22–7, the team's only twenty-game winner. Moore won his nineteen in relief and as a starter, while Pennock was 19–8, Urban Shocker 18–6, and Dutch Ruether 13–6. The Yankee pitching staff did not provide the American League with a strikeout leader, an innings-pitched leader, or a shutout leader, and only Hoyt and Pennock are in the Hall of Fame. But, with the great lineup that Huggins put in place, the pitchers were able to prevail almost daily. Their staff ERA of 3.20 was the best in the league.

Shocker, not well remembered today, was one of the tragic figures from that legendary team. Long before Gehrig died, it was Shocker whose courage was best remembered from the '27 Yankees. Late in the season, he developed a respiratory problem, and left the team to live in Denver for recovery in that city's "healthier air." He had an enlarged heart, and to relieve strain on it had to sleep sitting up. He came back considerably weakened in 1928 to make a single, two-inning relief appearance, but on July 4, he collapsed in the dugout, and on September 9, he died in Denver at age thirty-eight. He had been aware, even during the 1927 season, that he was a doomed man.

So stable was the Yankee starting lineup that by 1929 the Yanks became the first team to use uniform numbers, and they assigned the numbers to correspond with their regular batting lineup. Center fielder Earle Combs was 1, third baseman (in 1929) Mark Koenig was 2, right fielder Babe Ruth was 3, first baseman Lou Gehrig was 4, left fielder Bob Meusel was 5, second baseman Tony Lazzeri was 6 and so on. (Joe Dugan, third baseman in 1927, was gone; number 7 went to shortstop Leo Durocher). The catching spot was the only one that might be called "weak," in 1927, as it was a three-man platoon, with Pat Collins catching 89 games, Benny Bengough 30, and Grabowski 68. (Bill Dickey would not arrive until late in 1928, and while he is often thought to have been part of Murderers' Row, he was not there in '27.)

The team batted .307 to lead the league. It also led in runs, hits, triples, home runs, slugging average, runs batted in, walks, and strikeouts. But in comparison to today's statistics, the strikeouts were few. Ruth, the game's greatest slugger, led the league with eighty-nine, about half a season's total for today's big bashers.

Gehrig, at twenty-four, was only in his third season as a regular. His consecutive-game playing streak was under five hundred and hardly noticed. He had hit sixteen home runs in 1926, two fewer than Lazzeri. In 1927, Lazzeri hit another eighteen—but Gehrig belted forty-seven, finally developing a Yankee Stadium swing. As was often the case in his career, his forty-seven—the third-highest total in the game's history at that point—was barely noticed because his flamboyant teammate, Mr. Ruth, was on his way to breaking his own mark of fifty-nine, set in 1921.

Yankee Stadium, with its short right field, was labeled "The House That Ruth Built," but in his first four seasons there, Ruth's best showing was his forty-seven in 1926. Now, however, buoyed by a remarkable September finish, Ruth was destined to break his record. As a matter of fact, if you were to ask baseball historians to name the one event that gave baseball its mystical appeal, it would have to be the Babe's sixty home runs of 1927.

That same year, Gehrig became a hero to countless young boys in the country. He played the game hard and true, but he was polite and respectful, embodying all the qualities parents wanted to see in their children. It was his misfortune to play in Ruth's shadow, but he did not have the Babe's flair for headlines. He represented a more working-class ethic to followers of the game.

The tragedy that eventually befell Gehrig could not have seemed more unlikely in 1927. Magnificent of physique and strength, he batted .373 and drove in 175 runs, also leading the league with 52 doubles. To drive in 175 after Ruth had sixty times cleared the bases in front of him was an incredible accomplishment. When Gehrig's playing streak finally ended, it had reached 2,130 games. It was 1939, and he was the last of the 1927 team still with the Yankees. Even so, it seemed he would continue on forever.

Combs had been with the Yankees since 1924. He was the first in the succession of great center fielders on the club, and stayed with the team as a coach after his playing days ended in 1935. His 1927 season included a .356 average on 231 hits, 23 of them triples. Along with Ruth, Gehrig, and Lazzeri, he is a Hall of Famer, giving the 1927 Yankees six players, plus Huggins and general manager Ed Barrow, in Cooperstown.

Meusel was a grumpy but effective outfielder who hit .337 and was one of four men in the lineup with over a hundred RBIs. Meusel was the source of a great line by a sportswriter. Always surly to the press,

Babe Ruth hits his 60th home run of 1927. Muddy Ruel is the catcher and Bill Dinneen is the umpire. (National Baseball Library, Cooperstown, N.Y.)

he showed up in spring training in his final season, 1930, suddenly personable and cheery. Wrote Frank Graham, in the *New York Journal*, "Bob Meusel learned to say hello, just when it was time to say good-bye."

Mark Koenig, who would be the last survivor of the '27 Yanks, played a great shortstop and hit .285. Joe Dugan, the third baseman and Ruth's closest run-around friend, hit .269.

Ruth himself was a .356 hitter in 1927, and while everyone thinks of his home runs and his combined 107 homers with Gehrig, he also drew 138 walks, scored 158 runs, and drove in 164 batters. He had a .772 slugging percentage. To put this in perspective, no one has reached .700 in the American League since 1957. Roger Maris, in 1961, slugged .620. In the National League, the last .700 slugging average was in 1948. Hank Aaron's best ever was .669.

It is said that not much fuss was made over Ruth's assault on his own home-run record of fifty-nine, and certainly it did not compare to the Maris-Mantle chase of 1961. But everybody always followed the Babe, and whatever he did was discussed. By the end of August, however, he had only forty-three home runs, and no one was thinking of a record. But in September, with the pennant already assured, the Babe got hot. He clobbered seventeen homers in the month's twenty-seven games, two of them grand slams. On September 30, the next-to-last day of the regular season, he faced Tom Zachary of Washington in Yankee Stadium, having tied his own record of fifty-nine the day before.

Zachary was a left-hander, but such things never bothered Ruth, who was certainly never platooned. He had already hit two homers off Zachary during the season, and eighteen of his fifty-nine had been off southpaws.

Ruth came up in the eighth inning with the score 2–2. Koenig, who had tripled, was on third. Ruth took a 1–1 pitch and sent it halfway up the right-field bleachers, about ten feet fair. It was caught by a forty-year-old Manhattan resident named Joe Forner. The Babe circled the bases slowly, to tremendous cheers, and as he touched home plate, the fans tossed their hats into the air and staged a confetti celebration with torn scorecards. (How much would a scorecard from that game auction for today?) When he went to his position in right, the fans waved handkerchiefs, and Babe responded with military salutes to them all.

The Washington catcher, Muddy Ruel, who had been behind the plate for the Yankees when Ray Chapman was killed seven years earlier, called the pitch a low, inside fastball. Number sixty would have been a fitting climax to a great season, but there was still a World Series to come.

The Yankees met the Pittsburgh Pirates in the Series. Shocker, back from Denver, threw batting practice and the Yankee sluggers sent tremendous drives over the walls in Forbes Field. It was said that they had already won the Series in batting practice, intimidating the Pirates before Game One began.

As it happened, the Yanks hit only two homers in the Series, both by Ruth. But they beat the Pirates in four straight, Pittsburgh getting only ten runs in the four games. The season ended with Game Four on October 8, as Wilcy Moore, the relief star, got the start and won 4–3. In the last of the ninth, with the score 3–3, Combs walked and Koenig beat out a bunt. They advanced on a wild pitch, and Ruth was intentionally walked to load the bases.

Now your name is Johnny Miljus and you are standing on the mound in Yankee Stadium in the last of the ninth. The 1927 Yankees have the bases loaded and no one out, and if you give up a run, the World Championship belongs to the Yankees.

In a terrifically heroic performance, Miljus struck out both Gehrig and Meusel, and got one strike on Lazzeri. But then, he let loose another wild pitch, Combs scored, and the 1927 Series was history. Johnny Miljus just wasn't able to halt the inevitable.

The Series was really an anticlimax in 1927. It's still the Babe's sixty home runs that define that season. To this day, one of the biggest thrills of all young players who walk into Yankee Stadium is the visit to the monuments in left-center field. It evokes an eerie sense of history. And the first monument they always look for belongs to Number 3.

15

Connie Mack
at the Summit

Had Connie Mack not owned the club he managed, the Philadelphia Athletics, he would have met the fate of almost everyone else in his profession—getting fired. It could have happened at any time, after any horrid season, but he was the boss, and he elected himself manager for fifty seasons, a mark unlikely to fall.

He managed the A's through 7,878 regular-season ball games, losing two hundred and fifty more than he won and usually suffering through second-division years. He had no source of income other than his ball club and the meager sale of concession items at the games, so whenever his team got good, he'd have to sell off his players to raise cash. What could have been a long and proud franchise existed humbly instead until the team eventually moved to Kansas City, then later to Oakland.

Born Cornelius McGillicuddy in 1862, Connie was a major league catcher during a career that began in 1886 and lasted until 1896. He became a manager in Pittsburgh in 1894 and then a 25 percent owner and founder of the American League franchise in Philadelphia in 1901. Eventually he became the sole owner, and employed his sons as coaches and executives to run one of the last mom-and-pop shops on the major league map.

He was known as Connie Mack, and his players all called him Mr.

Mack. Even in print, thirty-six years after his death, it seems wrong to say "Mack" without "Mr." He had the bearing of a gentleman who had earned the formality, and his players respected that. Even those who played for him late in his life—he managed until he was a remarkable eighty-eight—never laughed behind his back or showed any disrespect. What if his attention span was lacking or if he moved the other team's fielders with a scorecard when his own team was at bat; he was still held in high esteem. He brought a dignity to American League baseball and respect to a poor franchise, even if he couldn't bless it with long-term success.

Things started off well for the Athletics, who won three pennants in the league's first nine years and four more between 1910 and 1914. These were colorful and exciting years for Philadelphia.

That team was said to have a $100,000 infield, which was something like having a $15 million infield today. Stuffy McInnis played first, Eddie Collins second, Jack Barry short, and Home Run Baker third. Collins later starred for the White Sox, and Baker the Yankees, and both made it to Cooperstown.

The pitching staff included such great names as Chief Bender, Eddie Plank, Herb Pennock, Joe Bush, Jack Coombs, and Bob Shawkey. Coombs won 31 games in 1910 and 28 a year later. Between 1910 and 1914, the A's won 488 games, an average of 98 a season. They were the class of the league.

Then, in 1914, a third major league emerged, promising higher salaries for the better players. Although the Federal League did not put a team in Philadelphia (where the Phillies also competed), it did stage successful raids on many major league teams. With the Federal League successful enough to launch another season in 1915, Connie Mack realized he was going to be losing players anyway, so he began to sell off his great stars, to the dismay of his fans. Both Plank and Bender elected to jump the A's and join the Feds. Coombs went to Brooklyn, Collins to the White Sox, Shawkey to the Yankees, Pennock and Barry to the Red Sox. Baker sat out a year and then was sold to the Yankees in 1916.

The short dynasty crashed to an end. The Athletics, with replacement players and twenty-seven different pitchers, finished fifty-eight and a half games out, in dead last. And there they sat for the next seven seasons, barely meeting the payroll, and drawing as few as 146,000 fans one season.

By the late 1920s, for those who'd had the patience to stay with him, Mr. Mack had reassembled a strong team. The Yankees were now in their Murderers' Row period, but the Athletics proved worthy competitors, with plenty of sock of their own.

Beginning with 1925, the team finished 2–3–2–2. In 1928, the A's finished only two and a half games behind the Yankees. And then, in 1929, they dethroned them. Fifteen years Mr. Mack had waited, but what a team he had pieced together!

Jimmie Foxx, twenty-one, who would go on to hit 534 home runs, was the first baseman. He, Al Simmons in the outfield, Mickey Cochrane catching, and Lefty Grove on the mound were all Cooperstown-bound. Other A's stars of the day included infielders Jimmy Dykes and Max Bishop, outfielders Bing Miller and Mule Haas, and pitchers George Earnshaw, Rube Walberg, and Eddie Rommel.

In the first game of the 1929 World Series against the Chicago Cubs, Mr. Mack bypassed all of his great pitchers to start thirty-five-year-old Howard Ehmke, who had made only eight starts in the regular season. The move would seem less surprising today, what with League Championship Series often overworking a pitching staff. The '29 A's, however, won their pennant by eighteen games, and everyone was well rested.

So all Ehmke did was beat the Cubs 3–1 with what was then a Series-record thirteen strikeouts! Connie looked like a genius—and perhaps he was.

Earnshaw, with relief from Grove, won the second game 9–3, but the Cubs took the third game 3–1, handling Earnshaw on just a days' rest. The fourth game, in Philadelphia on October 12, shines in the record books to this day, and was by most measures the single greatest game of Connie Mack's fifty-year reign.

The Cubs were poised to even the Series when they jumped to an 8–0 lead after six and a half innings, routing old Jack Quinn, age forty-five, and Walberg and Rommel in relief. Chicago needed nine outs, and had nineteen-game-winner Charlie Root working on a three-hit shutout.

Simmons, Foxx, and Miller were the first three hitters in the seventh. These were going to be the last at-bats for the A's regulars, with Connie planning to put in his bench for the final two innings. But Simmons broke the shoutout with a leadoff homer onto the roof, and four singles followed—by Foxx, Miller, Dykes, and Joe Boley. It was 8–3.

After a pinch hitter popped up for the first out, Bishop singled home the fourth run, and Root was gone, still holding an 8–4 edge. Art Nehf came in to hurl relief.

Haas drove a liner to center that Hack Wilson misplayed in the sun, and as it rolled to the wall, Haas turned it into a three-run inside-the-park homer. It was 8–7.

There were 29,921 fans in Shibe Park that day, but no record exists showing how many had remained for the seventh inning. Those who had were seeing history.

Cochrane walked, and Sheriff Blake came in to pitch. Simmons, the tenth hitter of the inning, singled over third. Foxx singled in the tying run, and Pat Malone became the fourth pitcher of the inning for Joe McCarthy's Cubs.

The Athletics were not finished. Miller was hit by a pitch to load the bases and Dykes doubled to the left-field wall, scoring two more runs for a ten-run inning.

Malone fanned the next two hitters, but the damage of the century was done. It was the biggest inning in World Series history, and the biggest comeback as well.

Dykes, in his excitement on the bench, slapped Connie Mack on the back so hard that he knocked him into the bat rack. I've seen rallies, and comebacks, and know the kind of excitement you feel in the dugout, so I can only imagine what was going on in Philadelphia that afternoon.

Lefty Grove pitched the final two innings in relief against the stunned Cubs and retired six straight. Two afternoons later, after a rainout, the Cubs somehow managed to build and hold a 2–0 lead through eight, but in the last of the ninth against Malone, Bishop singled, Haas hit a two-run homer to tie the score, Simmons doubled, and Miller doubled him home with the World Championship run. Game, set, match. The A's were the champs after two startling finishes in Games Four and Five.

The A's repeated their championship in 1930, and won another pennant in 1931, although they lost the Series to the Cardinals. The A's were second in 1932 and third in '33, but the Depression was hitting Connie Mack harder than other owners, and again, it was time to sadly sell off his best players to meet expenses. And so Cochrane

The Athletics congratulate Bing Miller, whose two-run double in the last of the ninth of game five won the 1929 World Series, two days after the ten-run inning had first shocked the Cubs. (National Baseball Library, Cooperstown, N.Y.)

left to run the Tigers; Simmons, Earnshaw, and Haas went to the White Sox; and Grove, Miller, and Bishop were sold to the Red Sox. The great Athletics were only a memory.

After 1933, the Philadelphia Athletics never contended again. From 1935 to 1943 they were last or next to last every year. Connie Mack retired after his fiftieth season in 1950, with the team in last place and only 309,000 paid admissions. By 1955, a year before Mack died at age ninety-four, they were the Kansas City A's, and then in 1968 they went to Oakland.

Under the ownership of Charles O. Finley, the franchise was once again successful in the early 1970s. It won five consecutive Western Division titles, and three consecutive World Series from 1972 to 1974. But Finley also operated on a shoestring budget, and had difficulty drawing fans. When free agency came around in 1976, he knew he would lose his big stars. So, like Connie Mack before him, he started to sell them off and get some value back in return before he lost them. In one swoop, at the June trading deadline in 1976, he sold Vida Blue, Joe Rudi, and Rollie Fingers, three of his biggest stars. Except this time Commissioner Bowie Kuhn voided the sales, and won his point in court, arguing that the commissioner, simply exercising his power under "the best interests of baseball," can prevent a team from discarding high-salaried players. Commissioner Landis never sought to halt Connie Mack, nor was it likely that Mack would have sued if he did. History repeated, however, when Finley lost his great players— Reggie Jackson, Sal Bando, Bert Campaneris, and the rest—via the free-agent route.

Today, Canseco, McGwire, Henderson, Stewart, and Eckersley can trace their roots back to a tall, thin man in a business suit who'd seen it all, including ten runs in a World Series inning.

16

The Called-Shot Home Run

If Babe Ruth had retired when the 1920s drew to a close, his reputation as the game's most towering figure would have remained intact; generations long after ours would still have been able to call him the ultimate baseball personality. What he accomplished in the twenties— taking baseball out of the dead-ball era—would have been accomplishment enough for anyone. The game became more exciting and infinitely more appealing to American tastes.

Overweight and slow in the 1930s, Babe still rang up three historic accomplishments to add to his glory: He hit his final three home runs in one game, while playing in Pittsburgh for the Boston Braves; he hit the first All-Star Game home run in 1933; and the year before, he hit what may be his most famous homer, the "called-shot home run" off Charlie Root of the Cubs during the 1932 World Series.

The problem with the called-shot home run, of course, was that he may or may not have really done it. He was smart enough to let the legend grow. Others who were present were not unanimous in their versions. So it was part myth, part oral history that made the homer a part of the game's lore. And indeed, it transcended baseball and became an American event.

I once met a gentleman who could only have been in his teens at the time of the blast. He was not a baseball fan, but he had a general awareness of the sport. In other words, he'd heard of Ruth and Cobb, but never of Hornsby or Speaker.

In speaking about Ruth one day, he remarked, "Oh, Ruth, he was special. Used to 'call' every one of his homers before he'd hit 'em.''

The Babe would have loved that story. Talk about creating a legend!

It was bench-jockeying that was at the "root" of the confrontation between Ruth and Root on that Saturday, October 1, 1932. The Yankees were meeting the Cubs in Wrigley Field in their first trip to the World Series since 1928. It was their first pennant under Joe McCarthy, who had been fired by the Cubs two years earlier. (We tend to think of the Yankees of that era as invincible, but this was their only pennant between 1928 and 1936.)

As often occurs in a World Series, one of the combatants was a former member of the opposing team. Mark Koenig, shortstop on the Murderers' Row Yankees of the twenties, was now winding down his career as a role player with the Cubs, who had purchased him from the Pacific Coast League in August. He was tapped to replace regular shortstop Billy Jurges, who had been shot by a showgirl in his hotel. During the season, Koenig had been a big contributor, hitting .353 in thirty-three games, and the Cubs had voted him a half share of their Series money. This being known before the Series even began, the Yankees decided that their old buddy had been cheated by the "cheap-skate" Cubs.

The practice of voting on World Series shares for players who spend only fractions of seasons with a team is still around today, and is just as controversial. On the surface, a half share for six weeks with a team seems adequate, but the struggle to quantify a player's actual contribution within a particular time frame has never been clearly resolved. Koenig had some key hits in the final days of the season. If the situation had occurred today, the same debate might have resulted.

Many of Koenig's former Yankee teammates were still around to lend support to their old buddy. Besides Ruth, there were Lou Gehrig, Tony Lazzeri, Earle Combs, Bill Dickey, and Herb Pennock. The identities of the principal bench jockeys are not important, however, because that's been part of baseball since the game began.

It was the return banter from the Cubs' dugout that seemed to get to Ruth. Because he was raised in an orphanage, his ancestry was a frequent source of taunts, and when it got personal, Ruth's fuse could be lit.

The Yankees had won the first two Series games in New York, and now the scene had shifted to Chicago. Nearly fifty thousand jammed into Wrigley Field; these were the days before strict fire laws were enforced. One of them was a fan named Matt Kandle, seated about twenty rows back to the left of home plate, with a perfect view of left-hand batters. Kandle, a printer, was armed with a new 16-millimeter home movie camera from Kodak. This was to prove fortunate. (Another fan that day was New York Governor Franklin D. Roosevelt, who would be elected president the following month.)

Ruth, age thirty-seven, came up with two on in the first and promptly put the Yankees ahead 3–0 with a drive into the Wrigley Field bleachers. The fans, caught up in the spirit of bad feeling, pelted him with lemons when he took his position in left field in the last of the first. Babe tossed them back good-naturedly.

In the fourth, Jurges, recovered and back in action, blooped one into left. Ruth tried for a shoestring catch and missed, further prompting jeers from the fans.

A few minutes later, Ruth came up with one out in the fifth. The score was now 4–4, with Root still on the mound. Root had been 15–10 in the regular season, his eighth in the majors. The players used to have fun with the names Ruth and Root, particularly since Colonel Jacob Ruppert, the Yankee owner, pronounced Ruth "Root" with a German accent. But this was no time for levity on the field. The Cubs were down by two games, and desperately needed a win.

The first pitch was a called strike. Like the Mighty Casey in "Casey at the Bat," Ruth treated it as if to say "that ain't my style" and held up one finger, apparently signaling, "That's one!"

After two balls, the fourth pitch was again a called strike. At this point, legend has it, Ruth again made some hand or finger gesture to acknowledge that he was in control. Lou Gehrig, on deck, said Ruth yelled something to Root about knocking the next pitch down his throat. If he did, it is likely the gesture was aimed at Root, not at the bleachers.

The next delivery was to Ruth's liking. As we have seen thousands of times on old newsreels (although never actually a newsreel of this particular homer), the Babe uncorked his torso and flung that heavy bat of his into the pitch with great authority. In an instant, the ball soared once again into the bleachers for his second homer of the game, and the fifteenth and last of his World Series career. He circled the bases

Lou Gehrig (number 4) congratulates Babe Ruth after his "called-shot home run" in the 1932 World Series. Gabby Hartnett is the catcher, and Roy Van Graflan is the umpire. (Wide World Photos)

with relish, gesturing toward the Cubs' silent bench. (Typically, Gehring followed with a homer, forgotten now by baseball fans, as was much of his work. The Babe always cast a long shadow. No doubt many weren't even watching Root pitch to Gehrig.)

Did Ruth actually point to the bleachers? Some newspapers completely ignored the event the next day. The players themselves, almost all of whom were interviewed on the subject over the years, gave conflicting stories. Root said, "No way," adding, "If he had pointed to the bleachers, I would have knocked him down on the next pitch."

Gabby Hartnett, the catcher, thought he *did* point. So did Gehrig. Joe Sewell, who batted in front of Ruth for the Yankees, thought he had pointed to the Cubs' bench. Charlie Grimm, the Cubs' manager, thought Ruth had pointed at the mound.

The Babe, ever the great showman, allowed the story to grow that he'd made the gesture to the bleachers. His own version of the tale became more dramatic with each telling. And so the question of "did he or didn't he" remained a lovable baseball tale for half a century.

And then in 1982, Matt Kandle's son Kirk, taking advantage of the ability of videotape to capture old home movies, had his father's old films converted. Sure enough, his father had captured the gesture from his seat in Wrigley. Kirk tried to interest *Sports Illustrated* in the film in the seventies, but the magazine couldn't capture a frame for reproduction. A decade later, the technology was in place.

The results of the film-to-tape transfer seem definitive. *The Sporting News* published the photos, which clearly show that the Babe pointed not once but four times, including two distinct gestures immediately prior to the pitch.

To find such photographic evidence after so many years is almost like finding film of John Wilkes Booth shooting Lincoln. Imagine that it existed for so long—precise evidence that this mythical event was not mythology!

Root went to his grave in 1970 denying that Ruth had ever showed him up so badly. I think it is safe to say that Ruth's greatest moment of bravado was backed up by performance. He rose to the occasion. The Yanks won the game 12–6, and the next day made it a four-game sweep. Gehrig hit .529 with three homers and eight RBIs in the four games, but wasn't that the story of Lou's life? The 1932 World Series will forever be the one in which Ruth called his homer.

Every young man who plays the game of baseball and is fortunate enough to make it to the big leagues lives, to one degree or another, with the legend of Babe Ruth. If he doesn't relate to the history of the game, he is shortchanging himself.

During my rookie season with the New York Mets in 1967, the team traveled to Pittsburgh for a series with the Pirates, and I visited the site where the Babe hit the last three home runs of his historical career.

A small plaque on the right-field wall of old Forbes Field commemorated the site of home runs number 712, 713, and 714, hit on May 25, 1935—providing a moving experience for the young athlete who takes the time to appreciate the history of his trade.

17

Gehrig Outdoes the Babe

The Lou Gehrig story, a tale that children still love to read about, is remarkable for the fallacies we hold sacred. The mythical Gehrig represents durability and longevity, but the whole truth lies elsewhere. His feat of playing in 2,130 consecutive games seems to span so many years that one forgets we are talking about only fifteen of them—a fleeting moment in most lifetimes.

But there he was, a teammate of Everett Scott, Babe Ruth, Joe Dugan, Aaron Ward, Bob Shawkey, and Herb Pennock at the start; Joe DiMaggio, Lefty Gomez, Joe Gordon, Tommy Henrich, and Red Ruffing at the finish. Always Gehrig, 1b, in the Yankee lineup.

He was the Iron Horse, the powerful, muscular gentleman whose body possessed the strength we associate today with weight training. But we know better; players of Gehrig's era did not work out with weights, because it was considered bad for them.

So Lou's fifteen years were, in their own way, meteoric. One day he was a New York street kid, the next he was a teammate of Babe Ruth, and then they were burying him before he was forty.

Born to German immigrant parents in the melting pot of New York City, Gehrig was academically gifted enough to attend Columbia University. But as they say that priests get "the calling," so too did Gehrig get a "calling," one that beckoned him into professional baseball. In 1921, at eighteen, he played a dozen games at first for

Hartford of the Eastern League under the name of Lewis. The alias was intended to protect his eligibility for college ball, while providing him with much-needed money for college expenses.

For a local product playing at Columbia to escape the eyes of Paul Krichell, the Yankees' chief scout, would have taken a miracle. These were the days before computerized scouting and a draft, when the best teams had the best scouts and a good scout could make the difference for a franchise for decades. It was a long era that ended just before I turned pro in 1966; the first draft of amateur players, signaling the end of the power of the scouting era, came in 1965. (I'm not implying that scouting is unimportant today. The human factor in talent evaluation is still significant, but it's now only one factor among many when a team makes a draft selection.)

When Krichell signed Gehrig to a Yankee contract in 1923, Gehrig was not joining a dynasty. He was coming to a team that had won two pennants and was about to move into its own ballpark, Yankee Stadium. The first baseman, Wally Pipp, was one of the best players on the team. He had been a Yankee regular since Jacob Ruppert had bought the team in 1915; he had led the league in home runs twice, and had batted as high as .329, for the pennant-winning Yanks of 1922. But Pipp was thirty, and it couldn't hurt for the Yankees to have a younger backup available at first.

The opportunity to move into the starting lineup came unexpectedly on June 2, 1925, when Pipp was unable to play, having been beaned during batting practice by a Princeton hurler named Charlie Caldwell. From that incident has risen a popular legend that Pipp had a "headache" or had even "claimed a headache but went to the racetrack." The fact was that he was out and that Gehrig, who had the good fortune to hit safely in his first three trips to the plate, was in. Manager Miller Huggins had seen the future and seized it. Pipp played a few more games in 1925, but never started at first, and went to Cincinnati in 1926, his Yankee career over.

The day before he replaced Pipp, Gehrig had begun his playing streak by pinch-hitting for shortstop Pee Wee Wanninger. (Just twenty-five days earlier, Wanninger had replaced Everett Scott at short, ending Scott's then record playing streak of 1,307.) Gehrig had been on the bench that day; now he was in the lineup, and although nobody knew it, he wouldn't leave until long after every 1925 Yankee had retired.

Lou Gehrig

Great as he was, Gehrig, of course, found himself in the shadow of the flamboyant Babe Ruth, who always seemed to dwarf his accomplishments, mighty though they were. Fortunately, Gehrig was as reserved as Ruth was outgoing, and jealousies never jeopardized their performances in the 3 and 4 spots in the lineup.

Gehrig's first two seasons as a regular produced 36 home runs to Ruth's 72. They were not truly spoken of as a one-two punch until that great 1927 season when Ruth hit 60 and Gehrig 47. From that point on, Gehrig topped the 40 mark five times and drove in countless runs, even with Ruth so often clearing the bases in front of him.

In '27 Gehrig drove in 175. In 1930 he had 174. In 1931 he ran after Hack Wilson's major league record of 190, set the year before, and drove in 184, still an American League record. And this he accomplished despite Ruth's batting in 163 runners in front of him.

Friday, June 3, 1932, or two days after the seventh anniversary of the start of his playing streak, can be loosely regarded as a midway point in Gehrig's career. It would be another year before he broke Scott's record, but frankly, no one was yet counting. It was an age before we lived and breathed baseball statistics by the hour.

The Yankees were in Shibe Park, Philadelphia, to face Connie Mack's Athletics, second-place finishers that season. The A's had won in 1929–30–31 and still had great pitchers like Lefty Grove, George Earnshaw, and Rube Walberg on the staff. This was Earnshaw's day to pitch.

In the first inning, with a man on, Gehrig belted a homer to right. It gave the Yanks a brief 2–0 lead, but the A's tied it in their half of the first. Gehrig came up in the fourth and did it again, also to right, also off Earnshaw. The Yanks led 4–2.

Philly scored six in the fourth for an 8–4 lead, and then Gehrig came up in the fifth, found another Earnshaw pitch to his liking, and belted his third homer to right.

He was now the first man in history to hit three in a game on four occasions. But this was only the fifth inning! The writers reached for the record books, where they found Bobby Lowe, Boston, N.L., 1894, four consecutive homers in one game. The only one. Ed Delahanty of the Phillies had four in a game in 1896, but not consecutively. Four in a game had not been recorded in the twentieth century, not even by Babe Ruth, who walked too much to get four swings in a game.

The score was now 8–7, A's, with relief pitcher Roy Mahaffey on the mound for Gehrig's fourth at-bat in the seventh inning. Like Earnshaw, Mahaffey was a right-hander. Gehrig hit left-handed.

Lou selected a nice fat one and sent it sailing to the opposite field. It came to rest over the left-field fence for his fourth home run of the game, the first time the American League had ever witnessed such a moment.

Lou grounded out in the eighth, but in the ninth, off Eddie Rommel, he belted one to deep center, where Al Simmons hauled it in at the wall, leaping high for the grab. Had Gehrig pulled it just a little, it could have been a fifth homer, a record that would still be standing alone today.

The Yankees won the slugfest 20–13, with Gehrig driving in six runs and additional homers coming from Ruth, Combs, and Lazzeri, with Tony's being a grand slam. Mickey Cochrane and Jimmie Foxx homered for the A's, meaning that nine home runs were hit that afternoon, and all nine were hit by future Hall of Famers. There were seventy-seven total bases (on thirty-six hits), a record that still stands. It was not a bad day to take in a ball game, although the attendance was barely five thousand.

But for Gehrig, the man who spent a career first in Ruth's shadow and later in DiMaggio's, here was a feat once again overshadowed. For back in New York, John McGraw, manager of the Giants for thirty-two years, unexpectedly resigned, turning over the team to Bill Terry. In the ultimate irony, McGraw's news knocked Gehrig out of the headlines on his greatest day at the plate.

Gehrig did ultimately manage to have the spotlight to himself, however briefly. Ruth left the Yankees after the 1934 season; DiMaggio arrived in 1936 (and had one of the greatest rookie seasons in history). So in 1935, Lou stood alone in the middle of the Yankee lineup, the stage all his. But he failed to have one of his biggest years, batting a "mere" .329 with thirty homers and 119 RBIs—numbers a player would ordinarily die for.

Since the Baseball Writers Association began balloting in 1931, no one has ever won four MVP awards. Gehrig won the MVP in 1936 and had earned an equivalent honor in 1927. He was also named Player of the Year by *The Sporting News* in 1931 and 1934. That sounds pretty close to four MVP seasons to me.

It all ended for Gehrig, of course, on April 30, 1939, in Detroit. Clearly ailing, his weight falling, his uniform ill-fitting, his batting average .143, he told Joe McCarthy to take him out of the lineup. The streak of 2,130 was over. No one knew on that date that he would never play again. But he was a doomed man, struck down by amyotrophic lateral sclerosis, "Lou Gehrig's disease," which remains to this day a mystery to medical science.

Lou Gehrig Appreciation Day, on July 4, 1939—the prototype of the modern Old Timers Day—was one of the most emotional events in baseball history. It was the day a dying Gehrig told baseball fans, "Today I consider myself the luckiest man on the face of the earth." He was talking about having had the opportunity to play baseball and be a part of so many great moments. No one has ever expressed a love for the game with such eloquence. Lou prepared the remarks himself, long before speech-writing became a function of public relations.

There are few historical moments in baseball that will bring a hush, an eerie quiet, to a clubhouse. One of those moments unfailingly occurs when players are lounging in their "office," maybe watching the "Game of the Week" (or game of every two weeks), and an old film clip shows Lou Gehrig speaking those thirteen words. It is as if time comes to a halt with a piece of history that's somehow more important than the game itself.

Lou's suffering ended with his death on June 2, 1941, sixteen years to the day that he'd replaced Wally Pipp. He was only thirty-seven years old.

18

Five for King Carl

Some sixty All-Star Games have been played since the first one in 1933, but remarkably few have been "memorable," although many have provided "memorable moments." Then again, sixty games is only about two months' worth of baseball over a regular season, and it is not particularly unusual to go that long without a memorable game. So those who feel that players just "go through the motions" in All-Star Games and don't play to win are wrong. In fact, having had the good fortune of being chosen for twelve of the games, I can assure you that a play-to-win attitude always exists once the game begins. No other sport puts on an all-star show like baseball does.

Probably the quintessential memory dates back to July 10, 1934— only the second All-Star Game. It took place in New York's Polo Grounds, where the National League's starting pitcher was the Giants' thirty-one-year-old left-hander Carl Hubbell. He was master of the screwball, as had been his predecessor in Giant history, Christy Mathewson. (In Mathewson's day, it was called a fadeaway.)

It was fitting that Hubbell should perform his All-Star magic in his own home ballpark, just as years later, Pete Rose would crash into Ray Fosse for the winning run in the 1970 All-Star Game in his. You can't tell me that playing in front of your own fans doesn't add something special. Hank Aaron homered in the 1972 game in front of his own fans of Atlanta, another example.

The starting lineup for the American League in 1934 was: Charlie Gehringer, 2b; Heinie Manush, lf; Babe Ruth, rf; Lou Gehrig, 1b; Jimmie Foxx, 3b; Al Simmons, cf; Joe Cronin, ss; Bill Dickey, c; and Lefty Gomez, p. Good lineup? Each of those players is in the Hall of Fame today. Mickey Cochrane and Red Ruffing, who also entered the game for the AL, are enshrined too.

The National League roster included future Hall of Famers Frankie Frisch, Pie Traynor, Travis Jackson, Bill Terry, Joe Medwick, Chuck Klein, Kiki Cuyler, Mel Ott, Paul Waner, Arky Vaughan, Gabby Hartnett, Al Lopez, Dizzy Dean, and Hubbell.

Twenty-five future Hall of Famers in one box score.

Of course, there was no Hall of Fame yet. The first election would not be held for another two years, with the building at Cooperstown, New York, dedicated in 1939. But it didn't take a genius to know there were an awful lot of "immortals" on the field that day.

Incidentally, the term "Hall of Fame" had been used before to describe a status reached by the game's earlier greats. In Florida one year I met old Roger Peckinpaugh, who played from 1910 to 1933. He showed me a yellowed, frayed newspaper clipping that identified him as a "Hall of Famer." That was good enough for Peck, who, although never voted into Cooperstown, considered himself to be in the Hall of Fame based on the newspaper column. And who could argue?

Getting back to that afternoon in 1934, 48,363 fans were expecting a display of American League power, the "junior circuit" having become the stronger of the two on the strength of the long ball. But Hubbell, who was 21–12 that season with a league-leading 2.30 ERA, was certainly the sort of pitcher who could stop the power hitters. His screwball was unlike anything they were used to seeing. (Twelve losses with a 2.30 ERA must have meant little hitting support on many occasions for Carl.)

But when Gehringer singled and Manush walked, it looked as if he could be in for a tough first inning. His infield, which included three player-managers at the time in Terry, Frisch, and Traynor, moved in to settle him down.

Up came Ruth, who had hit the first All-Star Game home run a year earlier. Babe was thirty-nine now, with 699 career home runs, but could, as they say in clubhouse meetings, "be pitched to." He'd batted just .288 in 1934, but had struck out only sixty-three times.

The screwball was not what he was looking for to power one out of

Carl Hubbell (Wide World Photos)

his old home ballpark. He took three in a row for called strikes and headed back to the dugout. Hubbell's catcher, Hartnett, laughed as he threw the ball back to the mound. Even Ruth smiled.

Gehrig was next. At thirty-one, he was at his peak. He would lead the league that season with a .363 average, and would strike out just thirty-one times the whole year, despite being a free-swinging slugger.

It only took four pitches to get him, the fourth being the low screwball, which Gehrig swung at and missed. There were two out, and the fans were loving it.

Muscular Jimmie Foxx stepped up. The runners were now on second and third with two out, a double steal having advanced them. As Gehrig passed Foxx, he said, "You might as well cut . . . it won't get any higher."

Foxx's mind was probably a little preoccupied that day, by virtue of his being positioned at third base so that both he and Gehrig could be in the lineup. Foxx played only nine games at third that year, and he did not want to embarrass himself. Only twenty-six years old, he was already in his tenth big-league season with the Philadelphia A's, and would hit .334 that year.

Now, with the screwball working wonders, Hartnett kept calling for it, and Jimmie went down swinging, too. The NL was out of the jam.

Frisch homered leading off the last of the first, so Hubbell had a 1–0 edge to work with as he took the mound in the second. The first hitter was Al Simmons of the White Sox. Al, thirty-two, was a tremendous hitter, despite a habit of stepping in the bucket, a propensity considered fatal for most hitters. He was a .344 hitter that year, with only fifty-eight strikeouts.

Simmons went down swinging. The players and the fans were really into what was happening at this point, not so much for the consecutive strikeouts as for the way in which the much-publicized screwball was baffling the hitters.

Cronin was up. He was the team's player-manager that day, having led the Senators into the 1933 World Series. At twenty-seven, he'd be a .284 hitter for the season and strike out only twenty-eight times. Good contact hitter. Hard to fool.

Strike three, swinging. Screwball.

Five in a row! Incredible!

Dickey, the next batter, hit an inside pitch for a single to snap the streak. Gomez, up ninth, struck out to end the inning.

Lefty was one of the funniest, most personable men who ever played the game. For years afterward he would get all over Dickey for the base hit. "If you'd only struck out," he said, "then it would have been Ruth, Gehrig, Foxx, Simmons, Cronin, Dickey, and Gomez. I would have been lumped in there with the great hitters!"

The magnitude of Hubbell's feat did not have to grow over the years. It was appreciated right at the moment and became the hallmark of his great career from that time on. The eventual Hall of Fame elections only confirmed what everyone knew at the time—these were legendary players who'd been cut down by this thin southpaw.

Although Hubbell's performance was the big story of the 1934 game, the American League did rally to win 9–7 once it got him out of there. How good the pitching of Lon Warneke and Van Lingle Mungo must have looked after Carl, as the AL scored eight runs off them in the next two innings.

Fifty-two years later, in the Astrodome, Hubbell's record of five consecutive All-Star Game strikeouts was tied by another screwball pitcher, the Dodgers' Fernando Valenzuela. Relieving Doc Gooden in the fourth inning, trailing 2–0, Fernando struck out Don Mattingly, Cal Ripken Jr., and Jesse Barfield. In the fifth, he fanned Lou Whitaker and pitcher Teddy Higuera before Kirby Puckett grounded out.

Although the record had been tied, Fernando's accomplishment was never heralded as Hubbell's had been. With all due respect to Fernando and to anyone who makes the starting lineup in an All-Star Game, the quality of his five hitters was clearly not the equal of those in the 1934 lineup. The exceptions were Mattingly and Ripken, who may well be Hall of Famers themselves someday. Higuera, victim of the record-tying fifth consecutive strikeout, had never batted before in the major leagues, with the possible exception of spring training. This was a case of creating a mismatched situation, sending pitchers out to hit when the league had a designated-hitter rule during the regular season. Higuera knew what was coming—he was a screwball-throwing Mexican just like Valenzuela—but he was helpless at the plate.

Hubbell was eighty-three and in failing health when Valenzuela matched his record, and watched the game on television at his Arizona home. After his career was over, he spent the rest of his life on the Giants' payroll, first as scouting supervisor and director of player development, then finally as an "honorary scout" in the years before his death in 1988. Whenever I think of him, I visualize a famous photograph that seems to say, "If you want to look like this, kid, with your pitching arm turned outward almost a hundred and eighty degrees, just go out there and throw screwballs for twenty years." There are few photographs in sports journalism that are as meaningful to a pitcher as that classic shot of Carl Hubbell.

19

Gashouse Gang Follies

For weeks, Carl Hubbell's All-Star strikeout feat was the talk of baseball, but then attention switched inevitably to the 1934 National League pennant race. It was a thing of beauty. Hubbell's Giants were playing so well that manager Bill Terry, asked about the Dodgers, said, "Are they still in the league?" They were, and they would be competitive for much of the season.

In St. Louis a wondrous team had come together, perhaps the most colorful in all of baseball history. The Cardinal players were blessed with nicknames like Pepper, Ducky, Dizzy, Ripper, Daffy, the Fordham Flash, Wild Bill, Sunny Jim, and Leo the Lip, and they were collectively called the Gashouse Gang because their shortstop, Leo the Lip Durocher, told a sportswriter that they were just a bunch of gashouse players—whatever that meant.

Without a doubt, the most flamboyant member of this remarkable ball club was Dizzy Dean, a character who might have fit in better in the 1890s than the 1930s. Years later, when I was just a kid, I think that my first physical association with baseball, other than reading the box scores and averages in the *Fresno Bee*, was probably not a player but Dizzy Dean on television. I can still see him wearing his cowboy hat and singing phrases from the "Wabash Cannonball." After that, baseball started to become a game made up of people, not just names and numbers in a box score.

Possessed of little education but loads of bravado and self-confidence, Dizzy boasted that he and his quiet brother Paul ("Daffy") would win forty-five games for the Cardinals in 1934. That Paul was an untried rookie hardly mattered. Dizzy won thirty and Daffy nineteen to top Dizzy's own expectations. (No one in the National League has since won thirty games in a season.) On September 21, they combined to beat the Dodgers twice in a doubleheader, Diz hurling a three-hitter in the opener, and Paul firing a no-hitter in the nightcap.

Said Dizzy, "If I'd a knowed that [Paul would pitch a no-hitter], I'd of pitched me one too!"

With two games left in the season, the Dodgers knocked off the Giants (naturally) and the Cardinals, who had trailed by seven on Labor Day, snuck in to win their first pennant since 1930.

In the American League, the Detroit Tigers were ending a twenty-five-year drought with their first pennant since the Ty Cobb days of 1909. They were led by catcher-manager Mickey Cochrane, Hank Greenberg, Charlie Gehringer, and Goose Goslin.

Anyone neutral about the World Series had to love the Cardinals. Radio had only in recent years begun to broadcast baseball games, and the Cardinals' antics had entertained the nation. Sportscasters loved telling, or inventing, tales of wonder out of St. Louis. If there were any Americans left who didn't like the Cardinals, it appeared they were all residing in Detroit, rooting for their own guys once the Series began.

Cardinal games had been on the radio since 1929, but the 1934 World Series would send this team over the nation's airwaves on both the NBC and CBS networks. The Cardinals were created, it seemed, to satisfy the nation's hunger for pleasure during the darkest days of the Depression. It was as though the madcap Gashouse Gang was somehow immune to cares and woes while on the baseball diamond. The Tigers, on the other hand, came from a factory town deep in unemployment, and the people lived the way Gehringer played second— without smiling.

The Series opened in Detroit with Dizzy Dean going all the way for an easy 8–3 win. After St. Louis lost the second game, Daffy, the rookie, stopped Detroit 4–1 in Game Three. Again the Tigers got even in Game Four. This was the game in which Dizzy was inserted as a pinch runner, then struck in the head and knocked out on a relay throw to first. Diz recovered after being taken to the hospital, then told the press, "They took X rays of my head and saw nothing."

The pattern broke in Game Five when Tommy Bridges defeated Dizzy 3–1, but Daffy kept the Cardinals alive in Game Six, winning his second, 4–3, with the go-ahead run scoring in the seventh on a double by Durocher and a base hit by Paul Dean himself.

So the stage was set for the seventh game, with over forty thousand people filling Navin Field, the same ballpark Cobb had played in, the same ballpark Al Kaline, Denny McLain, Mark Fidrych, and Cecil Fielder would later call home as Tiger Stadium. In left field, filling long wooden bleachers, were some eighteen thousand of the fans, witnesses to the game though a steel screen.

"Fordham Flash" Frankie Frisch, the second baseman and manager of St. Louis, had Wild Bill Hallahan well rested since the second game, but he chose to go with Dizzy on two day's rest, and Diz would have wanted it no other way. His baby brother having already won twice, the competitive juices were flowing.

What transpired in Game Seven would be called by Paul Gallico in New York's *Daily News* "the dizziest, maddest, wildest and most exciting World Series game played in recent years."

Eldon Auker pitched for the Tigers, and he and Dean were scoreless after two. In the third, however, the Cardinals exploded for seven runs, aided by two hits off Dean's own bat and a bases-loaded double by Frisch. It was a devastating inning for the Tigers and their faithful. One can only imagine the silence in the stands as Cochrane changed pitchers three times in the inning, all to no avail. It was apparent that the first World Championship for the city of Detroit would have to "wait till next year."

Still, down as they were, the Tigers had to keep playing. In the top of the sixth, with two out, Joe "Ducky" Medwick tripled off the right-center-field bleachers to score Pepper Martin and make it 8–0. Sliding into third, Medwick was apparently spiked by the Tigers' third baseman, Marv Owen. Whether the injury was intentional has never been determined, but Medwick answered back with a double leg kick at Owen. As would be expected, they soon came to blows, and when order had been restored by third-base umpire Bill Klem and some coaches, Medwick extended a hand toward Owen as though to apologize. Owen did not accept it and returned to his position. The inning continued and Medwick scored the ninth run, as Klem had not seen fit to eject either player.

As soon as Medwick reached his position in left field, the frustration of the fans turned to anger. A wave of booing erupted from the left-field bleachers. One fan threw a red apple onto the field. Medwick fielded it and gently lobbed it back toward the bleacher wall. Suddenly, as though prompted by the first apple, fans began hurling bananas, oranges, and more apples, plus bottles of beer and soda. It got very ugly.

In an era long before helmets, Medwick held his ground, but then moved toward the infield. After five minutes of continued pelting by the fans, he returned to left, only to find the fury still raging. Someone threw a full milk bottle. Obviously, the fans had come prepared with lunches and were using the contents of their brown bags to assault Medwick. To the fans' credit, it can be said that they had self-control to have all of this food left by the sixth inning.

Again Medwick headed for the infield, as workers tried to pick up the debris from left field. Fans were yelling, "Take him out! Take him out!" and the police were doing nothing to quiet them. Ironically, if St. Louis had been awarded the victory by forfeit, it would have gone in the books as a 9–0 Cardinal win, such being the forfeit rules—and the actual score at the time was 9–0 St. Louis.

Commissioner Landis, present at all World Series games, observed the action from his seat near the first-base dugout. He called for Medwick, Owen, and the two managers, Frisch and Cochrane. He asked Owen if the original action was intentional, and was told no. Medwick admitted kicking Owen.

Landis looked at the score and recognized the black eye baseball would receive if he awarded the World Championship to St. Louis on a forfeit. So he personally removed Medwick from the game, in what was probably the only time a player was ever ejected for his own protection. No one in St. Louis offered a protest.

The Cardinals went on to a lopsided 11–0 victory and the World Championship, as Dizzy joined his brother with two wins each in the Series. Medwick, eventually a Hall of Fame player, would forever be remembered for the bizarre episode that, after his departure, turned into a huge and laughable pillow fight, as the fans began hurling seat cushions at each other.

Strange to say, history almost repeated itself thirty-nine years later at Shea Stadium, in an era thought to be more civilized. It took an old-time type of player, Pete Rose, to bring it about. The event was the

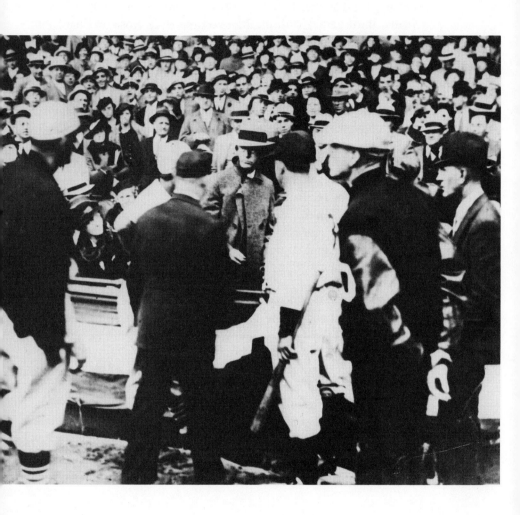

Commissioner Landis consults with managers and umpires before deciding to remove
Joe Medwick from the final game of the 1934 World Series.

1973 National League Championship Series between the Big Red Machine, the Cincinnati Reds, and my team, the New York Mets.

In the third game, with the Mets on top 9–2, Rose slid hard into Buddy Harrelson at second base, trying to break up a double play. The two came up fighting, with Rose getting the better of it, Buddy weighing only a hundred and fifty pounds. When the inning ended, Rose returned to, of all places, left field.

The Shea Stadium fans, not to be outdone by the long-departed faithful of Navin Field, began hurling garbage at Rose. There were paper cups and scorecards, but also a whiskey bottle and other hard matter. Rose headed for the dugout and Sparky Anderson ordered his team off the field, prepared to request the game be forfeited if the crowd could not be controlled.

We had a 9–2 lead, and that was the last thing we needed. League President Chub Feeney asked Yogi Berra and Willie Mays to walk toward left field and appeal for calm. Berra was our manager, and Willie, in his final season, our center fielder. I followed with Rusty Staub and Cleon Jones, and all we did was raise our arms a little as though to say, "Easy, easy." And somehow, it worked. Rose even managed to continue in the game in left field, but further enraged tempers the next day by homering and raising his arm in victory as he circled the bases.

Pete would be forever booed in New York afterward, but we beat the Reds that year after winning only eighty-two games in the regular season, and went seven games in the World Series before losing to Oakland. Just as people remember the '34 series for Medwick, so too do people remember postseason play in '73 for the Rose-Harrelson brawl.

20

Vander Meer, Twice

Johnny Vander Meer.

Oh yeah, the fellow who pitched two no-hitters in a row.

I suppose that's what Johnny has heard a lot since he performed that little bit of artistry more than a half century ago. Maybe it's taken too much for granted. Maybe it needs to be set in perspective.

No one did it before and no one has done it since. There have been more than 130 no-hitters since he did it, and each one set the stage for a duplication of the feat. You're talking about over a hundred pitchers (some had more than one no-hitter) coming off outstanding performances, "in the groove," and every one, including me, failing.

Can you imagine anyone ever breaking the record and hurling *three* in a row?

No-hitters, of course, involve luck as well as skill. Many pitchers who have thrown them will tell you it was not their best game. I never hurled one for the Mets, with whom I had my best seasons, but I came close a few times and finally got one with Cincinnati in 1978.

I didn't think it was the best game I ever pitched. I always thought that took place in the middle of the '69 pennant race against the first-place Cubs at Shea. The bottom line showed a one-hitter with no walks, ten strikeouts, and a 4–0 victory. My father had planned a business trip from California and "just so happened" to arrive in New

York that day, but the importance of achieving that kind of performance in a pennant race, at home in front of fifty thousand people, made it the number one game of my 647 big-league starts.

But, yes, it was Cincinnati where I pitched my no-hitter, and that was the city of Johnny Vander Meer.

Johnny was a kid from the suburbs of New York, who rooted for the Giants and Carl Hubbell as a youngster before signing with Brooklyn in 1932. He had some ordinary minor-league records during the Depression years, when the team would sometimes withhold part of his pay and ask him, "What do you need to get by?" A contract dispute over title to the left-hander found him freed from the Dodgers and made property of Scranton, Pa. Scranton sold him to the Boston Braves, who in turn sold him in 1936 to the Durham Bulls, property of Cincinnati. The deal was made by the Reds' general manager, Larry MacPhail. Ironically, Vander Meer's two no-hitters would come against Boston and Brooklyn, both former owners. And Brooklyn, by 1938, was run by MacPhail.

In 1936 Vander Meer was 19–6 with 295 strikeouts at Durham and the first winner of *The Sporting News* Minor League Player of the Year award. He started 1937 with the Reds but had to go back to Syracuse for more seasoning, so his rookie year in the majors showed a 3–5 record in nineteen games, certainly a disappointment after Durham.

During spring training of 1938, when Johnny was twenty-three, coach Hank Gowdy told him to watch Boston's Lefty Grove at work. Smart choice. Grove's style made an impression on Vander Meer, and he moved into the Reds' starting rotation with Paul Derringer and Bucky Walters. He was on his way.

On June 11, Johnny, with a 5–2 record and a league-leading fifty-two strikeouts, was named to start in Cincinnati against the Boston Bees, formerly and in the future the Braves and managed by Casey Stengel. The Saturday afternoon contest drew only 5,814 paying customers (plus 4,497 Knothole Day youngsters who'd been admitted free), but they were treated to a dandy performance, with Johnny walking only three batters as he moved easily through the Boston lineup. A close call came in the fourth when Vince DiMaggio, Joe's older brother, lined one off Johnny's glove, but third baseman Lew Riggs was able to throw DiMaggio out at first.

There hadn't been a no-hitter by a Red pitcher since Hod Eller had thrown one during the team's World Championship season of 1919, and the fans were cheering with every pitch in the ninth. Stengel sent up three pinch hitters, but Vander Meer got them all, including Ray Mueller, the last batter, who grounded to third. Johnny was now in the record books with the first no-hitter of the '38 season.

With three days' rest, Johnny got his next start at Ebbets Field in Brooklyn on Wednesday, June 15. Unlike the Saturday game, this one was played to an overflow crowd of more than thirty-eight thousand, with some fifteen thousand turned away. Seven hundred fans came from Johnny's hometown of Midland Park, N.J. But Johnny was not the only reason for the sellout; it was the first night game in New York history. The Dodgers were only the second team to install lights after the Reds (1935), and the common thread was the presence of Larry MacPhail, a master showman, who had moved from the Reds to the Dodgers.

MacPhail, typically, had created a circuslike atmosphere for the first night game, complete with pregame festivities featuring races with Olympic champion Jesse Owens. Babe Ruth, a coach with the Dodgers that season, was on hand. The game itself didn't begin until after nine-thirty, when the lights would have maximum effect, nor end until nearly midnight, a most unusual occurrence in 1930s baseball. Vander Meer's parents were even on hand, but they knew little about baseball.

Burleigh Grimes, the last legal spitballer, was the Dodgers' manager. He would be succeeded the following year by his scrappy short-stop, Leo Durocher, who batted eighth in the Dodger lineup that evening. The lineup also included former Pirate great Kiki Cuyler in right, Cookie Lavagetto at third, and slugger Dolf Camilli at first. But it was a seventh-place ball club, and welcomed the presence of lights and the ballyhoo that went with Vander Meer's "coming off a no-hitter" publicity. These were Depression times for attendance; the Dodgers averaged only about 9,300 a game that year.

Brooklyn fans being among the game's most knowledgeable, they were probably talking "no-hitter" by the third inning, after Vander Meer had gotten six outs without allowing a base hit. The Reds scored four times in the third, which put all the focus on Johnny's quest as the game progressed.

He was not sharp. Lacking his best stuff and his good control, he might have been lifted by manager Bill McKechnie under ordinary circumstances. But, he kept working out of jams and had his shutout intact after eight, with the Reds leading 6–0.

Johnny Vander Meer hurling his second consecutive no-hitter during the first night game at Brooklyn's Ebbets Field, 1938. (Wide World Photos)

"In both games," he would later say, "I was only thinking shutout through eight. Only in the ninth did I think about the no-hitters."

The first batter in the ninth was Buddy Hassett, who dribbled one down the first-base line. Vander Meer fielded it himself and tagged Hassett. One down.

Babe Phelps, Lavagetto, and Camilli were the next three hitters. Johnny walked them all, for a total of eight in the game. (Given another chance at breaking up a no-hitter, Lavagetto succeeded off Bill Bevens in the 1947 World Series).

You often find that a pitcher who has walked two or three in a row will lay one right down Broadway in an effort to find the plate and reestablish his control. That's usually fatal on the major league level, where even the worst hitter will jump on a mistake and hit a line drive between two fielders. It's part of the beauty of the game, unless you're the pitcher who's just made the delivery. Believe me, I've been there.

McKechnie went to the mound and told Johnny to just slow down. That break in his routine apparently worked. Ernie Koy grounded to third, and Ernie Lombardi took the throw to get a force-out at home and preserve the shutout. Two down.

The batter was Durocher, a .219 hitter but the sort of pesky player who often spoils no-hitters. Even a .200 hitter is going to be successful one out of five times, and you never know which at-bat is going to be the one of five. With two strikes, Johnny put one on the outside corner, over the plate with inches to spare. Umpire Bill Stewart called it a ball.

The savvy Dodger fans screamed at Stewart, one of the rare times they ever rooted against their own beloved "Bums." Durocher had another life. But he swung at the next offering and lofted one to Harry Craft in center, a routine fly that Harry pulled in for the final out.

The crowd went wild, and the first man to the mound was Stewart, who said, "John, I blew that other pitch. If you hadn't got him out I was the guy to blame for it." You don't get a statement like that from an umpire very often.

Cy Young once had a streak of twenty-four consecutive hitless innings, although it did not involve consecutive no-hitters. That record would be next on Johnny's agenda when he made his next start in Boston a few days later. But this time the Bees got a hit, although not until the fourth inning, and the streak ended at twenty-one and two-thirds. Young's major league record is still intact, and Johnny still holds the National League mark.

For a fellow in his first full season, Vander Meer was on a cloud. He started the All-Star Game on July 6 in Cincinnati against Lefty Gomez and was the winning pitcher. And although he wound up only 15–10 for the season, he was named *The Sporting News* Major League Player of the Year, just two years after winning the minor-league honor.

The Reds won pennants in 1939 and 1940, but Johnny was never as effective as he had been in '38. In 1940, in fact, he even went back to the minors for a large part of the season. He didn't pitch in the '39 Series and pitched only three innings in the 1940 Series.

But he never lost his halo as a Cincinnati Red and remained with the organization for many years. As a minor-league manager, he even served as Pete Rose's second-year skipper in 1961 at Tampa. In 1952, as a thirty-seven-year-old minor leaguer with Tulsa, he found the old magic one last time and no-hit Beaumont, managed by Harry Craft, before 335 customers.

Johnny knew baseball's ups and downs, but his "up" was probably higher than any other pitcher's has ever been. And for as long as baseball is played, every time someone pitches a no-hitter, he'll be "going after Johnny Vander Meer's record" his next time out.

21

Hartnett's Finest Moment

Fans have always enjoyed debating the question of "who's the best ever." All time: Ruth vs. Cobb. In the sixties: Mantle vs. Mays. Hardest thrower: Johnson vs. Feller vs. Ryan. It's great fun.

The choice for best all-around catcher of all time has never been easy. While the game has produced incredibly gifted athletes who have toiled for years under the physical burdens of the position, no one has ever emerged as clearly "the best."

By the 1920s and 1930s, experts polled on the question opted for old-timers like Buck Ewing, King Kelly, Roger Bresnahan, Johnny Kling, and Ray Schalk, who was Babe Ruth's choice. Bresnahan, Christy Mathewson's catcher and the man thought to define how the position should be played, selected a fellow named Marty Bergen when he picked an all-time team in 1936. Bergen (we looked it up) played four years for Boston from 1896 through 1899, caught over a hundred games only once, and batted .265. He must have been terrific calling pitches in '97 and '98, when Boston finished first. At least he made quite an impression on Bresnahan.

Today I believe the debate focuses on Mickey Cochrane, Bill Dickey, and Gabby Hartnett from baseball's "Golden Age," Roy Campanella and Yogi Berra from the postwar era, and my old Cincinnati battery mate Johnny Bench, who rewrote the book on how catchers

131

play the position. You might get some votes for a teammate of mine when I played with the White Sox, Carlton Fisk, whose durability has surpassed all of the others', and who set the career home-run record for catchers. Some might also vote for Josh Gibson, whose accomplishments were all recorded in the Negro leagues.

The combination of great offensive and defensive skills is the one thing that separates the men from the boys, the stars from the superstars. The perfect example is Bench, who during my era in the big leagues was a true offensive and defensive superstar.

Bench, the Hall of Famer who won the Most Valuable Player award twice in the National League, was like all good catchers in the sense that he seemed to be able to get on the same wavelength of any pitcher on the Reds' staff, especially late in the game in crucial situations. There were times when he would call for a pitch, knowing I would shake off the sign and go to the pitch I wanted, just so the hitter might have a shadow of a doubt as to what I might throw.

This "special" communication also took place with two other catchers I was fortunate to have pitched to during my career, Fisk of the Chicago White Sox and Jerry Grote of the New York Mets.

I won't pretend to put Jerry in their class, but he was an outstanding signal caller and defensive catcher, and a key to the success we had in developing pitchers on the Mets. The thing about catchers that no one in the stands or in the press box can ever understand is their pitch-calling ability. Pitchers probably spend more time singing the praises of men who "call a good game" than they do the catchers with great throwing arms or big bats.

Hartnett and Bench, who had line after line of magnificent statistical achievements in their careers, each had one premier moment that defined their ability to rise to the occasion, to take their team to a championship. For Hartnett it came in 1938, his seventeenth season in the league, only weeks after he had been named player-manager of a sinking Chicago Cub ball club. For Bench, it came in 1972, only his fifth season, but one for which he won his second MVP award in three years. Hartnett was thirty-seven, Bench only twenty-four.

Hartnett had been catching for the Cubs since he was twenty-one years old. Affable and very popular, he was a surprise choice to become manager in August 1938, after owner Phil Wrigley fired Charlie Grimm. Grimm had taken the Cubs to pennants in 1932 and 1935 and was as much "Mr. Cub" as Ernie Banks would later become. The change took place on July 20 with the Cubs in third, five and a half games out of first. Pittsburgh was on top of the league, with the Giants second. The managerial move paid no rapid dividends. The Pirates, under Pie Traynor, hung tough. A month after Hartnett took command, the Cubs had achieved only a 14–15 record. Although the Pirates' lead had grown to nine games, the Cubs had played well against the Giants and moved into second place.

After forty-eight games, Hartnett's team had played to a 26–22 record. By mid-September, if the Pirates won just seven of their final fourteen, the Cubs would have to go 10–3 to tie. Although Chicago was now hot, rolling up a 17–7 record in its last twenty-four games, the Pirates' chances seemed better than good.

The final week of the season brought Pittsburgh to Wrigley Field for three games. Few had thought these games would determine the pennant, but the lead was now shrunk to only one and a half, and indeed, there was a pennant on the line. It was time for the Pirates to put the Cubs to rest.

The initial game found Dizzy Dean, in a Cub uniform, making his first start in a month. Sore-armed and suddenly past his prime, Diz came through with a big 2–1 win to move the Cubs to within a half game.

On Wednesday, September 28, 34,465 fans jammed Wrigley Field to see Bob Klinger, a twenty-eight-year-old rookie, pitch for the Pirates against Clay Bryant of the Cubs, a nineteen-game winner that season who was leading the league in both strikeouts and walks.

The three o'clock starting time—common in those days to handle after-school crowds—was usually not a problem in summer months, when the sun still lit the field well past seven. That Wrigley Field had no lights was hardly an oddity in 1938; only Cincinnati and Brooklyn had them.

The Cubs scored in the second on an unearned run, but fell behind 3–1 in the sixth. In the last of the sixth, Chicago tied the game, helped by a double from Hartnett himself. Gabby, who had batted a career-high .354 in 1937, had dropped eighty points under the strain of both managing and catching, and had reduced his own playing time to eighty-eight games, the first time in nine years he had caught fewer than a hundred.

Both teams scored twice in the eighth to make it 5–5. A big hit for the Cubs this time was a pinch-hit double by Tony Lazzeri, the great

Gabby Hartnett celebrates the "homer in the gloaming." (UPI/Bettmann/Newsphotos)

Murderers' Row Yankee second baseman who was in his first year with Chicago.

Now came the ninth. It was past five o'clock, and the cloudy skies had made Wrigley Field dark with foreboding. Charlie Root, Chicago's sixth pitcher of the day, was on the mound. (We last heard from Charlie, of course, when he yielded Babe Ruth's "called-shot home run" in 1932.) Root set the Pirates down without a run, and the game moved to the last of the ninth.

It was clear to all that if the Cubs failed to score, this game was going to end as a 5–5 tie, and would have to be completely replayed.

Mace Brown, the Pirates' third hurler, was on the mound. He quickly retired Phil Cavarretta and Carl Reynolds, bringing Hartnett to the plate.

Brown got two strikes on Gabby. Conventional strategy called for a waste pitch at this point, particularly with vision obscured in the growing darkness. Hartnett was older, clearly slowing down at the plate, and might not react quickly to a breaking pitch out of the strike zone. But Brown, perhaps feeling pressure to get out of the inning and preserve the tie, broke one right over the plate. It was 5:37 P.M. Hartnett took a big swing—an everything-you've-got swing—and planted it over the ivy and into the left-field bleachers. The newspapers described it as a game-winning "homer in the gloamin'." Fans poured onto the field to accompany Hartnett around the bases. Photos of the event show how dark the skies were; the background appears black.

The Cubs moved into first place, and beat the Pirates again the next day, 10–1, sweeping the series and taking a one-and-a-half-game lead. A couple of days later, it was officially over; the Pirates never recovered and were eliminated on the next-to-last day of the season. The Cubs won it by two games. The Pirates wouldn't win again until 1960.

Thirty-four years after the "homer in the gloamin'," Johnny Bench, Hartnett's heir as the league's All-Star catcher, found himself in a tough League Championship Series against Pittsburgh. In 1972, Bench hit 40 homers and drove in 125 runs, a big comeback season for J. B., who had slumped to .238 with 27 homers and 61 RBIs in 1971.

The Reds had come back as a team, too. After a pennant in 1970, they had fallen to fourth in '71 before regrouping as the "Big Red Machine" in '72 with the addition of Joe Morgan at second base.

The best-of-five LCS opened at Pittsburgh with Steve Blass beating Don Gullett 5–1 in the opener. The Reds tied the series at 1–1 by winning Game Two, and then it was on to Riverfront Stadium in Cincinnati for the final three games. The Pirates won Game Three 3–2; the Reds took Game Four 7–1. Now, the pennant was on the line in Game Five, on Wednesday, October 11. (This would be the last game of Roberto Clemente's career; he was killed in a plane crash ten weeks later.)

It was Blass against Gullett again, and after eight innings the Pirates were hanging on to the slimmest of margins, 3–2.

Bench was the leadoff hitter in the last of the ninth. The Pirates were three outs from the World Series. Bill Virdon, the Pirates' manager, brought in his bullpen ace, Dave Giusti, to face Bench. It was a sound move. Giusti had won seven and saved twenty-two, and would be in a righty-vs.-righty situation. Everything about the move seemed correct—except that at that moment in history, Bench answered the call by hitting one of the game's most historic home runs deep over the right-field fence to tie the game.

Tony Perez and Denis Menke followed with singles, chasing Giusti for Bob Moose. Two outs later, the two men still on base, Moose let loose a wild pitch and the Reds were headed for the Series. It was another shocking loss for Pittsburgh, again the victim of a dramatic, career-defining home run by the league's best catcher.

22

The Streak

A half century after the Streak, the name Joe DiMaggio is still mentioned with the sort of reverence reserved for an actor like Barrymore or a writer like Hemingway. In fact, it was Ernest Hemingway who set the proper tone of awe when his fisherman in *The Old Man and the Sea* spoke of "the great DiMaggio." The book was published in 1952, the year after Joe retired. In 1954 he married Marilyn Monroe, another name that evokes awe and one that contributed further to his "mystique."

For all that he accomplished to earn the "Greatest Living Player" selection during fan voting in 1969, nothing was as impressive as his fifty-six-game hitting streak in 1941. Every major record we have seen fall in this half of the century was surpassed under less pressure. The lifetime records—Peter Rose in hits, Henry Aaron in home runs, Rickey Henderson in stolen bases—were set without the pressure of a ticking clock. They were remarkable achievements, each in its own way, but there was no deadline other than advancing age.

The single-season records—Roger Maris in home runs, Maury Wills, Lou Brock, and Henderson in steals, Nolan Ryan in strikeouts—had the pressure of the end of the season, but not the daily pressure of performing every time out. If you didn't homer today, there was always tomorrow.

But a hitting streak allows for no such luxuries. It has to be accomplished on a day-by-day basis. No excuses for travel weariness, a touch of the flu, or a tough right-hander. You could take a day off (which Joe did not do), but you couldn't hide when you got back. And for DiMaggio there was the added burden of playing in a pennant race in America's media capital, where newspapers, radio, and newsreel cameras caught his every step.

He was twenty-six years old at the time and, one could argue, at the very peak of his brilliant career. While his lifetime average through the end of the '41 season would be .345, it was only .304 over the rest of his career, hurt no doubt by three seasons missed during World War II and by injuries later on. But suffice it to say, the DiMaggio of 1941 was as good a baseball player as the world had ever seen.

That he should embark on a hitting streak, one that captured the attention of the entire nation, was not without personal precedent. As an eighteen-year-old minor-league rookie in 1933, playing for San Francisco at the tough Triple A level of the Pacific Coast League, he overcame whatever pressures one might associate with performing in front of hometown fans and batted safely in sixty-one games in a row. That piece of business put an initial spotlight on DiMaggio, and was one of the few baseball events on the West Coast to get national attention. He received a commemorative watch from the mayor of San Francisco, and the wire service photo of the presentation was his first national recognition.

No one ever questioned Joe's maturity. He fit into the Pacific Coast League at eighteen with no problems, and even when he broke in as a kid with the Yankees at twenty-one, he was a self-confident contract negotiator who knew his worth.

That self-confidence became evident years later. When laughingly asked what his worth would be in the modern, free-agent market, Joe would reply: "George [Steinbrenner], meet your new partner."

Joe had won the league's MVP award in 1939 when he batted .381, best in the majors, and in 1940 he finished third in the voting behind Hank Greenberg and Bob Feller after winning his second straight batting championship at .352. He had his usual abbreviated spring training, holding out for the first few days of '41 before signing for $37,500. He then hit safely in the Yankees' last nineteen exhibition games, an unusual feat because the regulars seldom played full games.

The Yankees split their first twenty-eight games and were in fourth place, five and a half games out, when the streak began on May 15 with an innocent 1-for-4 afternoon against Chicago. There being only seven opposing teams in those days, the hitters were more familiar with the pitchers than they might be today. (But so, too, were the pitchers more familiar with the hitters.)

The streak reached twelve straight when Joe went 4-for-5 against Washington on May 27, and it's possible that was the first time people paid much notice to it. (The day before, Jimmy Halperin of Norfolk had held Joe hitless in a minor-league exhibition game.) On June 2, when the streak reached nineteen against Feller, the day's big news was the sad death of Lou Gehrig at age thirty-seven. Everyone knew that death was coming for the former Yankee captain, stricken with amyotrophic lateral sclerosis, or "Lou Gehrig's disease," but the anticipation did not make the loss any less tragic. DiMaggio had been a teammate of Gehrig's for four seasons, and was now nobly carrying on the Ruth-Gehrig tradition.

On June 8, the streak reached twenty-three, equaling Joe's best previous performance in the majors. When he got to twenty-nine on June 16 against Cleveland, he tied Roger Peckinpaugh's all-time Yankee record, set in 1919. Peck was managing the Indians that day, and so witnessed the equaling of his record. When Joe broke it the next day and became the first Yankee to reach thirty, ahead of him lay the American League record of forty-one, held by George Sisler, and the major league record of forty-four, set in 1897 by Willie Keeler.

When he hit in his fortieth straight on June 28 against Philadelphia, he equaled the best Ty Cobb had ever done. The next day he played a doubleheader against Washington, had a hit in each game, and beat Sisler's record. In a July 1 doubleheader against Boston, he went 2-for-4 in the first game to set a new league record, and 1-for-3 in the nightcap to tie Keeler. Homering against Dick Newsome the next afternoon, he reached forty-five to break the record.

From then on the record was just Joe's to extend. And on he went, through three games with the Athletics, three with the Browns, and four with the White Sox. In between, he had a hit in the All-Star Game, which didn't count in the streak. The Yankees went to Cleveland on Wednesday, June 16, and Joe went 3-for-4 with a double to run the hitting streak to fifty-six. That game was at League Park, where Cleveland played its weekday games.

More than sixty-seven thousand fans turned up at Municipal Stadium on July 17 to see if Joe could be stopped and to enjoy the novelty of

Joe DiMaggio raps one out during his 56-game hitting streak. (National Baseball Library, Cooperstown, N.Y.)

night baseball. Only five American League cities had night ball in 1941—Chicago, St. Louis, Cleveland, Washington, and Philadelphia. The schedule was arranged so that each visiting team would play one night game in each park. Hence, the Yankees had only five night games in 1941, and this was the one in Cleveland.

The Indians started thirty-three-year-old left-hander Al Smith. Joe had not yet included Smith among his victims during the streak. In the first inning, Joe hit a hard shot down the third-base line, but it was backhanded by Ken Keltner, who fired to first and got Joe by less than a step.

Joe drew a walk in the fourth, and the fans booed. In the seventh, with Smith still on the mound, Joe again ripped one hard to third. Again Keltner made a good play, and again he just nailed him at first.

By the ninth, the Yanks had a 4–1 lead and Peckinpaugh brought in Jim Bagby, Jr. to pitch. Bagby, a right-hander, had been touched for a hit in Game Twenty-eight of the streak. Bagby's father had been a thirty-one-game winner for the Indians back in 1924. When DiMaggio's hitting streak at San Francisco had ended in 1933, the pitcher was Ed Walsh, Jr., whose father had been a forty-game winner for the White Sox in 1908. Baseball is great when it comes to such things—none of which could possibly have been on DiMaggio's mind as he stood now at the plate with the bases loaded and one out.

Joe swung at a 2–1 pitch and grounded hard up the middle. Shortstop Lou Boudreau made a clean pickup, he flipped to Ray Mack at second for a force, and Mack threw on to Oscar Grimes at first for a double play. Joe was 0-for-3, but he calmly picked up his glove, showing no emotion, and headed for center field.

What could have been going through his mind as the Indians rallied for two runs to make it a 4–3 game? Was he possibly hoping for a tie score, and one more chance to get a hit in extra innings? If the answer was yes, one thing certain was that Joe would never reveal it. Maybe he was just as happy to have the streak over.

Relief ace Johnny Murphy, who was my general manager years later with the Mets, came in to save it for Lefty Gomez, and the Yankees had a victory. For Joe, 56 would forever be the magic number.

He batted .408 during the streak as the Yanks moved into first place en route to a pennant. He had 91 hits, including 15 homers, and he drove in 55 runs. And as if that wasn't enough, he went out the next day and began a seventeen-game hitting streak, which, when it ended, gave him 73 out of 74.

Although Ted Williams batted .406 that season—the last major leaguer to hit .400—Joe easily won his second MVP award. The first sentence of his Hall of Fame plaque says: "Hit Safely in 56 Consecutive Games for Major League Record, 1941." There wasn't really anything else that needed to be said.

When might a seemingly unreachable record be broken? When might the legendary 56 fall? Many records in the history of baseball will never be approached. Cy Young and his 511 victories is one example, but 56 is within striking distance. When Pete Rose hit in 44 straight in 1978, it was the only time since Joe's big streak that anyone had made a serious challenge, and at that, Rose fell 12 short.

The 1993 expansion could provide the opportunity for such a feat. With the dilution of talent that will occur, especially when you consider the amount of pitching that will have to be force-fed into the major leagues, a contact hitter like Wade Boggs of the Boston Red Sox or the Reds' Barry Larkin could do the unthinkable.

Postwar Maturity

W HILE World War I had made the United States an international power, the nation remained innocent, and baseball was pretty much unchanged in terms of sophistication before and after the war. World War II was different. It was longer, of course, and more disruptive to American lives. Baseball emerged with a new social consciousness. It was also the dawn of the television age, when newfound audiences would discover major league baseball, nearly kill off minor-league baseball, and find that the black-and-white images on their TVs were just that—black and white, playing side by side.

It is true that there is no way to excuse organized baseball for having kept black players restricted to their own leagues for nearly half a century. It was white America's loss to have never seen Satchel Paige pitch against the best players of his age or Josh Gibson swing at a Bob Feller pitch in a major league game. But, if a saving grace could be found, the integration of Organized Baseball, which began with Jackie Robinson's contract to play for Montreal in 1946, put baseball in the forefront of the struggle. It came eight years before the Supreme Court turned its attention to the nation's schools, which really began the national civil rights movement. By then, baseball was already well into what may have been its greatest decade. That's a mathematical conclusion, not an emotional one. You still had only sixteen teams, and only four hundred jobs. The top four hundred players filled them. But in the 1950s, you now filled those positions from talent banks both white and black. Never before had available talent been so maximized. By 1961,

143

with the coming of expansion, there were more than four hundred jobs, and hence some watering-down of the game.

The 1950s were certainly a grand decade if you were living in New York. In the years 1950–1959, a New York team was in the World Series in all but '59, and in that year, the transplanted Los Angeles Dodgers made it, still carrying many of the Brooklyn players on their roster. In five of the ten years, both teams were from New York. Add onto this an all-New York World Series in 1949, and then six more Series with New York teams in them from 1960 to 1969, and it is easy to understand why people in New York felt this was a great time for baseball.

For those of us out of the area, the game was saved from this New York concentration of talent only by, it seemed, the continuous brilliance of Ted Williams in Boston and Stan Musial in St. Louis. For a while, Robin Roberts in Philadelphia was the best pitcher, then Warren Spahn in Milwaukee. The growth of television brought big-league baseball into all of our homes, and the glamour of wearing those uniforms and playing in those ballparks looked better than ever. Today, I am sure, parents and coaches talk about the riches to be gained by playing pro ball. For me and countless others who viewed the big time in the 1950s, it was the game itself, pure and simple, that beckoned. Many young men dreamed of pitching to Willie Mays, Mickey Mantle, and Duke Snider. By the 1960s, they were doing it.

23

The War Over, the Game Is Back

Could there have ever been a happier time for baseball than the third week of April 1946?

Never mind who won; never mind who lost. It was the first Opening Day following the end of World War II, and after four long years, the sixteen major league teams were back to full strength. Back, too, were millions of fans, whose love for the USA included their hunger for baseball.

As a morale booster, President Roosevelt had ordered baseball to continue during the war, but by 1945, the rosters were depleted, and what passed for the major leagues was a sorry substitute. Most able-bodied players, including most of the game's top stars, were in action overseas. Among those on the field in '45 were Pete Gray, the one-armed outfielder of the St. Louis Browns, who batted .218 in seventy-seven games, and Bert Shepard, who hurled one heroic effort for Washington after losing a leg in combat.

Fifty-seven professional players had given their lives during the war. All were minor leaguers, although one, an outfielder named Elmer Gedeon, had played five games for Washington in 1939 and another, Harry O'Neill, caught one game for the 1939 A's. Another casualty was Lt. Col. Billy Southworth, Jr., twenty-eight, whose father had managed the Cardinals from 1940 to 1945, winning three pennants and two World Championships. Billy Sr. asked for his release after the 1945 season so that he could manage the Boston Braves. For him, as for a lot of other Americans, the 1946 season would be a fresh start.

A total of fifty-four big leaguers had missed four complete seasons, the best known being Fred Hutchinson, the burly Detroit pitcher who later managed the Reds, and Billy Cox, the Pittsburgh infielder who later starred for the Dodgers. But the list of those who missed three seasons or parts of four is long and impressive: Ted Williams, Joe DiMaggio, Bob Feller, Dom DiMaggio, Johnny Pesky, Phil Rizzuto, Ted Lyons, Bob Lemon, Hank Greenberg, Tommy Henrich, Warren Spahn, Johnny Sain, Pete Reiser, Ewell Blackwell, Enos Slaughter, Terry Moore, Johnny Mize, and Hal Schumacher. In the cases of those who went on to the Hall of Fame and proved themselves among the greatest players of all time—Joe DiMaggio, Feller, Williams, and Spahn—the lost seasons robbed them of the opportunity to record lifetime statistics far more impressive than they ultimately posted. DiMaggio would have topped four hundred home runs; Williams six hundred. Feller would have been a three hundred-game winner and perhaps the all-time strikeout leader. Spahn would probably have become only the third four hundred-game winner in the game's history, joining Cy Young and Walter Johnson.

Greenberg, one of the first discharged when the war in Europe ended in the spring of 1945, returned to the Tigers in July. He was thirty-four years old, but he batted .311 with sixty RBIs in seventy-eight games, and on the final day of the season, his home run against the Browns gave the Tigers the 1945 pennant. Such heroics were only a preview of what might be expected of the returning players.

The war in the Pacific ended in August with the dropping of atomic bombs on Japan. In September 1945, five months after President Roosevelt's death, Harry Truman took in a game at Griffith Stadium in Washington, marking the first postwar appearance by a president at a ballpark. Normalcy was slowly returning to America.

Spring training of 1946 saw the sixteen teams with their 640 players and prospects headed south for Florida, after having trained for three years in northern sites, often in the snow, to conserve fuel. The players were full of war tales: those who had relatively "easy hitches," playing service ball far from the front lines, and those who had fought with valor, including Williams and Feller.

Throughout the land, everyone was talking baseball. The defending champions were the Cubs and the Tigers, but that seemed insignificant with rosters restored and questions raised about players' abilities. The best pitcher of the war years, Detroit's Hal Newhouser, would have to prove that he could still be a star against the top players. Newhouser, who had been classified 4F due to a heart ailment, had won MVP awards in 1944 and 1945, with 29–9 and 25–9 seasons.

Night baseball, halted by blackout regulations, would return in 1946, with Yankee Stadium getting lights for the first time as part of a complete face-lift under new owners Dan Topping, Del Webb, and Larry MacPhail.

There was a new commissioner in place, Albert "Happy" Chandler, a former Kentucky governor and U.S. senator. Chandler had taken office in April 1945 after the death of Judge Landis, who had reigned for twenty-five years. There was a similarity in his succession to the move of former Senator Harry Truman into the White House. Both had replaced towering figures who were seemingly in office forever. In 1946, Chandler would face a challenge to organized baseball by an outlaw Mexican League, which was luring away such American players as Sal Maglie, Max Lanier, Mickey Owen, and Danny Gardella. It failed to lure Stan Musial and Phil Rizzuto, who resisted huge contracts and remained loyal to the major leagues.

And then it was April 16, 1946, and 236,730 paying customers walked through the turnstiles of the eight parks to record the highest Opening Day attendance since 1931. Flags were flying everywhere to welcome home the troops and celebrate the Allies' victory.

In Washington, at the traditional presidential opener, Harry Truman did the first-ball honors before 30,372 fans, who saw Ted Williams belt the longest home run in Washington in fifteen years, a 430-foot shot that led the Red Sox to a 6–3 victory.

In Philadelphia, 37,473 turned out to see Connie Mack's Athletics host the Yankees in what would be Joe McCarthy's final Opening Day as Yankee manager. Joe DiMaggio belted a home run, Spud Chandler pitched a five-hit shutout, and the Yanks won 5–0.

At Chicago, Bob Feller shut out the White Sox 1–0 with ten strikeouts, as center fielder Bob Lemon made a belly-flop catch to save the game. Two weeks later, Feller would no-hit the Yankees 1–0 at Yankee Stadium. Lemon, of course, later converted to a pitcher, and eventually followed Feller into the Hall of Fame.

At Detroit, 52,118 saw Greenberg homer to lead the Tigers to a 2–1 win over the Browns, with Newhouser hurling a six-hitter. The return of the stars didn't hurt Hal; he was 26–9 in 1946.

In the National League, Musial joined other returning veterans to the Cardinals' lineup under new manager Eddie Dyer, along with a twenty-year-old rookie catcher, a native of St. Louis named Joe Garagiola. The Cardinals lost to the Pirates 6–4 before 14,009, but would go on to win ninety-eight games and the National League pennant.

At Boston, Southworth's debut as Brave manager was a success, with the Braves beating Brooklyn 5–3 behind Johnny Sain. Billy Herman had four singles for the Dodgers, and three hundred fans found their clothing ruined by wet paint on the seats at Braves Field.

At Cincinnati, 30,699 turned out for the traditional National League opener and saw the Cubs win 4–3 despite a 3-for-5 performance by the Reds' rookie third baseman, Grady Hatton, a "$25,000 Bonus Baby."

Finally, at the Polo Grounds, Governor Thomas E. Dewey and UN Secretary General Trygve Lie watched the Giants beat the Phillies 8–4 before forty thousand customers. Mel Ott blasted the 511th and last home run of his career, a National League record. Major league baseball was back.

The pomp and ceremony of the other home openers later in the week included 31,825 at Ebbets Field in Brooklyn, where the Dodgers beat the Giants 8–1 as Pete Reiser stole three bases, including home.

Major league attendance went up 80 percent in 1946. Six of the eight American League teams set all-time season records, with the Yankees becoming the first team ever to top two million. Five of the eight National League teams set records as well.

The Red Sox, led by Williams's return season of .342 with 38 homers and 123 RBIs, won the American League pennant by twelve games. The Cardinals needed a two-game sweep in the first-ever playoff series to hold off the Dodgers and win under rookie manager Dyer. The Cardinals won a seven-game World Series, best remembered for a mad dash home by Slaughter in the seventh game. Enos, on with two outs in a 3–3 game in the eighth inning, scored all the way from first on a liner by Harry Walker, never hesitating around third and sliding home with the World Championship run.

As in 1909, when Honus Wagner and Ty Cobb faced each other in the World Series, 1946 provided the only matchup baseball would witness between two of the three best players of their time, Ted

The World War II years found men like Joe DiMaggio wearing a different sort of uniform.

The return to action in 1946 climaxed with Enos Slaughter's "mad dash" home in the last of the eighth of game seven. Al Barlick is the umpire. (Wide World Photos)

Williams and Stan Musial. (DiMaggio was the third.) Because of the league domination by the Yankees throughout Ted's career, 1946 proved to be his only World Series appearance. It was a disappointment. He managed only five singles and a lone run batted in, hitting .200 against Cardinal pitching. He played for fifteen more seasons but never returned to the fall classic.

Musial had appeared in the World Series of 1942, 1943, and 1944, so this was his fourth in five years. Little could he have imagined that it would be his last. He played for eighteen more seasons, but the National League in those years was dominated by the Dodgers and Giants, and St. Louis's turn did not come around again until the year after Musial retired. Although Stan hit four doubles and drove in four runs in the 1946 Series, he batted only .222 without homering. The Musial-Williams matchup was a dud. And save for spring training and All-Star Games, the two would never face each other again.

There was one other event in 1946 that bore watching. On April 18, at Jersey City, New Jersey, twenty-five thousand fans turned out for an International League game and saw Montreal defeat Jersey City 14–1 behind the heroics of Jackie Robinson, the first black to play Organized Baseball in the twentieth century.

America was back to watching baseball, but things would never be as they were before Pearl Harbor.

24

The Coming of Jackie Robinson

If you happen to pick up a 1947 Brooklyn Dodger yearbook at a collector's convention one day soon (no small investment), you will notice that while the entire book is printed on an old-fashioned pulp-quality paper, there is one page inserted on glossy stock containing the image of Jackie Robinson.

One could leap to the conclusion that the addition of Robinson to the yearbook was a last-minute decision, as was his addition to the Opening Day roster. In fact, the most recent evidence suggests that everything about the entry of Robinson was so well planned and calculated by Dodger general manager Branch Rickey, it was probably his intention to keep the decision about going north with Jackie a secret from the folks who printed the yearbook.

Apparently, only once did he veer from the course he had charted. And that was when he decided to bring up only Jackie, instead of a small group of players, from the Negro Leagues.

To backtrack, Organized Baseball had never seen a black player in the twentieth century. Cap Anson, the influential manager and first-base star of the nineteenth-century Chicago entry in the National League, was apparently a leader of the movement to make the game an all-white sport. This seemed particularly strange behavior for a man

151

who had been the first white child born in Marshalltown, Iowa, a town populated entirely by Native Americans.

But Anson's unwritten "rule" took hold. In the early part of the century, there was no strong pressure on private business to integrate, and the sixteen major league owners were happy to keep attracting their small white audiences, while denying they were making any attempts to keep blacks out. "They have their league, we have ours," they would say publicly, at a time when the policy of "separate but equal" had gained national acceptance.

"Their" league was the Negro League, or more properly the Negro American League and the Negro National League. It is impossible to judge their caliber of play, because travel conditions, equipment, and training were all inferior to those available to whites, and the keeping of statistics was not taken seriously. Still, it is obvious that there were men in those leagues who deserved to play for the bigger salaries and to achieve the fame and benefits of Organized Baseball. That white baseball never knew how far Josh Gibson might have hit a ball or what Satchel Paige could have done in his prime as a pitcher is a tragedy the game can never justify.

Commissioner Landis, who ruled the game from 1920 to 1945, was hardly an enlightened figure, and it is no coincidence that the integration of the game followed very shortly after his death. Landis, the all-powerful commissioner, either took no leadership in integrating the game, or quietly bowed to the wishes of the sixteen owners. We have no evidence as to whether the matter was ever even discussed at league meetings.

One could make an argument that if the Hall of Fame opened today, Anson might be excluded, and there is a chance Landis might be as well. Their respective roles in keeping the game segregated would hardly be applauded in American society today. There is also evidence to suggest that some of the great stars of the teens and twenties were members of the Ku Klux Klan, but the secret nature of that organization makes verification difficult.

It was in 1943 that Rickey moved from the Cardinals to the Dodgers and began thinking of integrating the game, a decision that would certainly help his gate in Brooklyn, with its large black population. He certainly would have met far more resistance in St. Louis, the league's closest thing to a Southern town and the city that was to give the Robinson experiment the most trouble.

Rickey confided his plans to a few close associates and to a few others not affiliated with baseball. He wanted to help the Dodgers, who had won only one pennant since 1920, and as his plans grew, he no doubt saw a place for himself in history.

The theory that Robinson had always been his clear choice held firm for many years, but evidence uncovered in 1989 by historians John Thorn and Jules Tygiel reveal that his original plan called for the signing of several black players at once. In addition to Robinson, he considered Don Newcombe, Roy Partlow, John Wright, and Sam Jethroe. He was apparently determined to not just open the doors, but knock them down.

Rickey discussed all of this with a *Look* magazine writer, Arthur Mann, who worked the Dodger beat. He helped Mann prepare an article that would reveal the mass signings, to be held on a date coinciding with the article's publication.

But in October 1945, Mayor Fiorello La Guardia of New York asked Rickey if he could announce that baseball was planning shortly to begin to sign Negro players. Rickey, sensing that his moment of glory would be swept away by the politicians, called Mann and told him to cancel the article. Then, on October 23, he signed Robinson to a Montreal Royal contract for the 1946 season. Montreal was the Dodgers' Triple A farm team.

In ability, Jackie was no minor leaguer, but the year in the International League, in the safe haven of Canada, was a good preparation for Rickey's plan. Jackie was, in fact, a twenty-seven-year-old infielder who had batted .387 in 1945 with the Kansas City Monarchs. He had been a four-sport star at UCLA and a lieutenant in the army during World War II. His intelligence and the likelihood that he could deal with the pressures and publicity of being "the first" made him the perfect candidate. But as we see today, the original plan called for four or five black players at once, which would have taken a lot of the pressure off Jackie and made his entry into the majors much easier.

There was a famous meeting in Rickey's Brooklyn office on August 28, 1945, during which Rickey apparently shocked Robinson by telling him of his intentions. Robinson had been led to believe that Rickey was considering an all-black team that would play home games in Ebbets Field. Rickey lectured him on the verbal abuse he could expect and on the need to "turn the other cheek," rather than fight. Rickey understood that many would try to "get to him" and "break him" and prove that blacks couldn't cut it in the majors. Although his entire life had prepared him to be a fighter, Robinson recognized Rickey's logic in telling him to just take it.

And so Robinson reported to Montreal and had no trouble with Triple A baseball, batting .349, stealing forty bases, and leading the league's second basemen in fielding.

The Dodgers trained with Montreal in Havana, Cuba, in 1947, and Robinson batted .625 in his Montreal uniform in seven exhibition games against Brooklyn. But not until April 10, five days before the opening of the regular season, did the Dodgers announce that Jackie would go north with the team.

Opening Day—April 15, 1947—was more eventful for his presence than for anything that happened on the field. He was moved to first base. He wore a white sweatshirt under his uniform, almost to accentuate his dark black arms. He went 0-for-3 against Johnny Sain of the Boston Braves before 25,623, a rather disappointing crowd, all things considered. But the year itself worked out beautifully. Jackie hit .297, playing in all but three games. He overcame a threatened strike by the Cardinals, before league president Ford Frick and commissioner Happy Chandler stepped in and forced the Cardinals to honor their schedule.

The Rookie of the Year award was created that season, and Jackie was the first recipient. Forty years later, Commissioner Peter Ueberroth renamed the award the Jackie Robinson Award. To date, though, the name has not caught on like its predecessor, the Cy Young Award. Then again, you probably didn't know that the MVP award is actually the Kenesaw Mountain Landis Award.

The Dodgers clinched the 1947 pennant, their first in six years, and Jackie's teammates had to acknowledge that he was putting money in their wallets by helping the team win. Between 1947 and 1956, Jackie helped the Dodgers to six pennants. He was the league's Most Valuable Player in 1949, and there was a certain irony to him winning the "Landis Award."

After Jackie's retirement in 1956 with a .311 career average, it was time to speak out. For the rest of his life, while he had no official connection with baseball, he preached additional rights for blacks, particularly in managerial positions. Jackie died of diabetes in 1972 at the age of fifty-three, at the same age as the game's other high-impact player, Babe Ruth. Robinson did not live to see Frank Robinson

Jackie Robinson sits with his new teammates and awaits the start of his first game as a Brooklyn Dodger. Eddie Stanky is just to his right. (The Sporting News)

named as the first black manager three years later, but his widow, Rachel, was on hand for that occasion.

I lived near Jackie in Connecticut, played golf with him, attended banquets with him, and always found him a good companion. Two of his teammates, Gil Hodges and Rube Walker, were with me on the Mets, and you could see how much they cared for him as a man. It's hard to believe that when I signed a pro contract in 1966, blacks had been allowed in pro ball for only twenty years. Imagine what the game lost in the years before 1946. But look at what it has found since.

Jackie paved the way for what may well have been baseball's finest period, the years 1947–1960, when the major leagues were composed of only four hundred players and the talent pool was fully integrated. Thus, the fifties brought forth Willie Mays, Ernie Banks, Frank Robinson, Henry Aaron, and Roberto Clemente, none of whom would have been able to play big-league ball without Jackie. Expansion in 1961 diluted the talent on the major league level, but how thin that talent would have been without the pool of all races to draw from. Stars of the sixties, like Lou Brock, Reggie Jackson, Bob Gibson, and Juan Marichal, still knew they owed a debt to Jackie. Those feelings began to fade in the seventies, and by the 1980s, the Cardinals' Vince Coleman claimed to be unfamiliar with the name Jackie Robinson. It was a sad commentary on a player's lack of appreciation for the past, but perhaps Jackie would have been pleased with the ease with which black players now entered the majors, feeling no need to say thank you to anyone.

25

Veeck Brings a Flag
to Cleveland

The history of the Cleveland Indians is hardly laced with pride and tradition, and pennant races have been few. But their three pennants were memorable, and so was one of their owners, the colorful Bill Veeck.

The first pennant, after a twenty-year wait following the birth of the American League, came in the year the Yankees acquired Babe Ruth—1920. Despite the immediate impact of Ruth, Cleveland prevailed. And it won despite the horrible death of its vital shortstop, Ray Chapman (see chapter 10). The 1920 World Series then featured the only unassisted triple play in Series history, performed by Bill Wambsganss.

The Indians' most recent pennant came in 1954, when they set an American League record of 111 victories, a mark not bettered even since expansion (and its longer season) thirty years ago. It was the only time the Yankees failed to win the pennant between 1949 and 1958.

Cleveland also won in 1948, after a season that required the first playoff game ever to decide the American League pennant. That the league had gone forty-seven seasons without a tie for first seems rather amazing; equally amazing is that in all the years since, it has happened only one more time, in 1978.

The '48 Indians were owned by Veeck, son of the former president of the Chicago Cubs and a World War II veteran who later lost a leg as a result of combat in the Pacific. Although only thirty-two when he took over ownership of the Indians in June 1946, he was already renowned as a master showman whose gift for promotion had brought attention to the Milwaukee Brewers, the minor-league team he operated prior to the war.

Among those inherited by Veeck was his player-manager, shortstop Lou Boudreau, the handsome idol of Cleveland youth who had become manager at age twenty-five in 1942. Boudreau was somewhat like Cal Ripken Jr. today: a mature, steady player, a team leader not blessed with speed but very capable in the field, and a clutch hitter. He was the last of the successful player-managers—once a fashionable item among big-league teams who could save owners a salary by combining jobs. (Player-managers since Boudreau include only Eddie Stanky and Solly Hemus of the Cardinals, Hank Bauer of the A's, Frank Robinson of the Indians, Don Kessinger of the White Sox, Joe Torre of the Mets, and Pete Rose of the Reds.)

Before Veeck, Lou had not exactly set the league on fire as a manager, finishing 4-3-5-5-6-4 in his first six seasons. But when Veeck let it be known that he planned to trade Lou to the Browns for Vern "Junior" Stephens, Cleveland fans went crazy, forcing Veeck to cancel the deal and retain Boudreau. His near martyrdom gave Lou even greater popularity, and Veeck, by responding to the fans' appeal, reaped equal rewards. Bill was always a populist.

In 1947, shortly after Jackie Robinson joined the Dodgers, Veeck signed outfielder Larry Doby to a contract, making him the first black in the American League. (Years later, when he owned the White Sox, Veeck made Doby the major leagues' second black manager.)

In 1948, displaying his abilities as both showman and judge of talent, he signed legendary Negro League pitching star Satchel Paige to a Cleveland contract. He announced Paige's age at "forty plus," and subsequent research seemed to indicate that forty-one was about right. Paige was clearly the best pitcher in Negro League history, and one of the greatest pitchers of all time. He was deprived of a chance as a young man in the majors, but was successful in most exhibition games against white teams, where admittedly he had more to prove. It follows that he would have earned his rightful place in the Hall of Fame had he been permitted to work a full career in the majors.

Lou Boudreau, following the victory in the 1948 playoff game.

On the Cleveland staff, Paige joined the great Bob Feller, the team's most brilliant performer since 1936. And the Indians had another rookie on their '48 team, a twenty-seven-year-old pitcher from Arkansas named Gene Bearden, who threw a knuckleball and had a date with destiny.

The owner undoubtedly took a liking to Bearden because, like Veeck, he was a Purple Heart vet. Bearden's athletic prowess after World War II defied all odds. He had spent four years in the minors before joining the navy in 1942. During a battle on the high seas, he was knocked unconscious, his knee crushed, his skull shattered and filled with fragments. Hauled onto a life raft, he floated for two days before he was rescued.

Bearden's knee was slowly rebuilt with an aluminum cap and screw, and an aluminum plate was inserted in his head. He battled his way back, not only to health but to the minors, joining the Yankees' Binghamton team in 1945, where he was 15–5. He then moved to Oakland in 1946 under manager Casey Stengel, compiling a 15–4 record. In one of Veeck's first deals, he was traded to the Indians in December 1946, and made the team a year later. As is often the case in baseball, it's who you know. When Veeck operated Milwaukee before the war, Stengel had been his manager. Now it was Stengel who touted Bearden to Bill: "If [Larry] MacPhail is crazy enough to give him up," said Casey, "grab him!"

Veeck called Bearden the biggest surprise he ever had in baseball. Bearden spent the entire 1948 season getting batters to swing at his below-the-knees knuckleball, and his success translated into a big season. The rookie led the league with a 2.43 earned-run average and had a 20–7 record. Not surprisingly, in 1949, when Stengel joined the Yankees, he alerted his players to avoid the knuckleball and wait for strikes. Word got around the league fast. The pitch lost its effectiveness because no one was swinging at it, and Bearden became a one-year wonder.

But what a year it was! Boston, Cleveland, and New York battled into the final week of the season, until with two days left only the Red Sox and Indians remained. The National League's pennant belonged to the Boston Braves, winners of their first flag since 1914, and the prospect of an all-Boston series excited the fans tremendously. Cleveland fans were no less enthusiastic about their first pennant possibility in twenty-eight years; that season a record 2,620,627 of them turned out for Veeck's promotions, fun, and success. It would remain an American League attendance record for thirty-four years.

The Indians could have clinched the pennant with a win on the final day of the season, but Detroit's Hal Newhouser beat them while the Red Sox stopped the Yankees, and there was a tie for first after 154 games. A coin toss determined that the playoff game would be held in Fenway Park the next day, Monday, October 4.

The starting pitchers were difficult to select, both teams having gone with their best on the final weekend. Boudreau, having made the right moves all season long, openly discussed the situation with his players, and went with Bearden, who was 19–7. Although he was a lefty working with just one day's rest, and Fenway Park was usually a horror for southpaws, Bearden was the hot hand at the moment, even more so than Feller or Bob Lemon, both future Hall of Famers. Had Feller not pitched the day before, he might have started, but the Indians had had to play to win against Newhouser.

Boston's choice was equally surprising. Denny Galehouse, a thirty-six-year-old veteran who had started his big-league career in 1934 with Cleveland, was Joe McCarthy's selection. He was only 8–7 for the season, but had had some success against the Indians.

The fans packed Fenway Park on short notice for the Monday afternoon game and quickly saw Boudreau put the Indians ahead 1–0 with a first-inning homer. Talk about leading by example! It was Lou's seventeenth homer of the year, his career high, and it went with a .355 batting average, 116 runs, and 106 RBIs. In addition, he struck out only nine times in 658 plate appearances.

A single by Junior Stephens tied the game 1–1 in the last of the first. In the fourth, Boudreau opened with a single that led to a four-run inning, including a big home run by Ken Keltner to finish Galehouse and give the Tribe a 5–1 lead. Boudreau's eighteenth homer and second of the game, in the fifth, made it 6–1.

The Red Sox got two in the seventh on a home run by Bobby Doerr, but that was all they managed for the afternoon. A fourth hit by Boudreau was a fitting climax to the season, and Bearden stopped the Red Sox on only five hits, holding Ted Williams to a harmless single in four trips.

So the rookie hot-hand Bearden had his twentieth win and the Indians had their second pennant. For Veeck, Bearden, Doby—all the young ones—it had come fast and furious. For Paige, who had toiled

outside of organized baseball for decades, it was a glorious moment
that rewarded Veeck's faith. For Boudreau, it was a way of thanking
the fans for their loyalty. For Feller and Lemon, it was the first pennant
in brilliant careers, and they were fortunate to still be around when the
Indians won again in 1954.

The '48 World Series went to Cleveland in six games, with Boudreau hitting four doubles and Lemon winning twice. Bearden hurled a
five-hit shutout in Game Three and saved the final game in relief of
Lemon with another one and two-thirds innings of shutout baseball.

Baseball is like that. You can have major stars destined for the Hall
of Fame on a team, but you might also have a one-year wonder who
just happens to be the man of the moment. A manager has to recognize
that and play his card.

Bearden was 8–8 in 1949, and by 1950 was off to the Washington
Senators. He was bitter with the Indians for "not being used" enough,
an obvious result of his inability to get hitters out anymore. Beating
Cleveland became an obsession, but he wasn't especially successful at
that either. By 1953 he was out of the majors, having won only twenty-
five more games after his rookie season. He finished up with four
seasons in the Pacific Coast League and is seldom heard from today.

Boudreau managed Cleveland through 1950, then led the Red Sox,
Athletics, and Cubs, without much success. He became a longtime
broadcaster in Chicago and was elected to the Hall of Fame in 1970,
largely on the basis of his 1948 season.

Veeck continued to be a mischievous and maverick owner, stopping
at St. Louis, where he once sent a midget up to bat for the Browns
(Eddie Gaedel, who walked), and twice at the Chicago White Sox,
winning another pennant in 1959. He died in 1987, having lived a rich
and full life. He was the first to put players' names on uniforms,
erected an exploding scoreboard in Comiskey Park, removed its artificial surface, restored its name when he reacquired the team in 1975,
and generally had a fine time tweaking the noses of various commis-
sioners and league presidents.

The baseball establishment never cared much for Veeck, or for his
latter-day successor, Charley Finley. But they were the "thinkers" of
the game, the men of vision who knew that baseball could not stand
still and continue to attract the American public. They hustled, they
promoted, they offended the old-timers, but they made things interesting, and many of their innovations eventually found their way into the

baseball mainstream. Veeck, a lovable rogue, actually made it to Cooperstown. Finley, a much crueler man, will probably never get such an honor. But their contributions to the look of today's game should not be minimized. Baseball adapted to changing American culture with a little more razzle-dazzle, and it was Veeck who took the game there, kicking and screaming.

26

The Shot Heard Round the World

It was a Wednesday afternoon, and a game played on just a day's notice. So it was not altogether surprising that there were twenty thousand empty seats in the Polo Grounds on October 3, 1951. Still, the National League pennant was to be decided, in what had come down to a one-game playoff. And the two combatants were both New York teams—the Brooklyn Dodgers and the New York Giants.

What *is* surprising about those twenty thousand empty seats is that just about every New York baseball fan over the age of forty-five can tell you what he or she was doing at the moment that Bobby Thomson hit "The Shot Heard Round the World" to cap off "The Miracle of Coogan's Bluff." Plenty of people outside of New York still vote it baseball's most memorable moment. It seems to hold its own with Pearl Harbor, FDR's death, JFK's assassination, and men walking on the moon as an indelible twentieth-century memory.

This really was baseball's ultimate pennant race. The Giants were managed by Leo Durocher, who used to pilot the Dodgers. The Dodgers were managed by Charlie Dressen, who had served Durocher as a coach. The Dodgers had won pennants in 1947 and 1949, and had just missed in 1950. The Giants, a once-proud outfit steeped in the tradition of McGraw, Mathewson, Hubbell, Terry, and Ott, had not been in a World Series since 1937. The Dodgers had surpassed them as

New York's premier National League team. Durocher wanted to win the glory back; Dressen wanted to prove that he was Durocher's equal at the helm.

In addition, the Dodgers had won over all the black fans in town since the signing of Jackie Robinson in 1947. Now the Giants were poised to win them back with their own special find, a twenty-year-old center fielder named Willie Mays, who had hit twenty home runs in 464 at-bats in his rookie campaign after a .477 performance at Minneapolis early in the year.

This day, however, would belong not to Robinson or Mays, but to lesser players whose names would become indelibly engraved on baseball history.

The Giants' "miracle" finish of 1951 was not forged simply in the Polo Grounds that October afternoon. It really began in August, when the team went on a 37–7 tear, including twelve wins in its final thirteen games. This burst overcame a thirteen-game Dodger lead in the standings, as Brooklyn went just 26-22 in that span. Both teams finished at 96–58, forcing a best-two-of-three playoff for the National League pennant. On the basis of who was hot and who wasn't, on who was destined and who wasn't, all indicators seemed to favor the Giants. But this was playoff ball, when anyone could win a short series, and when both teams would be pumped up beyond ordinary playing levels.

The Yankees having already clinched the American League pennant, there was no need for the baseball world to alter travel plans and scramble to the playoff. This would be an all-New York affair. The first game was scheduled for October 1 in Ebbets Field, Brooklyn. As their starter, the Dodgers named Ralph Branca, who had a 13–10 record following a twenty-one-win season in 1947 and a 34–23 record in the three seasons between then and now. He lost Game One, 3–1 to Jim Hearn, after giving up home runs to Monte Irvin and the third baseman, one Bobby Thomson. It was Thomson's thirty-first home run of the year, seventh against the Dodgers, and second off Branca.

Game Two moved to the Polo Grounds, where the Giants could have wrapped it up, but the Dodgers won 10–0 behind rookie Clem Labine and a thirteen-hit attack. So neither team had been able to use the home-field advantage—if, in fact, the advantage was as strong as usual, given that half the people in the ballpark were rooting for the visiting team.

Then came the deciding third game. With television still in its infancy and few homes equipped with this electronic novelty, many people crowded in front of appliance-store windows to watch the action. Many more were tuned in to the radio broadcast, selecting either Red Barber of the Dodgers or Russ Hodges of the Giants.

The Dodgers were without the services of catcher Roy Campanella, soon to be voted the league's MVP. A bad leg injury, which kept him from running, put him on the bench in this most crucial of games. Rube Walker, who had homered in Game Two, would catch again.

Brooklyn tapped its ace, twenty-game winner Don Newcombe, and the Giants went with Sal Maglie. Maglie started wild, walking two in the first, and giving up an RBI single to Robinson: 1–0 Dodgers.

The Giants tied it in the last of the seventh, finally getting to Newcombe on a double by Irvin, a sacrifice by Whitey Lockman, and a sacrifice fly by Thomson.

But in the top of the eighth, the Dodgers scored three times, helped by a wild pitch and two walks from Maglie. Pee Wee Reese, Duke Snider, Andy Pafko, and Billy Cox all singled in the inning, and it began to look bad for the Giants. In the visiting clubhouse, the champagne was being set up on the center table. When the Giants went down without scoring in their half of the eighth, it looked as if the end was near. (So much so that Yogi Berra, a spectator that day, left early, convinced the Dodgers had won. This, from the original "It ain't over till it's over" guy.)

Although 1951 is part of baseball's modern era, the game was still played differently. Today, a team that had gotten as far as the playoffs would have a "stopper" in the bullpen, a "closer," someone to get the last three or six outs. That Maglie stayed in for the entire eighth was something we would not see today. That Newcombe would soon be relieved by a starting pitcher was also something that is not a part of 1990s baseball.

And so it was that Newk was on the mound as the last of the ninth arrived. The first Giant hitter, Alvin Dark, got an infield single. Now Dark represented neither the tying nor the winning run, but Dressen signaled Gil Hodges to hold him on at first. And that gave Don Mueller the opportunity to single past Hodges's glove into right, sending Dark to third.

Suddenly the Polo Grounds fans began to sense that this game could yet be won by the Giants. But they still needed three runs to tie and four to win.

Those little hopes fell a notch when the tough Monte Irvin fouled out. One down.

That brought up Lockman, who took Newcombe's second pitch and slammed a double to left, scoring Dark. Mueller, barreling into third, injured his ankle and had to be removed on a stretcher. Clint Hartung, "the Hondo Hurricane," once considered the game's top prospect but just an occasional role player now, went in to run at third.

Convinced that Newcombe had run out of gas, Dressen phoned bullpen coach Clyde Sukeforth and asked how his relievers were looking.

"Erskine's not at his best," said Sukeforth. "Branca's popping the ball."

In came Branca. And up to the bat came Bobby Thomson, the only Scot-born major leaguer in history. And here was a classic baseball dilemma: Should Thomson be walked intentionally, given his success against the Dodgers and against Branca? Or should Branca pitch to him?

There's a baseball adage that you never put the potential winning run on base. Reinforcing that line of thought at the time was the sight of Willie Mays on deck. Today, in light of Mays's fame, one naturally assumes that you would not have wanted to pitch to him. But back in his rookie year, he was a .274 hitter, whereas Thomson, who had moved to third base in July to make room for Willie in the outfield, had batted .357 since the shift. Nonetheless, still leading by two runs, Dressen wanted to pitch to Thomson.

The first pitch was a called strike. The second one was high and inside to the right-handed hitter, and Thomson went after it. He drove it toward the friendliest part of the field, toward the 315-foot sign in left.

For a moment, Russ Hodges thought Andy Pafko might catch it. Then Hodges's voice began to rise to the occasion: "It's gonna be . . . I believe . . . the Giants win the pennant . . . the Giants win the pennant! The Giants win the pennant! The Giants win the pennant! Bobby Thomson hits into the lower deck of the left-field stands! The Giants win the pennant! I don't believe it! I don't believe it! I do not believe it!"

Bedlam! The fans poured onto the field, third-base coach Eddie Stanky jumped on Durocher's back, and Thomson, hopping and jumping, could barely find home plate to touch it. Then came the long run

Bobby Thomson, greeted at home plate by his Giant teammates following his pennant-winning 1951 home run. (UPI/Bettmann Newsphotos)

to the center-field clubhouse, followed by a curtain call to appease all the fans on the field, and Bobby Thomson was forever baseball history.

Branca, understandably dejected, moaned "Why me?" over and over again in the Dodger clubhouse. All he could do was watch the World Series on television, watch the Giants lose to the Yankees, watch Thomson hit .238 in the Series with no homers, and somehow hope that he would be redeemed. Of course, he never would be.

They've done all right for themselves, those two. They were both great sports as the years went by, often appearing together at old-timers' gatherings for "reenactments."

Thomson played through the 1960 season. In 1954 he was with the Milwaukee Braves when he broke his ankle in spring training. That opened a spot on the roster for a rookie named Hank Aaron. So in a span of four years, Thomson had yielded his position twice—first to Willie Mays, then to Hank Aaron. His lifetime average was .270 with 264 home runs, and in 1969 he joined Mays and Mel Ott in the all-time Giant outfield, as voted by fans during baseball's centennial.

Branca had only twelve victories left in his career, finishing 88–68. On October 20, 1951, seventeen days after the playoffs, he married Ann Mulvey, whose family was part owner of the Dodgers. Branca became a wealthy insurance executive, Thomson a successful businessman with a paper company.

Today, what with high-tech communications, prime-time night games, and the vast commercial endorsements certain to follow it, one wonders how this quintessential baseball moment would have played out in the nineties. But then again, one wonders if it could possibly be more memorable than it was.

27

Milestones for The Man

There may have been no finer hitter in the National League in the last half century than Stan Musial. And to think that he achieved what he did with a batting stance so incredibly unorthodox that it couldn't be demonstrated by anyone other than "The Man" himself. But as the old axiom goes: It makes no difference where you start; it's where you end up that counts. In his case, it was where he ended up just before going for the ball.

Stan the Man got that nickname from New York baseball writers. It probably traces back to a series in 1948 in Ebbets Field when Musial went 11-for-15 with four doubles, a triple, and a home run. It included a 5-for-5 game and proved that no matter how big you are in your home city, if you come to New York and have a big weekend, you can go home with a brand-new nickname.

Stan spent his entire twenty-four-year career with the St. Louis Cardinals. He wasn't in many pennant races and never had more than two or three writers covering the team. It was an idyllic situation for the mild-mannered slugger, who was able to relax throughout a joyous career.

Now that free agency has facilitated the changing of teams, the idea of a player spending twenty-four years with one club seems like a relic from another century. In recent times we have seen Mike Schmidt, Carl Yastrzemski, and Johnny Bench spend whole careers in one city,

170

but they are the exceptions to the rule. When the 1990 season ended, Terry Puhl of Houston was the senior player among those who had spent an entire career with one National League club. But he left after the season, passing along the honor to the Dodgers' Mike Scioscia, who had merely twelve years in one place. Times have certainly changed.

Musial hit .331 in his career and won seven batting titles, but he had no better season than the year of his Ebbets Field explosion, 1948, leading the National League in runs, hits, doubles, triples, RBIs, batting average, on-base percentage, and slugging percentage. The only major department he failed to lead in was home runs—although he hit a career high of thirty-nine, had one rained out, and missed tying Ralph Kiner and Johnny Mize for the league lead by one.

Stan had 475 career home runs, making him sixth on the all-time list when he retired, yet he never had forty in a season and never led the league. What's more, he never considered himself a home-run hitter. In fact, he claimed that anytime he tried to homer, it would mess up his stroke. He thought of himself as a line-drive singles hitter whose natural stroke was such that he could lift the ball out of the park "on occasion."

Such an occasion came on May 2, 1954, in his home park of Busch Stadium, which had just been renamed after years as Sportsman's Park. The Busch brewery had just purchased the team, given Musial an $80,000 contract, and put him in an unquestioned position of team leadership, casting aside the last "Gashouse Gang" link from earlier Cardinal glory days.

The '54 season was the first in which Stan was the Cardinals' senior member, Enos Slaughter having been traded to the Yankees to make way for rookie Wally Moon. (There was also a day that April when Musial played right field and watched a kid named Henry Aaron belt his first major league home run, off the Cards' Vic Raschi. Little did Musial realize that afternoon that the skinny kid wearing number 5 for the Milwaukee Braves would one day break many of his own National League records.)

The Cardinals were hosting the New York Giants for the May 2 Sunday afternoon doubleheader. The Giants, who would emerge World Champions that season, started Johnny Antonelli in the first game. After walking in the first inning, Musial hit a slow curve onto the right-field roof for a homer in the third. In the fifth he swung at one of Antonelli's fastballs, down and in, and again hit the right-field roof, for his second homer.

In the sixth he singled off reliever Jim Hearn. With the score 6–6 in the eighth inning, Musial faced Hearn again, picked a slider, and again deposited it on the roof in right, for the first three-homer game of his career.

In the fifth inning of the second game, Stan faced knuckleball artist Hoyt Wilhelm, waited him out for a slow curve, and hit one over the stands and onto Grand Avenue for his fourth home run of the afternoon. In the seventh inning he got only knuckleballs, Wilhelm's specialty, but he sent one of those even farther out onto Grand, becoming the first player in the history of baseball to hit five home runs in one day.

That streak started a sensational month for Musial, and by the beginning of June, he had twenty homers in fifty games, causing the fans to talk about Ruth's record of sixty homers and Mel Ott's National League mark of fifty-six. All this over a man who had never led the league in homers. Musial, however, continued to insist that he was only a singles hitter, and eventually he found his level and wound up the season with thirty-five home runs, well behind the league leaders.

Although the power burst in 1954 was out of character for The Man, he was still the master at the plate when he found his usual stroke. He batted .330 that year, and when he followed with a mere .319 and .310 in 1955 and 1956, people thought he was an old warrior just hanging on to reach three-thousand hits. But in 1957 he returned to form, hitting .351 for his seventh batting title, and he entered the 1958 season forty-three hits shy of three thousand.

Although we have seen a number of players reach three thousand hits in the last twenty years or so—Hank Aaron, Willie Mays, Pete Rose, Carl Yastrzemski, Roberto Clemente, Rod Carew, Lou Brock, and Al Kaline, with Robin Yount on the way—in 1958 this club still had a very limited membership. There were Ty Cobb, Tris Speaker, Honus Wagner, Eddie Collins, Nap Lajoie, Paul Waner, and Cap Anson. Seven in all, and none since 1942, when Waner got his three thousandth.

Thus, the potential achievement brought a great deal of attention to St. Louis. On May 13 the Cardinals were in Chicago. Musial had 2,999 hits, and Fred Hutchinson, Stan's manager, told the press that

The Man would sit out the game in hopes of getting number three thousand in St. Louis before his hometown fans.

This sort of decision has always been met with a host of second-guessing, most notably when the Braves sought to have Aaron hit his record-breaking homer at home in 1974 and commissioner Bowie Kuhn ordered him to play in Cincinnati. But not much fuss was raised in 1958 over the decision to "rest" Musial in Chicago.

Fewer than six thousand people were in Wrigley Field that afternoon. The Cardinals were trailing 3–1 in the sixth when Hutchinson decided that he needed Musial to pinch-hit for pitcher Sam Jones. The Cubs' pitcher was Moe Drabowsky.

So on a day when only a handful of fans turned out to see him, when few expected any records to fall, Stan went out and drove a double down the left-field line for the Big Hit, thus becoming only the eighth player in history with three thousand.

Stan hit .337 that year, but when he fell under .300 for the next three years, it seemed clear that his day had passed. Then in 1962 he came back to hit an amazing .330, third in the league. He played one more season and retired with 3,630 hits, the most in the National League, and second only to Cobb lifetime. It was Pete Rose who would finally pass his league hit record.

Stan missed a Cardinal pennant by a single season, watching from the crowd as St. Louis won for the first time since 1946 the year after he retired. I came along in 1967 and was sorry I never had the opportunity to face The Man, because I always got a kick out of looking in at guys like Aaron, Mays, and Clemente, who were boyhood heroes.

When I was about fourteen, I went to San Francisco to see Stan play a game against the Giants. This was the first year of major league baseball in California. He hit four routine grounders that day at old Seals Stadium, but he sprinted on every one and showed everyone how the game is supposed to be played. I still have that image of him in my mind.

I actually met him one afternoon when I was about nineteen years old. The University of Southern California, my college team, was in Hawaii for a summer baseball tournament, and obviously we spent most of the time on the beach soaking up the Pacific sun.

One afternoon there was a tidal-wave warning and everyone was

Stan Musial collects his 3,000th career hit, Wrigley Field, 1958. (National Baseball Library, Cooperstown, N.Y.)

ordered to get off the beach and into the hotels above the ground floor. Some of my teammates and I went to our hotel and took an elevator up to a top floor to watch the wall of water, which never did come.

As I was walking down the hall of the hotel, I glanced into a room whose door was open. Who was sitting there, near the balcony, waiting to see the no-show tidal wave? You guessed it—number 6.

I took two more steps, stopped, and said, "I can't pass this up." Turning, I walked into Stan Musial's room, introduced myself and my teammates, and told him we were there for a tournament. We chatted for five minutes or so about baseball, USC, and, of course, Rod Dedeaux, my SC coach. Stan the Man. A nicer man I never met. When I left I felt we had been friends for years.

Musial continued his association with the Cardinals long after his retirement, but he really became a great ambassador for baseball, bringing good fellowship and charm to any gathering. With Joe DiMaggio and Ted Williams, he represented the last of the "legendary" modern players whose era drew to a close before the introduction of artificial turf and superstructure ballparks.

As for his records, some will be passed, as Aaron and Rose proved, and one has been equaled. Nate Colbert, playing for San Diego in 1972, hit five homers in a doubleheader to put his name alongside Stan's in the record book. I don't know about Nate, but I think I'd rather have my name with Stan's in a record book than alone. Adds a little to the record, if you know what I mean.

28

Mays, Center Field

Baseball is offense, pitching, and defense, with defense always mentioned last and least appreciated. It's almost the unnoticed element, except when it's missing. On the major league level, outstanding plays can look routine. "A major leaguer makes that play" is commonly heard around the ballpark when the slightest miscue occurs. But find a team with glaring defensive weaknesses and you'll find a team that won't be able to win without a struggle. And you won't find a team that can go all the way.

So good was Willie Mays as a defensive outfielder that he was one of the few sluggers in baseball history whose fielding was discussed in the same breath as his offense. He was simply spectacular, partly because of his instincts, partly because of his speed, and partly because of his showmanship. His "basket catch" and flying cap became trademarks. He was a joy to watch, not only for his ability to make the impossible possible but for the way he approached the game, with such zest and love.

I was his teammate on the Mets for the final year and a half of his career, when his skills had slowed but his enthusiasm was still genuine, and he was just a delight to behold. There was a biography on Mays called *Born to Play Ball*, and what an apt title it was.

When he was with the Mets, Willie would come to me before a game and ask me how I was going to pitch to each hitter. He'd write my responses down on a slip of paper that he'd keep in his uniform pants, then consult and position himself in center field accordingly. It was just a little edge, but he took advantage of it. He had slowed down in speed, and maybe his instincts weren't as sharp, but his approach to the game was still businesslike and exemplary. He helped us win a pennant in 1973, even though he played only sixty-six games and batted .211. He would do things on the bases to get other runners into scoring position, or he'd score runs when other men would have held at third. He knew how to play the game of baseball.

Looking back to the fifties, I often think how fortunate were New Yorkers to have three good baseball teams to choose from, to be virtually assured of a pennant race every year. And on an individual basis, how lucky were New Yorkers to have four of the best all-around players of all time, and all center fielders: Joe DiMaggio, setting the stage at the start of the decade, and then Mantle, Snider, and Mays, all playing the same position at the same time. What riches!

Willie made many brilliant plays in his long career, but none more famous than the spectacular running catch in the deep regions of the old Polo Grounds in the 1954 World Series. This great play occurred when television had arrived in most households, so that audiences in the millions were now viewing the games. But newsreel cameras were also on hand to provide highlights in movie theaters, and they too captured the play for all eternity. In a career of 660 home runs and honors too numerous to list, this was Willie's play for the ages.

The 1954 World Series produced as shocking a result as would the 1990 Series, in which underdog Cincinnati not only won but swept the Oakland Athletics. In 1954, the Giants found themselves facing the Cleveland Indians, whose 111 victories were not only an American League record for one season but also one that is still standing, three decades after baseball expanded the regular season by eight additional games. And as for the theory that good pitching always prevails in a short series, it was Cleveland, not New York, that had the celebrated pitching. Its 111 games were mostly the result of one of the finest pitching staffs ever assembled, a staff so strong that Bob Feller was the *fifth* starter.

Bob Lemon and Early Wynn were both twenty-three game winners for the Indians that year, with Mike Garcia adding nineteen and Ray Narleski fifteen. Feller, who made nineteen starts, was 13–3. The bullpen included Hal Newhouser, Don Mossi, and Art Houtteman, and

Willie Mays's catch off Vic Wertz at the Polo Grounds, 1954 World Series (Wide World Photos)

everyone on the staff had a role and played it perfectly. The pitching staff's earned-run average was 2.78, with Garcia leading the league at 2.64, while Lemon and Wynn tied for the most wins and Wynn led in strikeouts. The 111 victories were no fluke; the Indians had to beat the Yankees, winners of five consecutive World Championships, and they beat them by eight games. They really cleaned up by taking season series from Boston, Baltimore, Washington, and Philadelphia, going 75–13 against those clubs, an .852 percentage.

The Giants won ninety-seven under Leo Durocher, and while it was a great year for them, they simply were not expected to beat Cleveland. The Giants had won in 1951, Mays's rookie season. Then Willie went into the service in '52 and '53, and the Dodgers won both years. Mays returned to baseball in '54, and again the Giants prevailed. Apparently there was a correlation.

Mays hit .345 in the regular season to win his only batting championship. He led the league with 13 triples, belted 41 homers, and drove in 110 runs. At twenty-three, in only his second full major league season, he won the MVP award.

The regular season ended early by the calendar, and the first game of the World Series was played in the Polo Grounds on Saturday, September 29. Those without television sets gathered in front of "radio stores" to watch the games on display-model TVs. They saw Bob Lemon start for the Indians and Sal Maglie for the Giants, "The Barber" getting the nod over the staff's leading winner, 21–7 Johnny Antonelli.

Cleveland scored two in the first when Vic Wertz, the Indians' slugging first baseman, tripled home batting champ Bobby Avila and Al Smith. Wertz also singled in the fourth and the sixth.

The Giants tied the game 2–2 in the third, Hank Thompson singling home the tying run. And that's how it stood into the eighth when Larry Doby led off for Cleveland with a walk and Al Rosen singled him to second.

Wertz, now 3-for-3, headed for the plate, but Durocher went to his bullpen and brought Don Liddle in to replace Maglie. Wertz, a powerful left-handed hitter, took Liddle's very first pitch and hit it as hard as he'd ever hit anything.

Center field in the horseshoe-shaped Polo Grounds went back 490 feet to dead center, the farthest stadium distance in baseball.

In an instant, Mays turned and raced at full speed to the far reaches of right-center. Fans saw the number 24 on Willie's back racing ever deeper as the two runners considered whether to tag up or just take off.

About 450 feet from home plate, Willie peeked over his left shoulder and picked up the ball. He raised his arms and timed the catch perfectly, about twelve feet in front of the wall. Had he merely made the catch, we would still be talking about it. But he did more. In what seemed like a single motion, he made the catch, whirled, and fired it toward second base, where Davey Williams took the throw, fired home, and held the runners. What should have been two or even three runs had been turned into none. It simply broke the backs of the Indians.

There were no instant replays. It was left to word of mouth to share the wonder of what had just been seen. To catch any baseball over the shoulders is a tough play. To do it at full speed while approaching a wall, and then to execute such a perfect throw, made this a miracle catch.

The game went to the tenth inning, with Lemon still pitching. Mays led off the last of the tenth with a walk. He stole second. Thompson was walked intentionally, and Durocher sent Dusty Rhodes up to pinch-hit. Rhodes had hit fifteen homers in 164 at-bats during the season, and he responded to this call by belting the first pitch 270 feet into the right-field stands, far enough for a game-winning homer.

If that wasn't enough, the very next day Rhodes got a pinch-hit single in the fifth to tie the game 1–1. He stayed in to play right field, and in the seventh, homered again to insure a 3–1 Giant victory. He pinch-hit a single in Game Three to drive in two runs as the Giants won 6–2, and the sweep was completed the next afternoon with a 7–4 New York triumph before seventy-eight thousand fans in Cleveland's Municipal Stadium.

Rhodes, 4-for-6 with seven RBIs, was the toast of New York, but the fans were still talking about Mays's brilliant catch in the first game, a catch that has grown to mythic proportions over the years to become probably the most famous defensive play in baseball history.

To Mays, it was not the best catch he ever made, but he acknowledges its importance due to the World Series spotlight. In his autobiography, he cites a play for Trenton in 1950, when he was in the minors, a bare-handed, homer-robbing catch in dead center that included a throw all the way to home plate, a distance of 405 feet. He talks of a clutch catch of a ball hit by Brooklyn's Carl Furillo during the hot '51 pennant race, and another diving catch in Ebbets Field when he was knocked cold but held on to the ball.

At Candlestick Park, in 1960, he made a play against the Cubs in which he raced to his left, intending to cut off a sinking drive and hold it to a single. Instead, he was able to stretch and reach back to catch it on a fly *after* it had actually gone past him.

Over the years, Willie made many, many plays that left both seasoned major leaguers and longtime fans in total awe. Because he was such a complete player, blessed with such offensive and defensive skills and the flair for the spectacular, he did very little that wasn't memorable. But the World Series catch of 1954 will forever be his trademark performance.

29

Perfection in October

The list of baseball's fifteen perfect games includes some fairly well-known names—Cy Young, Sandy Koufax, Jim Bunning, and Catfish Hunter, as well as some obscure names generally lost to history, like Lee Richmond (who threw the first one, in 1880, a year in which he went 32–32), Charlie Robertson (who never had a .500 season), and Ernie Shore, who hurled his game in relief after Babe Ruth, the starting pitcher, was ejected for arguing over a base on balls (see Chapter 8).

Don Larsen is neither obscure nor an all-time great. But the only reason he does not land on the obscure list and, in fact, draws votes at Hall of Fame election time, is that one beautiful fall afternoon in October, he chose to pitch a perfect game in the World Series.

The year was 1956, and this was a matchup between the New York Yankees and the Brooklyn Dodgers, the sixth World Series between these two foes in ten years and the only one in which the Yankees were seeking to avenge a loss, the Dodgers having won it all in 1955.

Larsen, hardly the ace of a staff that also included Whitey Ford, Bob Turley, and sixteen-game winner Tom Sturdivant, had won his last four decisions of the regular season, and was thus the starter in Game Two. His response to Casey Stengel's confidence was a second-inning knockout following four walks.

To the writers who had covered the Yankees all season, this was hardly astonishing. The four straight wins in September were the surprise. Larsen was, after all, the same fellow who had gone 3–21 just two years earlier with the old St. Louis Browns, and who was only 30–40 lifetime. At age twenty-seven, he still had "promise," having gone 20–7 in two seasons with the Yankees, but was hardly a dominant force.

His training techniques were not classic examples of self-control. He was known to miss curfew on more than one occasion, including the night before the fifth game of the '56 World Series, even though he was scheduled to pitch again that day. He had been out celebrating life with sportswriter Arthur Richman and got home after midnight. It is hard to imagine, even today, how he could have broken curfew the night before pitching a World Series game, but you would have to conclude that Larsen was just a free spirit.

Stengel, a free spirit himself during his hell-raising days as a player, tended toward leniency with his truants, even if the front office considered it acceptable to hire private detectives to follow Yankee players on their nightly rounds.

Larsen's assignment on October 8 would be to face a Brooklyn lineup of Jim Gilliam, Pee Wee Reese, Duke Snider, Jackie Robinson, Gil Hodges, Sandy Amoros, Carl Furillo, Roy Campanella, and Sal Maglie. Reese, Snider, Robinson, and Campanella are all in the Hall of Fame today; many think Hodges belongs as well. So these were not exactly the '62 Mets out there. To beat them, and to outpitch the skilled Maglie, would be a task. To pitch a complete game seemed unlikely; to hurl a shutout (Larsen had five to this point in his career and would finish with eleven), a long shot. Any talk of a no-hitter would be saved for others—there had never been one in a World Series. If anyone deserved that kind of whisper it was Maglie, who had tossed one against the Phillies just two weeks earlier. The glamour of that feat was still very much the talk of the baseball world. Furthermore, Maglie had beaten Ford in the Series opener five days earlier, striking out ten Yankees in the process. Those who studied the pitching matchup gave it all to Maglie.

And Maglie *was* on that day. He got the first eleven Yankees in order before Mickey Mantle homered just inside the right-field foul pole to make it 1–0. Meanwhile, Larsen was setting down the Dodgers in order, no doubt causing lovers of offensive baseball to bemoan the dull pitching duel that was unfolding. The first twenty-three batters in the game—both sides—had been retired before Mantle's homer.

Maglie was still sharp, but in the sixth, a sacrifice bunt by Larsen helped to build the Yankees' second run, when Hank Bauer drove in Andy Carey. That would be all the scoring in this game.

No doubt by the sixth inning, the fans were talking about a no-hitter. Those keeping box score in their seats would add to the drama by informing those who weren't that no Dodger had in fact reached base—not on a walk, not on an error. Even the Yankee fielders later admitted they were unaware of the perfect game in progress, only the no-hitter, in part because Larsen worked from a stretch position, coming set at the waist without bringing his arms over his head. Weeks earlier he had abandoned a full windup. Players tend to remember when pitchers work from a stretch—strategies and defensive respon-sibilities change accordingly. But with Larsen always in a stretch position, the "no runners" mode wasn't as obvious. And, of course, in observance of a time-honored tradition, no one mentioned the work-in-progress to Larsen between innings. No one, in fact, even cared to sit with him on the bench, for *fear* of saying something inappropriate.

The Dodgers had a few close ones. Robinson had been retired by a step in the second on a liner off Carey's glove at third, which had to then be fielded by Gil McDougald at shortstop. Hodges flied deep to left-center in the fifth, but Mantle, in his MVP and Triple Crown season, rose to the occasion and ran it down. Amoros, the weakest hitter in the lineup, followed that play by hitting a long foul to right before grounding out.

The fans at Yankee Stadium—all 64,519 of them—were into every pitch by the seventh inning, counting down the nine outs Larsen had left. Even the *talk* of a perfect game was something that just didn't happen in baseball. The last one had been Robertson's, thirty-four years earlier. Perfect games now seemed as extinct as gloves without the fingers or forty-game winners. And besides, although it was the seventh inning, Larsen still had to get through the tough Dodger lineup one more time.

In the seventh, Gilliam grounded to short, Reese flied to Mantle in center, and Snider flied to Slaughter in left.

In the eighth, Robinson grounded back to the box, Hodges lined to third, and Amoros flied to center. In the last of the eighth, the Stadium rocked with a standing ovation for Larsen, who led off for the Yankees. (Another element of baseball sadly missing since the designated-hitter rule is that grand opportunity for fans to applaud a pitcher when he comes to bat late in a game, having won their hearts with his day's work on the mound.)

Now, the ninth inning. Larsen went 1-and-2 on Furillo, then got him on a routine fly to right.

Campanella was up next. A foul for strike one, then a grounder to Billy Martin at second. Two down.

Maglie, due to hit, was of course brought back for a pinch hitter—Dale Mitchell, who had spent his entire eleven-year career with the Indians, save for his last nineteen games. He had been purchased on July 29 but had had only twenty-four at-bats in the season's final two months. Sharp he wasn't. This would be the next-to-last at-bat of his career, and probably, despite a .312 lifetime average, his most famous. Hit or out, he was certain to go down in history with this appearance at the plate.

The first pitch was outside for a ball, and the crowd groaned. Next Larsen threw a called strike to even the count. Then came a swinging strike, and then a foul into the left-field stands. The next pitch may or may not have covered the black, but umpire Babe Pinelli, working his final game behind the plate, yelled "strike three" and was running off the field before Mitchell could protest. Pinelli wasn't about to blow his part of history.

That was it! A no-hitter, a perfect game, only the fifth of the century, and of course, the first and still the only in World Series play.

Yogi Berra, who caught Larsen, ran out and jumped with glee into Larsen's arms, like a little boy greeting his dad after a business trip. To know the low-keyed, grunt-for-an-answer Yogi, and to see the film of this burst of excitement, is truly to realize the emotion of the moment. Given the situation, and given the rather ordinary tools with which Larsen had to work, it was probably the greatest game ever pitched.

Larsen had thrown ninety-seven pitches. It was the first time I remember ever hearing a pitch count. For a long time I assumed that must have been some sort of record, too, but I've since learned that although anything under a hundred is impressive, ninety-seven has been bettered many times. Still, Larsen made all of America aware of things like "pitch count," "no windup," and "perfect game" that day.

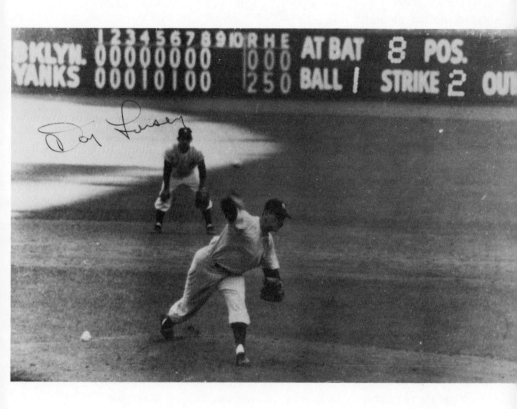

Don Larsen delivers the final pitch of his perfect game in the 1956 World Series. Billy Martin is the second baseman. (UPI/Bettmann Newsphotos)

Larsen's burst of fame was brief by major league standards. He was 10–4 in 1957 and in 1960 was traded to Kansas City, for whom he went 1–10. He bounded around with a number of teams until his retirement in 1967, the last St. Louis Brown still active. He was 81–91 lifetime, and probably added years to his career on the strength of the perfect game. Imagine how many Old Timers Day invitations it has resulted in after more than thirty-five years.

In 1962, it happened that Larsen was with the pennant-winning San Francisco Giants. He got into three games in the World Series that year against the Yankees. Game Four was played in Yankee Stadium. In the sixth inning, with the game tied 2–2, he ambled in from the bullpen to face Yogi Berra, batting for Ford. He walked him. But he got the next batter, and when the Giants scored four in the seventh on a grand slam by Chuck Hiller, Larsen ended up the winning pitcher.

It was not his most famous World Series win in Yankee Stadium.

30

The Majors Move West

When I was growing up in Fresno, California, in the 1950s and 1960s, St. Louis was the nearest major league city. We would never travel there just to take in a ball game. For generations of kids on the West Coast, the Pacific Coast League (PCL) meant pro baseball, and all the other guys—the real big leaguers—were what you read, heard, or dreamed about.

The PCL was based in cities that have for the most part made their way into the major leagues. Los Angeles, San Francisco, Seattle, San Diego, and Oakland all started out as PCL franchises, and when the major leagues topped out at four hundred players before expansion, you had some great talent performing on a very high level in Triple A. Today there are six hundred fifty big leaguers (and there will be seven hundred by 1993). If you ranked them in order of ability, you would find that numbers 401 to 700 played Triple A ball before expansion—a level at which many of them should still be playing.

In my hometown we had the Fresno Cardinals, and I well remember the summer of 1952, when Larry Jackson was 28–4 with 351 strike-outs. Jackson later became a top-flight major leaguer, and was particularly tough against the Mets.

I happened to be a Milwaukee Brave fan. I liked the team's uniforms and its power hitters. Maybe there was something about the Braves' "newness" that attracted me, but I don't remember that with certainty.

188

They had moved to Milwaukee from Boston after the 1952 season, the first franchise shift in the majors since the Baltimore Orioles had become the New York Highlanders in 1903. For a half century, Major League Baseball had been a model of stability, with three teams in New York, two each in Boston, Philadelphia, Chicago, and St. Louis, and one each in Cleveland, Detroit, Washington, Pittsburgh, and Cincinnati. Most of the excitement of the "national pastime" was confined to those ten cities. The sport may have been stable and charming, but it left a lot of people on the outside looking in.

The Braves' move to Milwaukee caused no great consternation among baseball fans. Although the Boston franchise had drawn over a million fans during its pennant-contending years in the late forties, interest in the Braves had fallen quickly. In 1950 they drew 944,391. In 1951 they were down to 487,475. In 1952, they drew a horrid 281,278, which came to about 3,900 a date. In a town that belonged to the Red Sox, the announcement that the Braves were moving to Milwaukee did not arouse lasting protest, certainly nothing like the furor that would result when the team moved from Milwaukee to Atlanta for the 1966 season.

Then, following the 1953 season, the St. Louis Browns shifted to Baltimore and restored the Oriole name to the major leagues after a half century. The Browns had never been a successful American League franchise, by any measure. In the 1930s, they drew 1,184,076 for the entire decade. They had one championship to show for their history, a 1944 pennant won under war conditions. Even in that season, they had drawn only 508,644. By 1947 they were back in last place, with an attendance of 320,474. From 1949 to 1953, they topped three hundred thousand only once, and in '53 finished last, with a hundred losses, forty six and a half games out of first, averaging four thousand paying customers a date. And so they left St. Louis to the Cardinals and headed for Baltimore. Again, no loud protests of any lasting nature were heard.

After the very next season, 1954, the once-proud Philadelphia Athletics abandoned their home for Kansas City. Connie Mack had retired as manager after 1950, but the team was still dismal in the standings, weak at the gate, and empty in the bank. In 1953 it finished sixty games out of first, having drawn 304,666 fans. Philadelphia now belonged solely to the Phillies.

So after half a century of stability, three franchises shifted in three

years. The concept was now accepted with little more than a murmur.
The game, it was felt, could not only survive the moves, it could
prosper with them: Wouldn't the "abandoned" cities be better off with
only one team? Wouldn't fans still have big-league baseball, but a
team that would draw better? The new markets were rewarding,
particularly Milwaukee, where the Braves soon became National
League champions. Franchise maneuvering didn't have to hurt, did it?

But what would come next? The other franchises were all relatively
successful—with the exception of Washington, but moving out of the
capital was not a viable idea. After all, could you imagine a "major
league" in Russia without a Moscow franchise? Or England without a
London team or France without Paris? It just couldn't be.

Festering in New York, however, were concerns in the minds of
Horace Stoneham, owner of the New York Giants, and Walter O'Malley, owner of the Brooklyn Dodgers. Both franchises were among the
most historically sacred in the game. They both belonged deep in the
game's ties to its past. The Giants' legacy included John McGraw,
Christy Mathewson, Bill Terry, Carl Hubbell, Mel Ott, and Willie
Mays. The Dodgers' greatest era was in motion just as these concerns
were developing. The great "Boys of Summer" players of the 1950s
(a term coined much later by writer Roger Kahn) included Duke
Snider, Gil Hodges, Roy Campanella, Pee Wee Reese, Jackie Robinson, and Carl Furillo.

But there were problems. Both the Polo Grounds and Ebbets Field
were aging parks, and New York City showed little enthusiasm for
building replacement facilities. As populations shifted to the suburbs,
parking became a major issue at both inner-city facilities.

The Giants had won pennants in 1951 and 1954, and in Mays had
the league's most exciting player and in Leo Durocher its most exciting
manager. But in 1951 the team drew only 1,008,876, and in 1952 just
a little more. Then, between 1953 and 1957, the Giants topped a
million only once, falling under seven hundred thousand in both 1956
and 1957, when they had sixth-place teams. Worse, a large percentage
of that attendance was registered on the dates in which Brooklyn was
the visiting team. Subtracting those dates left embarrassingly low
totals for this proud franchise.

On the other hand, the Dodgers always drew over a million fans into
their small and uncomfortable Ebbets Field, but these were low figures
for one of the greatest teams ever assembled. Over their shoulders,

O'Malley and Stoneham could watch the Milwaukee Braves draw over two million every year between 1954 and 1957. Think of it: Milwaukee!

Not until 1957 did whispers become outright rumors that both teams were looking west. The city governments in San Francisco and Los Angeles could not keep secret their desires to make their cities "big league." Los Angeles in particular was poised to become the nation's third-largest city. Having major league baseball seemed not just a dream, but almost a necessity.

When denials turned into "wait and sees" in New York, the fans knew the situation was serious. Dodger fans had always been among the most loyal in baseball history. While they may have found a visit to Ebbets Field less and less comfortable as the park aged, they were still ardent supporters. In fact, they were as much a part of the Brooklyn mystique as were the great players of the fifties. Rooting for "Dem Bums" helped create a Brooklyn identity that the nation recognized immediately. The fans' loyal "Wait till next year" cry after losing to the Yankees so many times became part of the national idiom.

As a California teenager, I was thrilled by the prospect of having big-league baseball come west. I had no particular feelings for the Brooklyn fans, three thousand miles away. It took me a long time to understand the depth of their loss. I have lived in the New York area for more than twenty years, and I still meet so many people who feel Brooklyn lost its identity when the Dodgers left that I can't help but take a new, sociological view of the event. Certainly, I feel more sympathy today than it ever occurred to me to feel back then.

To tell the truth, it was not until my sixth or seventh year with the Mets that I learned what their colors meant: The blue and orange were borrowed from the Dodgers and Giants, respectively, in order to retain the link to National League baseball in New York and to appeal to both Dodger and Giant fans. Who would have ever imagined that the two sets of fans would someday be sitting side by side, rooting for the same team?

At any rate, in 1956 and 1957, the Dodgers gave every indication that they were serious about moving by playing fifteen home games in Jersey City, New Jersey. It was O'Malley's way of telling New York that it just wasn't working in Brooklyn. In February 1957, the Dodgers and Cubs swapped minor-league franchises, the Cubs taking Fort Worth and the Dodgers taking Los Angeles.

On August 19, 1957, the Giants turned rumor to fact when their directors voted 8–1 to permit the move to San Francisco. Although the Dodgers had not yet made such an announcement, it seemed illogical that the Giants would move alone and forfeit their rivalry with the Dodgers. Besides, without them, travel would be absurd for the other teams, who would have to go to California for only three days.

So on October 8, while the Milwaukee Braves were playing Game Six of the World Series at Yankee Stadium, while all the nation's sporting press was in New York, the Dodgers' directors voted unanimously to move to Los Angeles.

It was devastating news for National League fans in New York, and cause for joyous celebration on the West Coast. As the railroads had once linked the nation and made it whole, now Major League Baseball was a coast-to-coast affair.

The first big-league game played in the Pacific Standard Time zone was on April 15, 1958, at Seals Stadium in San Francisco. The Giants beat the Dodgers 8–0 on the pitching of Ruben Gomez and home runs by Daryl Spencer and rookie Orlando Cepeda. Three days later, 78,672 fans, a major league record, headed for Los Angeles Memorial Coliseum, where a forty-foot screen had been built over a 251-foot left-field wall. They saw the Dodgers hold on for a 6–5 win behind Carl Erskine and Clem Labine. Missing from the Dodgers' lineup was their lovable catcher, Roy Campanella, who had been paralyzed in a car accident over the winter.

West Coast baseball inevitably brought change to the game. A casual style took hold in the West and worked its way east. Fans no longer wore neckties and hats to games. Eastern fans had to learn to live without knowing all the scores in the majors before they went to bed. Players added Hollywood to their list of "places to go" when they went on the road.

The Dodgers won a pennant in 1959, the Giants in 1962. The Dodgers became the game's most financially successful franchise. On the other hand, the Giants got the short end of the move, because of a difficult ballpark in windblown Candlestick and the relocation of the A's from Kansas City to Oakland in 1968, which complicated attendance and created a situation exactly like baseball had tried to pull itself out of in the early fifties. The Dodgers were joined by the Angels in 1961, but both franchises managed to thrive at the gate, particularly

Seals Stadium in San Francisco, 1958.

after the Angels got their own ballpark and moved down the freeway to Anaheim.

The borough of Brooklyn had taken its loss hard, but the Mets arrived in 1962 and won back the hearts of New York's National League fans in a city that could obviously support two teams. It was a painful growing process for Major League Baseball, but in retrospect, a necessary one. The time had come to reach out to cities deserving of big-league baseball and to recognize that the United States was truly a coast-to-coast country.

Expansion Years

THE HALF-CENTURY of stability for Major League Baseball, when sixteen teams remained in place, none farther west than St. Louis, ended with the move by the Dodgers and Giants to the West Coast in 1958. Two years later, the "pre-expansion era" concluded with two thundering farewells—Ted Williams's final at-bat to finish the 1960 regular season, and Bill Mazeroski's historic homer to close the World Series. And that was it: the end of sixteen-team, four hundred-player baseball.

The events that unfolded in the coming years were monumental, and not necessarily attributable to expansion. Certainly, with fifty new jobs open in 1961 and another fifty in 1962, the level of play changed. Not only did the expansion teams employ players who might otherwise have been in the minors, but so too did the existing teams, who had to surrender established players to stock the new clubs and replace them from their farm systems.

An immediate result was the 240-homer season of the 1961 Yankees, led by Roger Maris's record 61. In 1962, the first year of National League expansion, Maury Wills broke Ty Cobb's stolen-base mark. In 1963, Sandy Koufax threw the first of four no-hitters he would hurl over four years, and his feats set the standards by which Juan Marichal and Bob Gibson proceeded to work toward the "Year of the Pitcher" in 1968. The Yankee dynasty crumbled in 1965, the first year of the free-agent draft for amateurs. In 1967 the Boston Red Sox won a pennant with an "Impossible Dream" season from Carl

Yastrzemski, and in 1968 Denny McLain won thirty-one and the Tigers came back from a 3–1 deficit to win the World Series. The decade ended with the World Championship of the "Miracle Mets." In the span of history, the 1960s will be a speck; but the baseball events of the decade make one think that it may have been the most historic of all the periods the sport has experienced.

The sixties was a time for great sluggers. When the decade began, the top ten home run list read Ruth, Foxx, Ott, Williams, Gehrig, Musial, Snider, Hodges, Kiner, and DiMaggio, Joe bringing up the rear with 361. Joe barely makes the top forty today. Most of the list is dominated by players who played during the power years of the 1960s, when the strategy was "three-run homer and say good night." And still, some of the greatest pitchers of all time performed in that decade.

The game was blasted by business publications for being overtaken in its appeal by football and for ceasing to be the national pastime. And baseball responded with a greater flair for promotion. The result, as the mid-seventies approached, was a well-packaged entertainment for the masses that would break attendance records yearly and emerge from the growing pains of expansion healthier than ever.

This was the major leagues I entered in 1967. I would see the game's great sluggers from sixty feet, six inches away. I saw the balance of power switch to the mound. John Fogerty of Creedence Clearwater Revival described a road "where the neon turns to wood." I was there when the flannel turned to double knit and a new baseball explosion hit.

31

Farewell to The Thumper

When the greatest of the greats play their final game, somehow the earth ought to shake or the skies lighten, or there should be some other supernatural sign that this particular athlete will play no more.

But it doesn't happen that way. In fact, very few of the game's "greats" willingly retire. As with ordinary players, they are either released, injured and unable to continue, unclaimed as free agents, or cut in spring training. Few choose just to walk away.

It's understandable. To quit is to acknowledge that you've become old, that the skills you thought you could call upon are no longer sharp enough. That's hard for anyone to accept. And the money is so enormous today, how does one say "no thanks" to a million bucks? But even when it was $100,000, it was, after all, your living. Players have always had trouble walking away from their jobs.

When DiMaggio and Mantle and Jackie Robinson retired, they made their announcements in the offseason or the following spring. Pete Rose never could bring himself to say he had quit. Johnny Bench turned down a million-dollar salary, saying, "I've had it." Brooks Robinson, Carl Yastrzemski, and Willie Stargell let everyone know it was a final year, but Jim Palmer hung it up in mid-season, as did Mike Schmidt.

After Jim retired, I was really pulling for him to make it in '91 during spring training with the Baltimore Orioles, from a couple of perspectives. First, as a broadcaster, how great it would have been if I could've done a pregame show for the New York Yankees and said, "Pitching for the Orioles, Hall of Famer Jim Palmer."

And second, I could relate entirely with Palmer's attempt to make a comeback. I was very fortunate in my career to get past the three hundred-win, three-thousand-strikeout plateaus, making "retirement" all that much less difficult to accept. If I were sitting home with 280 wins, I think it would be fair to say that sometime after my "retirement" I would have tried to come back and finish what I'd started over twenty years before.

But in my mother's words, "Enough is enough." A few months after I left the game, I considered a comeback with the Mets. But after the layoff, I knew the attempt would have taken too long, and it would have been unfair to the Met organization and the players on the field. I had accomplished my goals; it was time for others to play the game.

No one else, however, retired with the style that Ted Williams did. And that's appropriate, because no one else ever played the game quite his way. If ever there was a man who did it "his way," it was The Thumper, Teddy Ballgame.

To best illustrate how I learned about this John Wayne figure of a man, I go back to the year I hosted the TV program, "Greatest Sports Legends." Ted was one of my guests. Before filming, the format was being explained to him when Ted looked at me and said, "Don't worry, kid, I'll take care of you."

After the show was completed, we went to dinner with my mother and father. He put his arm around my mom and said, "Hiya, Betty, how are you!" During dinner he'd tap my dad on the leg and start an argument with me. Finally, my mother turned to me and said, "Are you sure you know what you're talking about?"

He could be the most convincing man you'd ever meet, as well as the most opinionated and argumentative. And if you liked that style, Ted was your man.

A case could also be made for calling him the best hitter of modern baseball, if not the best ever. He had a lifetime .344 batting average, which put him ahead of names like Ruth, Terry, Sisler, Gehrig, Lajoie, and Wagner. In fact, the only twentieth-century players ahead of him are Cobb, Hornsby, Joe Jackson, Lefty O'Doul, and Tris Speaker. Wade Boggs is also there, but his career has a way to go yet, and Boggs is still not the hitter Williams was; like Carew and Gwynn, other high-average hitters of recent times, he does not hit for power.

Williams did that, too. He hit 521 home runs, which was third on the all-time list when he retired, despite his having missed five seasons to military service, covering two wars, while he was at the peak of his skills. If he had hit two hundred home runs in those five years—not impossible—he would have hit more than Babe Ruth.

. Ted won seven batting titles, one at the age of twenty-one, in his rookie season of 1939, and one at the age of forty, in 1958. In 1941, he batted .406, the last player to top .400, and he played in the final two games of the season (a doubleheader) when he could have sat out to insure the .400 average. (In those days, there was no sacrifice-fly rule, either—that is, an at-bat was charged for a fly ball that scored a runner. What is now a sacrifice fly and no at-bat, was then scored as an out on a batter's record. It is estimated that Ted had fourteen sacrifice flies in 1941, or fourteen fewer at-bats by today's scoring—which would have given him a .419 average!)

He could have reached .400 again in 1957 with just five leg hits over the course of the season, but at thirty-nine, he didn't have youthful speed on his side. So he settled for .388.

After those final batting titles of 1957 and 1958, a neck injury turned the '59 season into a nightmare. Ted fell to a mortal .254 with only ten home runs in 103 games. It was the first time in his career he had fallen under .300, and he did so with a thud.

After the season, Ted told the Red Sox that if they didn't want him back he would understand. But Boston was a second-division team in the fifties, and Ted was their hero. "Don't be silly," they told him, and they shoved a contract at him for the same pay—$125,000—as he'd received in 1959. Ted wouldn't take it until they cut him down to $90,000, which he figured better represented his worth after the bad season.

Ted got off fast in 1960, a season that made him a four-decade player but one in which he was supposed to play about a hundred games and do a lot of pinch-hitting. He hit eight home runs in his first fifteen starts, including the five hundredth home run of his career, a total that only Ruth, Foxx, and Ott had then reached.

He made the All-Star team for the sixteenth time (he missed out only during his rookie year), but as 1960 wound down, with the Red Sox barely finishing out of last place, Ted admitted it would be his final season. He shunned "Ted Williams Days" in different ballparks and just went about his business, keeping his average over .300 and belting home runs.

September 26, a dreary, drizzly, dark Wednesday, would be Ted's final game in Fenway Park. Remaining on the schedule were three weekend games at Yankee Stadium. Before the game, Ted told his manager, Mike "Pinky" Higgins, that he didn't want to go to New York, that he would call it a career that afternoon. This announcement was not made to the press.

Only 10,454 fans filed into Fenway Park that afternoon to see the Sox take on the exciting "Baby Birds" of Baltimore, who had given the Yankees a good run at the pennant that season. Ted was not exactly surrounded by super talent on his own roster. In the outfield with him that day were Willie Tasby and Lu Clinton. The infield had Don Gile at first, Marlan Coughtry at second, Pumpsie Green at short, and Frank Malzone at third. Jim Pagliaroni caught and Billy Muffett pitched. Mike Fornieles made his seventieth relief appearance of the year that afternoon, setting a new American League record.

Before the game began, a little ceremony took place at home plate, at which it was announced that Ted's number 9 would be retired after the game. Ted made a few remarks, thanked the fans, and knocked the sportswriters, few of whom he ever held in esteem.

Sport magazine and *The New Yorker* each assigned writers for special coverage, and every movement of Ted's final game at Fenway was recorded. He gave the writers and photographers little courtesy. It wasn't his style. Nor was it his style to acknowledge the cheers of the fans during a game. He was famous for never tipping his cap after their applause, figuring they were the same ones who booed him when he failed.

Ted walked off Steve Barber in the first inning, and Barber was replaced by Jack Fisher, later a teammate of mine on the Mets. (Fisher would gain additional fame the following season by giving up Roger Maris's sixtieth home run.) Ted's second at-bat produced a drive deep to center, where Jackie Brandt hauled it in for a long out. In the fifth, he really got hold of one, but the air was heavy with a mist, and right-fielder Al Pilarcik caught it four hundred feet from the plate. At this point the lights were turned on.

Ted came up again in the eighth, with Boston trailing 4–2. The fans stood for one last ovation. The first pitch was low for a ball, and the

Ted Williams crosses the plate after his 512th and final home run, 1960. The on-deck hitter greeting him is Jim Pagliaroni. The umpire is Ed Hurley. (The Sporting News)

fans booed Fisher. The next one was a fastball, the kind Williams had destroyed for years. He swung and missed, not a common sight. But he had made a career out of studying pitchers, whom he generally loathed as a group and considered dumb. (It was too bad he chose not to hang around for 1961, an expansion season, loaded with even more "dumb" pitchers.) He figured Fisher would throw him the same pitch again. Jack did.

In deepest right field are the bullpens Boston erected in 1950 to give Ted a closer home-run target. Fittingly, that's where this one headed. There was no doubt in anyone's mind that he had connected. The ovation from the small crowd seemed deafening, but Ted wouldn't tip his cap, wouldn't betray his principles. The fans pleaded for a curtain call. Higgins asked him to go out; so did the first-base umpire. But he stayed in the dugout. Higgins sent him to left field for the ninth inning, only to pull him out immediately so he could have one last trot off the field. The fans roared, but Ted wouldn't acknowledge them.

It was after the game, a 5–4 Boston win, that the Sox announced that Ted would not be going on to New York with the team. So at the moment the home run was hit, it was assumed to be his final at-bat in Fenway Park; now it turned out to be the final at-bat of his career. It was home run number 521, and number twenty-nine for the season. No one else has ever hit that many in his final year.

But no one else has ever approached the game quite like Ted Williams.

32

Mazeroski to the Rescue

Virtually every baseball season ends the same way. It's the last game of the World Series. The team about to win the World Championship is in the field. The pitcher faces the year's final hitter, retires him, and everyone mobs the pitcher. Between 1935 and 1990, covering fifty-six years, you could put all the endings back to back and they would all look the same.

Except for one.

The 1960 season was the only one to ever end with a home run. It brought tears of joy to Pittsburgh, a city that had not been in a World Series in thirty-three years.

The thrilling conclusion of the '91 World Series, with Minnesota winning game six on a Kirby Puckett homer in the eleventh inning, and game seven with a ten-inning, 1–0 win behind Jack Morris over Atlanta, captured only a sampling of the dramatic season-ending clout that brought the reign of Casey Stengel to a close more than three decades ago.

There was much in the 1960 Series to recall, for those old enough. Another World Series had been held here, also against the New York Yankees. Those '27 Yankees—Murderers' Row—were legendary even as they played. They didn't need history to make believers out of ordinary people. And when they went to Pittsburgh for the first two games of that Series, they took batting practice and, legend has it, scared the hell out of the Pirates before the game even began. Babe Ruth, Lou Gehrig, Tony Lazzeri, Bob Meusel, Earle Combs, et al., practically tossed their bats into the batter's box and won the Series in four games, so they say. The Pirates were no slouches; they had Pie Traynor and the Waner brothers, but they got knocked out before they knew what hit them.

It's stretching the point to say that the 1960 Pirates were out to settle that score, but certainly the newspapers reminded them of it prior to the start of the Series, and certainly beating the Yankees was as fashionable as ever. The Yanks were entering their tenth World Series in twelve years under Casey Stengel.

While the 1927 Yankees had hit 158 home runs (to the Pirates' 54), the 1960 Yanks had smashed 193 homers to lead the majors. Principal among their sluggers were Mickey Mantle, who led the league with forty, and first-year Yankee Roger Maris, who just missed sharing the lead with thirty-nine but who would edge Mantle for the league's MVP honors.

The pitching seemed talented but somehow out of whack. Whitey Ford, one of the game's most respected hurlers, was a meager 12–9 for the year. The team's top winner, Art Ditmar, had fifteen, not a high total for a team that won ninety-seven games. Few people in baseball looked at Ditmar as the ace of the staff—most people still saw the veteran Ford in that role.

Still, on the basis of his victory total, Stengel started Ditmar in Game One, upsetting from the outset the theory that you wanted your ace available for Series Games One, Four, and Seven. (Ever since division play began in 1969, the importance of winning the League Championship Series has become uppermost; you go with your best and let the World Series rotation fall out any way it does. But prior to 1969—assuming that teams had the luxury of a few days to put their rotations in order—you always had your ace prepared to start three times.)

Despite the possible screwup of Stengel's pitching rotation, however, the Yankees looked unbeatable in 1960. Ford did rise to the occasion, winning Game Three 10–0 and Game Six 12–0, and in Game Two, the Yankees blew out the Bucs 16–3, with nineteen hits off six Pirate pitchers, including two homers by Mantle. So although the Pirates hung in with wins off Ditmar in Games One and Five, and beat Ralph Terry in Game Four, the seventh game seemed to pit

Yankee power against little more than a home-field advantage for Pittsburgh. Ah, but was that to be a big advantage!

Bob Turley was the Yankee starter. He had won the Cy Young Award in 1958 and was a World Series hero that year as well, but now, two years later, he was only a nine-game winner in the regular season, walking as many as he struck out. "Bullet Bob" Turley had only eighty-seven strikeouts for the year.

The Pirates went with Vern Law, who, at 20–9, was soon to win the Cy Young Award for 1960. This was Law's third start of the Series, and he had won Game Four with relief help from Elroy Face.

Turley did not hang around for long. Rocky Nelson tagged him for a two-run homer in the first, and after he gave up a leadoff single in the second by Smoky Burgess, Bill Stafford came in to relieve him. A walk to Don Hoak, a bunt single by Bill Mazeroski, and a two-run single by Bill Virdon, and the Bucs were up 4–0.

But the Yanks fought back. A homer by Bill Skowron gave them a run in the fifth, and they scored four times in the sixth to knock out Law and take a 5–4 lead. Yogi Berra's three-run homer that inning had all the makings of a World Series clincher.

The Yanks poured it on in the eighth, adding two more on a walk to Berra and hits by Skowron, Johnny Blanchard, and Clete Boyer. It was 7–4 Yankees. They were just too much.

But in the last of the eighth, with Bobby Shantz on the mound, pinch hitter Gino Cimoli singled to right. Up came Bill Virdon, who sent a double-play grounder to Tony Kubek at short. Except that instead of being turned into a DP, the ball hit a pebble and took a crazy hop right into Kubek's Adam's apple, knocking him to the ground, with his hands clutching his neck. So rather than two out, nobody on, the Pirates had the tying run at bat.

Up came Dick Groat, who would win the MVP award in a few weeks. His base hit zipped past third and a run scored, Virdon stopping at second.

Out of the dugout came Casey Stengel. Shantz had pitched well and should have had an easy inning, but Stengel motioned to the bullpen for Jim Coates. Casey took the ball from Shantz in what would be the Ol' Perfessor's last appearance on the field for the New York Yankees.

A sacrifice by Bob Skinner moved the tying runs into scoring position. Rocky Nelson flied to Maris in right and the runners held. Two out.

Then up stepped the great Roberto Clemente, a .314 hitter in the regular season, a .310 hitter in the Series. He hit a slow chopper to first and beat it out for a single, Virdon scoring, and the Pirates now trailed 7–6.

Hal Smith now came up. Smith had gone in to catch in the eighth after Burgess had been removed for a pinch runner the previous inning. Good move by Buc skipper Danny Murtaugh.

Smith proceeded to belt a three-run homer over the left-field wall and the Pirates led 9–7. Pandemonium erupted throughout Forbes Field.

Bob Friend, the team's number two starter, came in to work the ninth. Three outs and the Pirates would have their first World Championship since 1925.

But this was not a Series in which one of the teams rolled over and played dead. Bobby Richardson, who already had a grand-slam homer and six RBIs in Game Three, as well as twelve RBIs for the total series (both marks still stand), delivered his eleventh hit of the series, a single to left-center, to open the ninth. Dale Long smacked a pinch-hit single to send Richardson to second, and Harvey Haddix came in for Friend.

The move looked good after Maris fouled out, but Mantle singled to make it a 9–8 game, Long going to third. At this point, Gil McDougald, playing his final game before retiring, ran for Long. There probably haven't been many players whose final appearance before retirement was pinch-running. (Why hadn't Stengel pinch-run him when Long was still at first? The answer didn't matter and was probably never asked—except, possibly, by the Yankee owners.)

Haddix got Berra to ground out, but the tying run scored. Skowron then hit a grounder to short, where Groat tossed to Mazeroski to end the inning. Mazeroski had no way of knowing what he was holding in his hand as he tossed the ball onto the pitcher's mound and headed for the dugout. He would lead off the last of the ninth.

Bill Mazeroski was a brilliant second baseman. His quick and sure hands were already legendary in the league, although he was still only twenty-four years old. He had won a Gold Glove Award in 1958 and would win again in 1960. He was a clutch hitter, but it was his glove that earned him his reputation. In the 1960 series, he was seven for twenty-four so far, and had homered off Coates in Game One, sending one over the left-field scoreboard. But Coates was no longer pitching, having been relieved by Terry in the eighth.

Bill Mazeroski approaches home plate following his game-winning home run in the final game of the 1960 World Series. (Wide World Photos)

There are moments that live in a youngster's mind forever because of their relative importance at a certain age. Growing up in California and not being a Yankee fan, I was always on the side of the underdog. I rooted for the Pirates, I pulled for the Braves, I cheered for the Phillies, and I prayed for the Dodgers to dethrone the mighty Yankees, even though I lived three thousand miles away from Yankee Stadium.

And every time David toppled Goliath, there was hope for the eternal underdogs in the world. The giant had fallen when Johnny Podres and the Dodgers beat the Yankees in 1955, and again in 1957 when the Braves got the job done with Lew Burdette and Henry Aaron. Now it was up to the Pirates and Bill Mazeroski.

On Terry's second pitch, two hours and thirty-six minutes into this most memorable of seventh games, Maz took his cut and sent the ball to familiar territory, that left-field wall. Yogi Berra, playing left, ran back but had to watch it sail over for a dramatic game winner. Mighty Goliath had been toppled by Pittsburgh.

Mazeroski danced around the bases, escorted by a handful of fans who had eluded security. In comparison with future hometown celebrations, it was a calm field. But the city rocked with pleasure that night. The Yanks had outscored the Pirates 55–27 in the Series and had outhit them .338 to .256. The Yankee pitching had an ERA of 3.43, the Bucs 7.11. But the Pirates had found a way to hang in there until the blast by Mazeroski made the World Championship a dream come true.

Stengel was fired. Would he have kept his job had he won? No one knew. They told him he was too old, but he went on to manage the Mets in their first years and turned them into a lovable team who outdrew the Yankees.

Mazeroski was a hero throughout his entire major league career, all seventeen years spent with the Pirates. He won eight Gold Glove awards; no major leaguer ever won more at second base.

Terry, although the goat of the game for allowing the homer, came back in 1962 to win the World Series MVP award and experienced the thrill of being on the mound for the final out. That's the way those things are supposed to end, aren't they?

33

Roger Conquers the Babe

The passage of time has made Roger Maris's feat of sixty-one home runs even more magical than it was when he hit them, back in 1961.

He had to overcome the fans, the writers, the commissioner of baseball, the legend of Babe Ruth, and the glamour of Mickey Mantle. For an unassuming twenty-six-year-old from North Dakota, that was one tall order. That he did it made you realize that Roger Maris was quite a man, and not just the mighty home-run hitter he became for a brief period of time.

Truth to tell, he wasn't viewed as a home-run hitter.

Maris's first three seasons were spent with the Cleveland Indians and Kansas City Athletics. He hit fifty-eight home runs over those years, and while that was a good performance, no one mentioned his name when the subject of sluggers came around. There were Mantle and Willie Mays, Rocky Colavito and Ernie Banks, Willie McCovey and Ted Williams, Eddie Mathews and Orlando Cepeda, Frank Robinson and Harmon Killebrew and, well, a lot you would have named before Roger. In fact, Maris hit 133 home runs in three seasons, 1960–62, but only 142 during the rest of his career, for a total of 275. More than seventy men have exceeded that sum.

So, in many ways, 1961 was a bit of a fluke. Today, the term "career year" is used to describe a player who puts everything together in one season, reaching a performance level he is unlikely to ever reach again. That was the case with Maris in 1961, when everything went just right for him and he hit 22 percent of his career home runs in one season. Roger would have been the first to acknowledge the unlikelihood of his ever repeating such an accomplishment.

But Maris was not a fluke. He was a solid, professional baseball player and a skilled hitter. I faced him in the final two seasons of his career, when he was with the Cardinals. He was then playing in Busch Memorial Stadium, which is death to power hitters. Instead of flailing away at the fences, Maris adjusted his swing and became a very successful hitter and a strong RBI man. No one ever said, "Where did Maris's power go?" Instead, everyone admired the adjustment he had made to suit his new surroundings.

In any case, the Yankees felt that Maris had a good "Yankee Stadium" swing—that is, that he was a lefty who could reach the short right-field seats fairly regularly. So they traded four players to Kansas City (as they often did in those days) and obtained Maris prior to the 1960 season.

He really came through, belting thirty-nine homers and winning the league's Most Valuable Player award. He should have been the "toast of the town," finishing as he did just one home run behind Mantle for the title. But the Yankees had Mantle, Whitey Ford, Yogi Berra, Ellie Howard, Bobby Richardson, Tony Kubek, and others who had deeper "roots" in New York and more established followings. That was all fine with Roger. If he could eat in a restaurant unnoticed and unbothered, it suited him perfectly.

Perhaps Maris's problem with the fans began that November 1960 when he narrowly beat Mantle for MVP. It marked the first time Mantle had been edged out of anything, and for Maris—this upstart from the Kansas City Athletics who was just lucky to be a Yankee—to do it, well, somehow it didn't seem right.

Up to that point, the fans had been fickle when it came to Mantle. He had succeeded Joe DiMaggio in center field nine years earlier, and to many, he couldn't carry Joe's glove. So they booed him fairly regularly as he rang up big strikeout totals (which appear almost modest by today's standards).

Then along came Maris, a genuine threat to Mantle, and suddenly Mickey was able to inspire the fans' adulation. From the moment Maris arrived until his retirement after the 1968 season, Mantle would be the most popular player in baseball.

Maris did not hit his first home run of 1961 until the eleventh game of the season. When he and Mantle started belting them, the newspapers took notice and began running daily charts comparing their progress to Ruth's mighty record of sixty, set in 1927.

In July, commissioner Ford Frick stepped in. It should be mentioned that Frick was a sportswriter during the Ruth era, and in fact was a ghostwriter for Ruth and his close friend. He was now placed in the awkward position of dealing with an assault on Ruth's most famed legacy in what was the very first year of expansion, and with it, a 162-game schedule. Whereas Ruth had performed his feat in a 154-game season, Mantle and Maris would be playing in eight extra games.

But which were the extra eight? The first eight? The last eight? If the first eight were designated, the M&M boys would be fine. But Frick ruled that the record had to be established by game number 154. Ignoring all other records, he limited his ruling to home runs. He called for a "distinctive mark" to be used in the record book to describe a home-run record set in those extra games. The writers labeled the distinctive mark an asterisk, although no asterisk was ever used. (Frick's autobiography was even called *Games, People and Asterisks.*)

So Maris and Mantle had the commissioner's ruling to contend with by mid-July. For Maris, the problem was compounded. He was not only chasing Ruth's "ghost," but also stealing Mantle's limelight. Although the two were friends and, in fact, lived together (along with Dale Long) in a Queens apartment during the season, the fans were all for Mickey. The competition was fueled in part by the veteran New York writers. Mantle, who could be surly with them, was suddenly more personable, enjoying as he was a sensational year while the Yankees were rolling to a pennant. So a lot of pressure was off him. He had a smile for the writers and for the front-office people. They, in turn, would whisper to each other that "if anyone should break the record, let it be Mickey. He's paid his dues, he's come close before, he proudly wears the legacy of Ruth, Gehrig, and DiMaggio."

Maris told the writers in no uncertain terms what they could do with what he perceived as their dumb questions. A wise man once said, "Never pick a fight with anyone who buys ink by the barrel." Translation: You can't win an argument with a newspaper. And as the summer wore on, Maris was getting hammered in the columns. They said that clumps of his crew cut were falling out due to worry. If it was true, it was because Roger kept a lot bottled up inside him. He never knocked the people in the Yankee front office, but he surely felt they were against him.

Years later Bob Fishel, perhaps the game's top publicist, who worked for the Yankees at the time, confessed that he could have done more to help Maris. "We could have set up an interview room under more controlled circumstances, as they later did with Pete Rose," he said. "But it was unheard of at the time, and Roger would get cornered in his locker and feel deprived of dignity. I wish we had taken more control of things."

Going into Game 154, Maris needed two home runs to tie Ruth. Although pretty disgusted with Frick's ruling, he gave it his best shot, hitting number 59, and just missing number 60. The fans in Baltimore applauded his effort.

Back home in New York, with the pennant clinched and the team on the way to its nineteenth World Championship, Maris tied Ruth at 60 on September 26 in Game 159. Mantle, injured, had finished with 54, his career high, but not good enough to match either Ruth or Maris.

Now it was the final game, number 162. The Yankees were hosting arch-rival Boston, and you would have thought the game would sell out, but only 23,154 were present to see history made. As many as possible crowded into the lower right-field seats, hoping to catch number 61 and receive the $5,000 from a Sacramento restaurant owner who was offering to trade the cash for ownership of the baseball.

Tracy Stallard was on the mound for Boston. Maris, who had just turned twenty-seven a few weeks before, flied out to rookie Carl Yastrzemski in left in the first inning. In the fourth, he took two balls. The fans booed, not wanting to see a walk.

The next pitch, a fastball down Broadway, sent Maris's bat into that now-classic level swing. For a moment he stood in silence and watched the arc of the ball. And then he and the twenty-three thousand fans knew that baseball history had been made, the kind that leads off the front page of the morning papers. Maris had become the first man in history to hit 61 home runs in a single season, asterisk or no asterisk. They could never take it away from him.

He rounded the bases with his head down, not wishing to show up the pitcher. When he reached the dugout, his teammates pushed him out to take a shy bow, as they had with number 60. (Curtain calls were most unusual then.) The Yankees, by the way, won the game 1–0. It

Roger Maris's 61st home run was a classic study in the perfect swing. The catcher is Russ Nixon, the umpire Bill Kinnamon. (The Sporting News)

was the team's 240th homer of the year, an all-time record. (The Yankees did not lead the league in home runs again in that decade, or in the seventies, or in the eighties.)

In 1962, Maris hit a respectable 33 homers and drove in 100 runs, but the Associated Press named him "Flop of the Year." In 1963 and 1964, he played with an injured hand and his game fell off further. The fans booed him even more. By 1967, the Yankees could barely give him away, trading Maris to St. Louis for Charley Smith, a lifetime .239 hitter. There Maris found peace and helped the Cardinals to two World Series in his final two years.

Maris retired to Gainesville, Florida, where he ran a beer distributorship. He became estranged from the baseball fraternity, bitter with the Yankees, and loath to return to New York for more booing.

But time heals many wounds. His absence made hearts grow fonder. Mantle always spoke well of him. And as the years passed, his accomplishment—both the number sixty-one and all it implied—was finally appreciated. At long last he returned to Yankee Stadium to hear the ovations that were due him in the sixties.

Maris died of cancer in 1985 at the age of fifty-one. (Ruth had died of cancer at fifty-three.) By then he had made peace with himself and with the baseball world.

One last note: Ruth's sacred record of sixty homers stood for thirty-four years, and Maris's mark has already reached thirty-one in 1992. Frick had guessed wrong—the extra games did not play havoc with the record book. And in 1991, Commissioner Fay Vincent removed the "asterisk," or dual listing.

34

Speed Returns
to the Game

Nothing in modern baseball history so seemed to catapult the game into a new style of play than the base-stealing exploits of Maury Wills of the Dodgers. Base stealing is more than speed and a quick start—it is cunning, daring, and a careful study of the motions of both the pitcher and the catcher. Wills had it all.

For decades, since the advent of the lively ball, base stealing had become a dormant art. Teams played long ball. The idea was to get a man on base and then power him home. Purists of the game's early days decried the loss of the hit-and-run, the double steal, and all the things you could do on the base paths to build runs. No less a purist than Ty Cobb claimed that only Phil Rizzuto and Stan Musial among stars of the 1950s could have found success in his time.

Rizzuto, the speediest of the Yankees during their glory days of the 1940s and 1950s, had a high of 22 steals and a career total of 149. I suppose Cobb admired Musial's bat control, for he was not an adept base stealer.

So embarrassingly low had stolen-base statistics fallen that in 1950, Dom DiMaggio led the American League with 15. I suspect that Rickey Henderson has had *weeks* when he approached that figure.

Actually, the dramatic increase in steals began in the American League, in the form of Luis Aparicio of the White Sox. Luis, the brilliant shortstop who went all the way to the Hall of Fame, arrived from Venezuela in 1956 to replace his countryman Chico Carrasquel, who had been dealt to Cleveland. Aparicio led the league with 21 stolen bases in his rookie season and proceeded to win nine consecutive stolen-base titles, a record. In the hearts of White Sox fans, he moved right in there with another Sox shortstop of like initials, Luke Appling.

Clearly the high point, the season in which Luis was thrust into the national spotlight, was 1959, when he stole 56 bases to form the heart of the "Go-Go Sox" pennant winners, as Chicago took its first pennant since scandal-ridden 1919. Teaming with second-base partner Nellie Fox, who batted right behind him at the top of the batting order, Luis helped the Sox fashion ninety-four victories out of the fewest homers and the third-lowest team batting average in the league. The 56 steals were the most in the league since George Case of Washington had 61 in 1943. (Ben Chapman of the Yankees also had stolen 61, in 1931. Why anyone needed to steal sixty-one bases batting in front of Ruth and Gehrig is quite a mystery, but it was Joe McCarthy's first season as Yankee manager, and maybe he hadn't gotten things quite right yet. Yankee historian Frank Graham wrote that Chapman ran "very often when there was no excuse for running.") White Sox fans spent the season shouting "go go go," and Luis "went went went" with their hearts. Baseball was changing. You could steal a pennant.

In the National League, Willie Mays represented a different sort of oddity: He was a power hitter who could also steal bases. He led the league in steals from 1956 to 1959 and was a forerunner of the "thirty-thirty" men who have become more common today—players who steal thirty bases and hit thirty home runs in a single season. When Mays began doing it, well, it just wasn't done.

By the time the 1960s unfolded, the respective stolen-base records of the twentieth century were very old. Cobb held the major-league record of 96, which he set in 1915. His own total of 68 the following year was the closest anyone had come to it. Aparicio's 56 was impressive, but it couldn't have made Cobb blink.

In the National League, a Cincinnati outfielder named Bob Bescher has stolen 80 bases in 1911. (Record books today accept new research and revise that to 81.) His 67 the next year was the closest anyone had come in that league. For someone holding such a long-standing record in such a major category, Bescher is remarkably forgotten by fans. He was a college football star who then became a career .258 hitter over eleven seasons with the Reds, Giants, Cardinals, and Indians between 1908 and 1918, and he won four stolen-base crowns while with Cincinnati. He died in 1942 at the age of 58.

Thus, Bescher and Cobb represented targets that no one ever gave much thought to. Their places in the record books seemed secure. No doubt Cobb died in July of 1961 feeling that way.

In his final years, Cobb did at least become aware of one Maurice Morning Wills of Washington, D.C. If ever there seemed to be a career minor-league infielder, Wills was that player. Maury had signed with the Dodgers in 1951 when they were still in Brooklyn. He played all over the field—second, short, third, even catcher and pitcher—struggling to move up the ladder. And it went slowly, from Hornell of the Pony League to Pueblo of the Western League, to Miami, back to Pueblo, to Fort Worth, back to Pueblo, to Seattle, and to Spokane, where he settled at shortstop in 1958 and 1959. He had batted .202 in 1955, but .302 a year later and .267 after that. No one knew quite what to make of him, other than the fact that he could steal you a base.

Then the Dodgers, by now located in Los Angeles, saw a chance for a pennant in 1959, and on June 1 called up the twenty-six-year-old rookie from Spokane. Don Zimmer, the team's regular shortstop, wasn't hitting a lick. Wills didn't exactly set the league on fire, hitting only .206 through September 7, but the Dodgers were playing well with him at short. In the seventeen games that followed, he batted .429 to finish at .260. The Dodgers won the pennant in a playoff with Milwaukee and faced Aparicio and the "Go-Go Sox" in the World Series, beating them in six games. Maury had earned his way into the majors.

In 1960 he led the league with 50 stolen bases, and then he led it again in '61 with 35. This set the stage for the 1962 season, the first one in beautiful new Dodger Stadium and the National League's first since having expanded to 162 games.

While Sandy Koufax was enjoying his first superseason, Wills was turning heads with his assault on the base paths. The Dodger fans loved Sandy and Don Drysdale, but Wills had them screaming "go go go" just as White Sox fans had done (for Aparicio) in '59. The Dodger attack was now tailored to speed and pitching. Gone were the sluggers of the Brooklyn days.

Since baseball had just gone through the Maris pursuit of Babe

Ruth's home-run record a year before, comparison charts soon popped up again in the daily papers. Maury's number 35, to equal his 1961 total, came in the Dodger's sixty-eighth game; by that game, however, Cobb had stolen fifty-one. Wills reached Aparicio's best mark of fifty-six in Game 110; Cobb had had seventy-one by Game 110. So, someone asked commissioner Ford Frick if another asterisk would be needed, and Frick said, "Yes."

In the first ten days of September, Maury stole sixteen bases, including four in one game against Pittsburgh to break Bescher's National League record. He reached eighty-nine steals in Game 145. He was just seven behind Cobb with seventeen games left, and now it looked as if the record was his for the asking. The steals seemed effortless. Cobb had been thrown out thirty-eight times in stealing his ninety-six; Wills would be nailed only thirteen times.

Maury got number 90 on September 11. The Dodgers played their 154th game on September 21, and his total went to 95. This was the theoretical cutoff for the total games in Cobb's 1916 schedule. But Cobb had played two ties, and the Tigers played 156 games that year. In fact, after 154, Cobb had only ninety-four.

Both 96 and 97 for Maury came in St. Louis on September 23, the Dodgers' Game 156, the same number that Cobb had played. And so the "unbreakable" record of Ty Cobb fell, fourteen months after his passing.

There would be three more stolen bases for Maury in the regular season, with number 100 coming in Game 158 in Dodger Stadium against Houston. He thus became the first player in the twentieth century to reach triple figures.

The Dodgers and Giants wound up in a tie for first, as they had eleven years earlier in New York, and a three-game playoff, won by the Dodgers, allowed Maury to play in 165 games to run his stolen-base total to 104. His final three thefts came in the third and deciding playoff game.

Little Maury Wills, who turned thirty during that playoff series, had been transformed from a career minor leaguer to the Most Valuable Player in the National League. He had batted .299 that year, with 208 hits.

Others have surpassed his accomplishments since 1962. First it was Lou Brock, stealing 118 in 1974 and going on to break Cobb's lifetime total. He finished with 938. Then came Rickey Henderson in the

Maury Wills steals third in the 1962 playoffs against the Giants. Jim Davenport is the third baseman.

American League, with 130 stolen bases in 1982. Then Vince Coleman rolled off three consecutive seasons of over a hundred, in 1985–86–87.

Henderson was probably the most amazing of them all. In only his thirteenth season, 1991, he broke the record it had taken Brock nineteen seasons to accomplish. The record breaker for Rickey came on May 1 when he dove headfirst, his normal style, into third base in Oakland against the Yankees. Brock was present for the brief ceremonies that halted the game.

Oh, how the game has changed with respect to team speed since I broke into the big leagues in 1967.

There used to be one or two players on a team who would cause you to worry about the stolen base. But with the introduction of artificial turf and the bigger ballparks, there was an immediate need for defensive speed in the outfield to cut off the ball, which never seemed to slow down going across the playing surface. This defensive speed broadened into an *offensive* weapon, and the number of players who would even *attempt* a stolen base rose dramatically.

Johnny Bench, Cincinnati's Hall of Fame catcher who made his living throwing out those runners, has said the game seemed to change right before his very eyes.

As for Maury Wills, he so captured the spirit of Los Angeles that he seemed like a Dodger for life. But he could be argumentative and opinionated and march to his own beat. A dispute with management found him traded to Pittsburgh and then Montreal in the late 1960s, before "all was forgiven" and he went home to L.A. to finish out his final four seasons. He retired in 1972 at age forty, with 586 stolen bases, fifth in this century on the all-time list. (He has since been passed by Henderson, Brock, Joe Morgan, Bert Campaneris, Willie Wilson, and Tim Raines.) He became a broadcaster and, briefly, manager of the Seattle Mariners. His legacy may continue to fade as his totals are surpassed, but someone had to be a pioneer in this area, and it fell on the shoulders—or rather, the legs—of Maury Wills to fill that role.

35

The Mick

After Mickey Mantle retired in 1968, they must have broken the mold.

No other player since then has captured the public fancy through that special combination of raw talent and inspiring life story. Nor has any other player enjoyed such popularity at home or on the road as did The Mick in his final years as an active player.

Mantle himself admits that his alliterative name had something to do with it, like Mickey Mouse or Marilyn Monroe. His father deliberately gave him a name with a Hollywood sound, and Mantle's good looks and rippling muscles made him seem like something out of central casting.

His background had a Hollywood quality as well. Boy must make good in baseball or else he is doomed to a life in the zinc mines of Oklahoma. So Mickey's father and his grandfather taught him to bat from both sides of the plate and encouraged him to play sports at Commerce High. There he wrecked his knee playing football and developed osteomyelitis, the first in a lifetime of serious injuries that would forever raise obstacles on the path to fulfilling his potential.

He took to switch-hitting naturally and belted more home runs than any other switch hitter in the game's history. But as a Yankee rookie at age nineteen, playing right field while Joe DiMaggio patrolled center in his final year, Mantle had trouble adjusting to big-league pitching and had to be sent back to the minors. Dejected and tearful, he called home and said he was quitting. "Fine," said his father. "Come on back to the mines if that's what you're made of."

That talk forced Mantle back to the field. Recalled quickly, he helped the Yanks to the '51 pennant, only to suffer a major knee injury in the World Series when he tripped on a drain cover in right field. He was hospitalized in the same room as his father, who by then was dying of Hodgkin's disease. Mantle had lost his grandfather the same way. He was convinced that all men in the Mantle family would die before age forty.

Mickey's knee healed and he returned to play center field, where he found himself burdened with the label of being DiMaggio's successor and heir to the Ruth-Gehrig-DiMaggio legacy. Slowly he began to assume his place in the hearts of Yankee fans. They booed his many strikeouts, cheered his "tape-measure" home runs, and proudly watched him win a triple crown in 1956 and MVP awards in 1956 and 1957. Still, older fans who thought he wasn't DiMaggio's equal could never stand up and cheer—not until Roger Maris arrived to challenge Ruth's home-run record. Only then did fans embrace Mickey as the "rightful" one to mount such a challenge. From that time on, Mickey was awash in love (see chapter 33).

To say there's been no player like Mantle since he retired is to contend that no one else has become such a household name. He passed the "grandmother" test: "Has your grandmother ever heard of him?" He passed the talent test: "Did you ever see anyone so strong yet so fast?" And he passed the good-citizen test: "Did he ever say anything wrong in the newspapers about anyone?" He didn't. That wasn't the way it was done in the fifties and sixties. And although we later learned that he may not have been quite the All-American Boy off the field, his role in upholding the highest ideals of baseball was never questioned. He played hurt, he played hard, he gave the game everything he had, and he never embarrassed his profession. He was a great competitor who brought millions of new fans to the parks, and despite all of his injuries, he appeared in more games than any other Yankee in history, and was third on the all-time home-run list when he retired, with 536.

By as early as 1963, there were signs that the Yankee dynasty was starting to crumble, despite the team's fourth pennant in a row. Mickey had broken his foot and played in only sixty-five games that year, with fifteen homers and thirty-five runs batted in. In the World Series,

Sandy Koufax, Don Drysdale, and Johnny Podres of the Dodgers had swept the Yanks in four straight, a tremendous embarrassment. Their fabled broadcaster, Mel Allen—hated by all who rooted against the Yankees—had even lost his voice doing the Series on NBC.

In 1964, the Yankees struggled under their new manager, Yogi Berra. They did not play "inspired" ball, but were saved in the end by two new pitchers: rookie Mel Stottlemyre, called up in August, was 9–3, and veteran Pedro Ramos, obtained on September 6 and ineligible for the World Series, was a master of relief down the stretch.

Something else happened that was less than inspiring, something that has been made much of over the years. It seems that reserve infielder Phil Linz played the harmonica on a team bus after a tough loss—"Mary Had a Little Lamb," to be specific—and that an angry Berra smacked it out of his hands. Yankees simply didn't play music after a loss in Yogi's time. The incident, to the beat writers, was the first indication that Yogi meant business and was not just a simple "pal" who had been a teammate in '63 and suddenly a manager in '64. Much can happen on a team that may just be a quick over-and-done-with moment during a long season, but that seems poetic or literary to the newspaper reporters. Had the event not received such publicity, it might have been no big deal. But possibly the fact that it was in all the papers got the Yankees to thinking that they had better shape up or this pennant was going to get away from them.

Mantle had a good season in 1964, although not as good as his performances in the fifties and early sixties. He batted .303 with thirty-five homers and 111 RBIs, and it was a relief to see him back and productive after missing so much of the '63 campaign with that broken foot.

At season's end, the Yankees had prevailed. They won the American League pennant by one game, doing it with an eleven-game winning streak in mid-September and clinching it with one game left. They were 22–6 in September, as Ramos saved seven games in thirteen appearances. It was their twenty-ninth pennant. No one could have thought that it would be their last for a dozen years.

Mantle came into the World Series against the St. Louis Cardinals with fifteen Series homers, having equaled Babe Ruth's record. For all that Mantle achieved in his career, he actually set few records. So the '64 Series gave him a chance to put his name in the books all by himself, with the most home runs in World Series history.

The shot that would accomplish this feat was carried out in heroic style. There were 67,101 fans jammed into Yankee Stadium on Friday afternoon, October 10. Jim Bouton, the Yankees' eighteen-game winner, faced veteran Curt Simmons, one of the original Philadelphia Phillie "Whiz Kids" of 1950. The Cardinals had an outstanding ball club, but they too had struggled all season, finally winning at the end. St. Louis had Bill White, Julian Javier, Dick Groat, and Ken Boyer in the infield, Tim McCarver catching, and Lou Brock, Curt Flood, and Mike Shannon in the outfield. Bob Gibson and Ray Sadecki led the pitching staff and Johnny Keane was the manager. (Stan Musial had retired just the year before.)

The teams split the first two games in St. Louis, which was Yogi's hometown, and now they were locked in a tense 1–1 pitching duel in Game Three. The Yankees had scored in the second on a single by Elston Howard (another St. Louis native), a walk to Joe Pepitone, and a double by Clete Boyer, Ken's brother. Bouton, meanwhile, coming straight overhand so that he would frequently knock his cap off his head, stopped the Cardinals until the fifth, when McCarver singled and went to second after Mantle fumbled the ball in right field. (Maris was playing center, since Mantle had been hampered by a bad leg.) With two outs, Simmons himself singled off Boyer's glove to tie the score. And there it rested, 1–1, as the game moved quickly along. The Yanks loaded the bases in the sixth but failed to score, and in the top of the ninth, the Cards had the potential winning run on third when Bouton got Flood to fly out to Mantle.

Simmons had left after eight for a pinch hitter, and the Cardinals brought in veteran knuckleballer Barney Schultz for the last of the ninth. Schultz has been the Cardinals' top relief man all season with a 1.65 ERA and fourteen saves, and had saved the first game of the Series. Mantle, the leadoff hitter, watched him take his warm-up pitches and then stepped in from the left side of the plate. On the first pitch, Mantle powered one high and deep into the right-field stands, and the Yankees had a 2–1 victory. It was Mantle's sixteenth World Series home run, a new record.

With the joy of a youngster, Mantle circled the bases to meet the welcoming hands of his teammates. It was a classic Yankee moment. But there weren't to be many others for Mantle and the Yankees in the Series. He hit two more homers to give him eighteen, but the Yankees lost in seven games when Gibson beat Stottlemyre in the finale, 7–5.

Mickey Mantle crosses the plate to the welcome handshake of Elston Howard.

After the Series, the Yankees fired Yogi and hired Johnny Keane away from the Cardinals. But the dynasty was over. The players had aged and the farm system had dried up. The team fell to sixth in 1965 and last in 1966, and didn't win again until 1976.

Mantle played four more years, but they were mediocre seasons by his standards. The fans cheered his few remaining home runs, but in those final four years he batted only .254, with 82 homers and 211 RBIs. He saw his lifetime average fall under .300 and all of his old teammates retire or get traded, until he was the last one left.

I faced him in his final All-Star Game at-bat, striking him out on three pitches in Houston. Never mind that it wasn't the same Mantle I had admired growing up. The thrill of pitching against Mickey Mantle in an All-Star Game remains one of my fondest memories. There are a few players who have a certain presence about them, regardless of age or numbers on the stat sheet. Henry Aaron, Willie Mays, Sandy Koufax, and Mickey Mantle occupy that special niche in the game of baseball.

The tragedy of Mantle, as he himself explains today, was that he didn't keep in better shape. Perhaps he was guilty of thinking he would die before he was forty, so he stayed out late and did not condition himself the way today's athletes do. But not enough is made of the outfield-drain accident in his rookie season, an event at age nineteen that seriously hampered him throughout his career. Those of us who came along later can thank the Players Association for making the game safer. The association meant not only free-agent contracts, but padding on outfield walls and elimination of hazards such as the one that ultimately shortened Mantle's career.

Mickey was thirty-one years old when he had his last big year, and should have been a star for another decade. Still, he played more games than any Yankee: more than Gehrig, more than Ruth, more than DiMaggio. And he remains the standard for baseball "stardom" more than twenty years after his farewell.

36

Of Koufax, Marichal, and Gibson

The 1960s produced three of the greatest pitchers of all time, three stars who would have dominated any era. Each threw hard, although one was better known for a masterful screwball. All three cruised into the Hall of Fame.

The triumvirate included Sandy Koufax, Juan Marichal, and Bob Gibson, names that brought fear to any hitter. If the 1960s was an age of big sluggers, these three played to their weakness—their propensity for striking out. Ask most hitters what impresses them most about a pitcher and they say "good heat," baseball slang for a good fastball. Still, they generally love to sit back and wait for the fastball, the pitch they grew up with. It's straight and true and cries out with the challenge of "hit me." Anyone who has ever dropped a quarter into a batting cage can understand how a hitter likes to step up to a challenge.

When Koufax and Gibson stood on the mound, "good heat" took on a new dimension. Their fastballs moved, defying gravity. When Marichal stood there, he baffled 'em with deceptive screwballs and struck out over two hundred men six times. For the first time, in the 1960s television cameras brought you right behind home plate. You could see their pitches move: the fastballs rise, the curveballs break, the screwballs dance, and the change-ups fool the hitters.

Koufax was the first of the three to arrive in the majors, and for as long as baseball is played, he will remain the paradigm of a pitcher who is developed slowly by a patient management. You hear, even after four or five mediocre seasons, of pitchers who "can still mature—remember Sandy Koufax?" We will be hearing that comparison into the next century.

Koufax, a native of Brooklyn, was signed by the Brooklyn Dodgers and went straight to the major leagues in 1955 because of a rule that forced teams to keep big bonus players on the major league roster. Sandy's bonus was modest by today's standards, $20,000, which included his salary. In retrospect, it was hardly worth spoiling two years of minor-league development for that. Most players under this bonus policy did not benefit from the destructive rule, which was finally dropped. Koufax might have been just another failure without the patience shown by the Dodgers organization, one of the best in the game.

At nineteen, he found himself a rookie on the only World Championship team in Brooklyn history. He was surrounded by future Hall of Famers like Jackie Robinson, Duke Snider, Pee Wee Reese, Roy Campanella, Don Drysdale, and his manager, Walt Alston. He played in twelve games, had a 2–2 record, and mostly "observed." The same was true in 1956 and 1957, and as the Dodgers packed up and headed for Los Angeles, Sandy took with him a 9–10 record, plus 182 strikeouts in 205 innings.

He moved into the starting rotation in L.A., but after three years, he had only a 27–30 mark. After six big-league seasons, he was 36–40. Trouble was, while he threw hard, he also threw wild. There had been others who fit that description before, and there will be others to come, but Sandy turned out to be different.

In the spring of 1961, pitching a "B" game in spring training, Sandy's catcher, Norm Sherry, got him to relax and throw more curves and change-ups. What took root that day was a more confident, relaxed performer on the mound who learned to mix his pitches and enjoy his work. Sandy went through that season with an 18–13 record, leading the National League with 269 strikeouts. His ERA was 3.52, seventh best in the league. He was ready to take charge.

Beginning in 1962, Sandy put together five of the most spectacular seasons ever recorded, certainly in modern baseball. But his statistics, legendary though they are, hardly told the story of how dominant he had become. He was seemingly unhittable, even with all his pitches in the strike zone. It was, as someone said, as though he'd "come down from a higher league."

In each of the next five years, he led the league in ERAs, with marks of 2.54, 1.88, 1.74, 2.04, and 1.73. He won three more strikeout titles in that period, topping three hundred each time, and set a major league record with 382 in 1965.

He led the league in victories three times, with totals of twenty-five, twenty-six, and twenty-seven. Twice he struck out eighteen men in a game. For the second six years of his career, his record was 129–47. Sandy was named MVP in 1963 and won Cy Young Awards in 1963, 1965, and 1966, years in which, behind his dominating pitching, the Dodgers won pennants.

His string of four no-hitters, one each in 1962, 1963, 1964, and 1965, was a stirring accomplishment. The last one, which broke Bob Feller's record of three no-hitters, was a perfect game, only the tenth in major league history. In that game, on September 9, 1965, he and Bob Hendley, a 2–2 pitcher with the Cubs, locked up in a classic duel.

Hendley was also brilliant that day, pitching the finest game of his career. The Dodgers managed only one hit off him, a two-out double in the seventh by Lou Johnson, who had earlier scored the game's only run. Koufax however, was better; for five years, he almost always was. He stopped the Cubs cold, retiring all twenty-seven men he faced, fourteen on strikeouts.

When Sandy suddenly retired after a 27–9 record in 1966, he was only thirty years old. No one had ever quit at that summit, but he faced crippling arthritis if he continued, according to his doctors. By thirty-five, he was already a Hall of Famer.

Entirely different, but just as much a master of the art of pitching, was high-kicking Juan Marichal, who joined the San Francisco Giants in 1960. He was the third great product of the Dominican Republic (after teammates Felipe & Matty Alou), a nation that has since become a hotbed of baseball talent, particularly shortstops. No one really understands what in that small nation's baseball program has sent so many players to the big leagues.

By then, the Giants had added Willie McCovey, Orlando Cepeda, and Alou to their transplanted New York team and were making their own mark on the West Coast. Marichal quickly joined the franchise's long tradition of pitching greatness, which traces back through Carl Hubbell, master of the screwball, and Christy Mathewson, master of the fadeaway, its forerunner.

Expert observers might give Koufax the edge over Marichal, but it was Juan who was 24–1 lifetime in Candlestick Park against the Dodgers.

In his major league debut, on July 19, 1960, Juan went seven and two thirds hitless innings and wound up with a one-hit shutout. It was a sensational way to break in, and by 1962, a pennant-winning season in San Francisco, he was an eighteen-game winner.

A milestone performance took place against Milwaukee on July 2, 1963 in Candlestick Park. That night Marichal, twenty-five, faced Warren Spahn, forty-two, who, like Marichal, had a trademark high leg kick. It was the old guard against the new, a rite of passage in major league baseball. Spahn, the winningest left-hander of all time, was still effective and had a 23–7 record that year, his last big season. But Marichal was the coming star, en route to a 25–8 record, tops in the league and his first of six 20-win seasons.

After nine, the game remained scoreless. Both Marichal and Spahn stayed on, adding up the zeros. It was well past midnight in the East, and still they plowed away at each other's lineup. The Giants had Mays, McCovey, and Cepeda. The Braves had Aaron and Mathews. But no one could score.

Not until the last of the sixteenth, with both pitchers still in there, did the Giants earn a run. Willie Mays blasted a homer over the left-field fence to give Marichal the win at 12:25 in the morning, or 3:25 on the East Coast, where the morning papers had already gone to press. It was one of the great pitching duels of the twentieth century, especially coming in an era when pitchers no longer worked sixteen-inning ballgames. It was one for the ages.

Unfortunately, Marichal had a black mark on his career, and it came in the heat of a Dodger-Giant pennant race in 1965, when, as a batter against Koufax, he clubbed Dodger catcher John Roseboro with his bat. He had thought Roseboro was throwing the ball back to Koufax too close to his head. The ugly photos of a bloody Roseboro and the nine-day suspension cast a pall over Marichal's reputation. But when Hall of Fame election time arrived in 1983, he became the first Dominican ever elected.

As for Bob Gibson, he had about him a mystique of fearlessness and

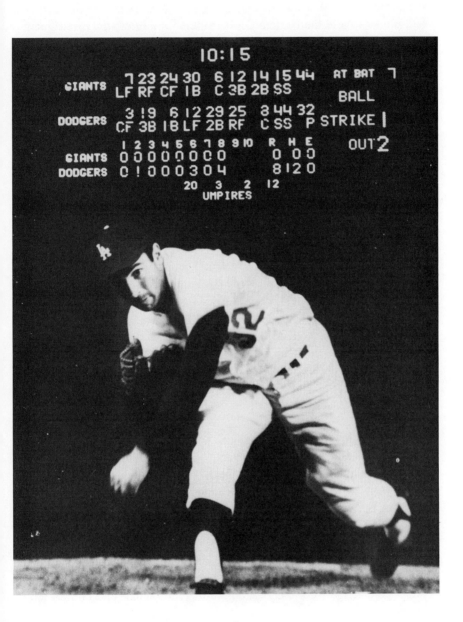

Sandy Koufax closes out his no-hitter against the Giants in Dodger Stadium, May 11, 1963.

indestructibility. A native of Omaha, Bob was a good enough basket-ball player to join the Harlem Globetrotters for a brief stint. He signed with the Cardinal organization in 1957 and was in the majors by 1959. In 1961 he became a regular starting pitcher for the Cardinals, and was their ace by 1964, leading them to a World Championship over the Yankees with a victory in Game Seven. The following season he had his first of five 20-win seasons.

In 1968, the "Year of the Pitcher," when only six batters hit .300, he was the "Pitcher of the Year," with a 22–9 record despite a 3–5 start. Thirteen of his twenty-two wins were shutouts, and in thirty-four starts he wasn't knocked out once, completing twenty-eight games. Over one long stretch, he allowed only two earned runs in ninety-five innings, with five shutouts in a row. For that season he had a 1.12 ERA, the lowest in the National League since ERA had become an official statistic in 1913.

Gibson was more intimidating than Koufax or Marichal, because hitters thought he was more apt to knock them down. This gave him a tremendous psychological edge. A fast worker who liked to get the ball back and fire it again, he never seemed to weaken, never seemed to tire. If he looked tough in the first inning, you figured he had you.

He won nine Gold Gloves for fielding and had a 7–2 World Series record with a 1.89 Series ERA. In nine starts, he was never relieved and struck out ninety-two in eighty-one innings. In the opening game of the 1968 Series against Detroit, he fanned seventeen batters, still a Series record.

While neither Koufax, Marichal, nor Gibson won three hundred games, they launched one of the game's most pitching-dominant eras. Steve Carlton, Don Sutton, Phil Niekro, Gaylord Perry, Nolan Ryan, and myself all followed with three-hundred-victory careers. Ferguson Jenkins, Tommy John, Jim Kaat, and Bert Blyleven narrowly missed, although Blyleven is still active as this is written. Mickey Lolich, Jerry Koosman, Catfish Hunter, Ron Guidry, and Jim Palmer all pitched sensationally. Relief pitchers like Rollie Fingers, Tug McGraw, Goose Gossage, Dan Quisenberry, Sparky Lyle, and Bruce Sutter shone. It was a golden age for pitchers, and Koufax, Marichal, and Gibson led the way.

37

McLain, Lolich Lead
'68 Tigers

In baseball's "modern" era, there seems to be little room for startling, bold managerial moves. If nothing else, the media can anticipate even the unorthodox, and by the time the unusual occurs, it is as though people seem to have been reading about it for weeks. The age of the sneak attack may be gone forever, but in 1968, Detroit manager Mayo Smith pulled some tricks out of his hat and wound up hoisting a World Championship flag on Opening Day the following year.

The 1968 season was the last for Mickey Mantle, Roger Maris, and Eddie Mathews, and also the last before divisional play began. It was, then, the last pure race for the pennant, with no League Championship Series required before the World Series. There were two ten-team leagues: two champions, eighteen losers.

Having narrowly missed the pennant in 1967 in the final weekend, the Detroit Tigers were determined not to fail in '68. They played throughout a tense summer of racial rioting in their city, and with their ballpark right in the downtown section of town, the pressures from outside the walls were a daily reminder of a troubled world. But the Tigers were a well-integrated club of white and black stars, featuring Al Kaline, Willie Horton, Jim Northrup, Bill Freehan, Mickey Lolich, Norm Cash, Earl Wilson, Gates Brown, and even Mathews, who'd come over the year before. And then there was the irrepressible Denny

McLain, free spirited son-in-law of Lou Boudreau, who was out to set the world on fire in '68 and have a helluva time in the process.

McLain had a won-loss record of 17–16 in 1967, not very impressive for a pitcher on a team twenty games over .500. But McLain possessed a smooth, easy delivery, a live arm, and a brashness that translated into confidence. The 1968 season would belong to Denny, who started winning and winning, keeping the Tigers on top. By midyear, attention began to focus on whether he could keep up the pace and become the first thirty-game winner in the American League since Lefty Grove in 1930.

To win thirty games meant stepping back into another era and accomplishing something thought to be impossible under current playing conditions. It was a landmark number that, like .400, seemed out of step with the times. For one thing, pitchers were usually getting only about thirty-five starts a year. McLain, however, made forty-one in 1968, in what was very much the "Year of the Pitcher" (see Chapter 36). In the National League, Bob Gibson rose head and shoulders above all others with a 1.12 earned run average, thirteen shutouts, and a 22–9 season.

The American League had only one .300 hitter, Carl Yastrzemski, .301. But take nothing away from McLain. At age twenty-four, he let none of the growing pressure of national television interfere with his glorious quest for thirty. Onward he went, leading Detroit throughout the summer, until he stood on the mound in Tiger Stadium on September 14 looking for history. Seated in the stands that day was the last major leaguer to win thirty games, the equally flamboyant Dizzy Dean, who achieved that record in 1934 in the National League. With television cameras recording his every move, McLain did indeed accomplish his goal. And then he won another one after that to finish the year at 31–6, with 280 strikeouts, a 1.96 earned-run average, and twenty-eight complete games.

What was not known at the time by the general population was that McLain was, in fact, hurting. During the season he was taking cortisone injections, perhaps more than would be administered today, when doctors are more cautious about the procedure. Cortisone, which can be painful to receive, masks the symptoms of tendonitis and permits normal pitching. But it isn't a long-term treatment. It wears off. So McLain continued receiving booster shots to keep himself going. By the time the World Series against Gibson and the Cardinals came to town, Denny was pretty much out of gas—or out of cortisone, at least. The season had indeed taken its toll.

Fortunately for manager Mayo Smith, he had another ace on his staff, the equally durable Mickey Lolich. Although eclipsed briefly by McLain, Lolich was in fact the more dependable Tiger hurler over the long haul. He had a much more impressive career and was probably the premier left-hander in the league during his era. A strikeout pitcher with a bit of a beer belly, he would emerge from McLain's shadow during the Series and establish his place in baseball history.

Smith had managed the season by juggling four outfielders in and out of the lineup. Injuries, especially to Kaline, had made the presence of the four quality players a real luxury. Jim Northrup had played 151 games in the outfield, Willie Horton 139, and Mickey Stanley 130. Kaline, one of the greatest Tigers ever, had been reduced to seventy-four games in the outfield and had contributed only ten home runs for the season. But by Series time, Smith found himself with four healthy outfielders, and knew that the skills of future Hall of Famer Kaline would be needed against the Cards. Although Kaline had been in the league for sixteen years, this would be his first Series.

In the days before the first game, writers asked Smith how he would work the four outfielders. He usually smiled and said they'd all be needed. But secretly, early each afternoon, he began working Mickey Stanley at shortstop. The regular Tiger shortstop, Ray Oyler, had given the team a steady defense all season but had batted a horrid .135. His backups, Tom Matchick and Dick Tracewski, had hit .205, and .156, respectively. Help was needed.

Stanley had impressed Smith with good hands, good range, and a good arm. Most major leaguers have enough instinctive athletic ability to successfully play another position; they probably tried all positions in Little League and high school. But the major leagues—and especially the World Series—seemed no place to "experiment" with such a theory. Still, Smith was determined to do it. He gave Stanley a late-season start at shortstop to get him acclimated, and Mickey wound up with nine appearances at the position before the year was over.

Not until the day of the opening game itself did Smith reveal that Stanley would be his shortstop. The brash, unorthodox move had all of baseball talking. Was Mayo out of his mind? This was the Tigers' first World Series in twenty-eight years. How could he?

Lou Brock, the Cardinals' very first batter, hit a grounder to short.

Mickey Stanley works out at shortstop days before the 1968 World Series. (Detroit Tigers)

Denny McLain (Detroit Tigers)

Stanley fielded it cleanly and threw him out. It was like a quarterback taking an early hit to get the butterflies out. Stanley relaxed and settled in, hurting the Tigers not at all and giving Detroit four strong out-fielders' bats in the lineup.

Meanwhile, Gibson beat McLain 4–0 in Game One, striking out seventeen to break Sandy Koufax's World Series record. The Tigers needed a lift in Game Two and Lolich gave it to them, winning 8–1 on a six-hitter. After the Cardinals won the third game, it was Gibson against McLain in Game Four, and again, Denny was overwhelmed by the brilliance of Gibson, who won 10–1. The Tigers were down three games to one.

There were now three "must-wins" coming up for the Tigers. Lolich was the man for Game Five, and he was up to the task, going all the way for a 5–3 win over Nelson Briles. This was the game in which Lou Brock tried to score standing up and was nailed at the plate on a great throw by Horton. It would have given the Cards a two-run lead. This match also required some snappy managing by Smith, The Tigers trailed 3–2 in the last of the seventh, with Lolich due to hit. Smith simply had confidence that with two innings left, his team was capable of scoring again. So he let Mickey bat, a move that could have been second-guessed for all time had the Tigers lost that day. And Lolich, a .110 career hitter, blooped a single to right. The Tigers scored three runs, Kaline driving in two of them, and won the game. It was one gutsy move by Smith.

McLain was due to pitch Game Six. But Denny was 0–2 in the Series and his arm was hurting. Everyone knew it. But he took himself to the hospital for another cortisone shot. Smith told everyone that Earl Wilson would work Game Six, but when the lineups were posted, there was McLain.

Denny shut out the Cardinals for eight innings before they finally scored in the ninth, giving the Tigers an easy 13–1 win and setting up a seventh game. He would not have to spend the winter thinking of a thirty-one-victory season and an 0–3 Series. But it could have happened.

The deciding game challenged Detroit to become the first team in a decade to come back from a 3–1 deficit. Now, on only two days' rest, Lolich was handed the ball by Smith. Mickey was his hot ticket, but it was a tall order. Gibson would be on the mound for the Cardinals, with two brilliant victories behind him, as well as a lineup that included

Brock, Curt Flood, Tim McCarver, Orlando Cepeda, and, in his final game, Roger Maris.

The game went scoreless through six. In the top of the seventh, with two out, Cash and Horton singled, and Northrup drove them both home with a triple. Freehan doubled and it was a 3–0 game.

In the ninth, the Tigers added another for a 4–0 lead. Then it was the last of the ninth. Smith moved Stanley to center and put Oyler at short. Lolich got Flood on a liner to Oyler. Cepeda fouled to Freehan. Two down.

Mike Shannon then belted a homer to left, and suddenly it was 4–1. But McCarver lifted a pop foul, also to Freehan, and it was over—a seven-game thriller for a Tiger championship!

Lolich had three Series wins, matching Gibson's 1967 performance. Kaline hit .379 with eight RBIs in his only World Series. Stanley had thirty-three chances at shortstop and made only two errors. The gamble had paid off. Smith was Manager of the Year.

McLain made forty-one starts again in 1969, winning twenty-four and copping another Cy Young Award. (He actually tied for the award with Mike Cuellar.) But allegations of gambling associations, three suspensions in 1970 by commissioner Bowie Kuhn, and a host of unsavory gossip virtually ended his brilliant career at that stage. Perhaps the cortisone, which may have been overdone, also contributed to bringing things to a close all too soon.

Lolich went on to win 217 games and record over 2,800 strikeouts. Kaline never appeared in another World Series.

It's a real shame there has never been interleague play. The strongest argument can be presented when you think simply about Kaline's position, right field. Consider a player of his stature, with his reputation and his place in history, along with two other great right fielders—Henry Aaron and Roberto Clemente—and you have an immediate argument on behalf of the people who never saw them play. Kaline, Aaron, and Clemente all played in isolated cities, when you compare them to New York, Chicago, or Los Angeles. Those living in Pittsburgh never got to see Kaline play; those in Detroit never got to see Clemente throw from the right-field corner or Aaron, in his prime, roll his wrists and hit one of his classic home runs. Let those three names represent my ballot for interleague competition.

38

The Miracle of '69,
and I Was There

To understand the 1969 Mets, one must first take a look at the 1968 Mets, the team that finished ninth in the final year before the major leagues broke into four divisions.

The '68 Mets were a 73–89 ball club in their first year under Gil Hodges, who had come over from the Washington Senators. Although the team finished twenty-four games out of first, it was only three out of seventh and eight out of the first division. The seventy-three victories were the most ever by the seven-year-old franchise, and a twelve-game improvement over the year before. More to the point, the team was 26–37 in one-run games. If ways could be found to reverse that statistic, the thinking went, the '69 team could be highly competitive.

It was our catcher, Jerry Grote, who first thought we could be in the hunt. He said so as early as spring training of '69. Few took him seriously, because players are somewhat influenced by media, and we had all been raised in the Met organization reading about the short, sorry history of the team and its laughable beginnings under Casey Stengel. But some of us did believe that we had the makings of at least a .500 team. And we had come to admire Hodges and his managerial abilities.

The Opening Day lineup in 1968 was composed entirely of players who would figure in the '69 success. The infield had Ed Kranepool at first, Ken Boswell at second, Buddy Harrelson at short, and Ed Charles at third. In the outfield were Art Shamsky, Tommie Agee, and Ron Swoboda. Grote caught and I pitched. And the nine of us were still there eighteen months later, hoisting champagne to celebrate all that happened in '69. We had come a long way in a short time.

That we were young and untested proved to be an asset. None of us were paid so much in those days before free agency that there was any jealousy. None of us had played for the stumbling Mets of the Stengel years, except for Kranepool. The veterans among us, the only players over thirty—Al Weis, J. C. Martin, Don Cardwell, and Ed Charles— were good team men. Charles was an especially joyful presence in the clubhouse. Donn Clendenon, thirty-three, was obtained in the only significant trade we made during the '69 season, and, if you recall, he went on to become the World Series MVP.

It was important that the Met organization had always stressed pitching and shown great patience with young arms. There we were in 1969: myself, Jerry Koosman, Nolan Ryan, Gary Gentry, and Tug McGraw, Koosman being the oldest at twenty-six. Jerry, Nolan, and I went on to win over eight hundred games in the majors, but we needed those nurturing years with the Mets to establish ourselves and get the opportunity to show what we could do. Another management might have used us differently and altered our destinies. Although Ryan achieved most of his success after the Mets traded him, his roots were in the Met organization, where pitchers were beautifully coached and skillfully allowed to mature.

True, the '69 Mets did not have a lot of hitting. Despite Cleon Jones's .340 season, we outscored only three teams—the two new expansion teams in Montreal and San Diego and the Cardinals. But once we began to believe in ourselves and realize that a pennant was possible, the batters' confidence intensified. The team ended up hitting .360 with two outs and runners in scoring position late in the game. This figure, compiled by the Elias Sports Bureau, was higher than any team between 1975 and 1987, the years in which they were regularly compiling such stats.

Day after day, Jones, Swoboda, Kranepool, Agee, Rod Gaspar, Grote, Clendenon, Boswell, Harrelson, Wayne Garrett, Charles, or Weis would deliver. And with each key base hit, we would slap each other's hands with growing assurance that we were making history.

We played the Cubs—a far better team "on paper"—sixteen times in 1969, and won ten. These were the first "big games" the Mets had played in their entire history. One of the wins was the famous "Jimmy Qualls game," in which I had a real shot at my first no-hitter, going to one out in the ninth, only to have Qualls get a base hit to spoil it. After the game my wife, Nancy, met me in tears, but the fact that I kept my composure and got the last two outs showed we were a team of maturity—a team ready to play more "big ones."

Beginning on August 16, the Mets were 34–10 with a 2.03 ERA. But during that streak we went twenty-nine consecutive games without scoring more than five runs, the longest such spell in the Mets' history. Pitching and defense, along with "amazin' " clutch hitting, were doing it for us.

The '69 Mets didn't reach .500 for good until June 3, and didn't get to first place until September 10. But we never stopped hustling and never stopped believing in the miracle. After all, it was the same year man walked on the moon!

While everyone has different memories of the "key moments," historically one would have to look back to a stretch of games with San Diego and San Francisco at Shea Stadium between August 16 and 19, a stretch that included two doubleheaders. We won them all, by scores of 2–0, 2–1, 3–2, 3–2, and even 1–0 in fourteen innings. Suddenly, we were a team accustomed to winning, not losing, the one-run games.

During that 34–10 streak, Koosman, Cardwell, and I were 19–1 with a 0.99 ERA, while McGraw was 4–1 with five saves, and we gave up only ten homers.

Helped by the Cubs' collapse, our gain of twelve and a half games in September was the biggest in major league history, surpassing the 1914 Braves, who had gained ten and a half in September.

We were also helped by incredible fans, who had stuck with us through woeful seasons, cheering our every small success along the way. It was poetic justice, I think, that all three of our "clinching" games in 1969—the division, the pennant, and the World Series— were accomplished in front of our hometown fans, whose joyful noise washed over us and reverberated across the field. In each case, an impromptu on-field celebration of love for the team followed the game, leaving the ground crew a massive cleanup job, which was always skillfully accomplished. It was all truly a "team effort."

We clinched the division title, the first in National League history, on September 24, with Gary Gentry beating Steve Carlton. Hodges was as pumped as the rest of us in the spirit of the moment, and here was a man who had celebrated success with so many great Dodger ball clubs over the years.

Five games remained in the regular season, and we needed four wins to make one hundred. And we did it! We had gone from seventy-three to one hundred wins in one magical season!

The League Championship Series against the Atlanta Braves was a best-of-five series. With Hank Aaron, Orlando Cepeda, Felipe Alou, Rico Carty, and Felix Millan, the Braves were a good club, but we had a date with destiny, and we steamrollered them in three straight. I beat Phil Niekro 9–5 in the opener, Koosman beat Ron Reed 11–6 in the second game, and Gentry and Ryan teamed up to stop Pat Jarvis 7–4 in the final game at Shea. The Mets had twenty-seven runs in three games! What was going on here?

Even those who had come to believe in the Mets figured it was all over in the World Series. We were facing a terrific Baltimore Oriole team that had won 109 games during the regular season under Earl Weaver. The team had Frank Robinson, Brooks Robinson, Boog Powell, Paul Blair, Dave Johnson, and Mark Belanger, and super pitching from Jim Palmer, Mike Cuellar, Dave McNally, and Tom Phoebus.

When Cuellar beat me 4–1 in Game One, most thought our luck had run out. But a strange thing happened. We didn't feel defeated in the clubhouse at all. It felt more like, "Hey! We can play on the same field as these guys. They weren't supermen out there. We can beat them!" Strange feeling, but contagious. By the time we were dressed, we all believed the Orioles could be taken.

Sure enough, Koosman beat McNally 2–1 in Game Two. Then Gentry and Ryan combined to beat Palmer 5–0, the game in which Agee made two fantastic running catches in center field. I got another chance in Game Four, and went ten innings to beat the Birds 2–1. This was the game in which Swoboda, no great outfielder, made one of the greatest all-time catches ever recorded in World Series history, robbing Brooks Robinson of a sure single that could have put the Orioles ahead in the ninth. His miracle catch kept the game tied at 1–1 until we scored in the tenth on a bunt by J. C. Martin. The throw to first hit Martin in the back and the winning run scored. One more victory, and we'd be World Champions!

The fifth game featured a long home run by Al Weis, his first of the

The Mets celebrate the final out of the 1969 World Series. I'm the first one to reach Jerry Koosman. (Louis Requena)

After the fans had left, Gary Gentry and I returned to the quiet of the late afternoon at Shea Stadium to reflect on what we had done. (Louis Requena)

season at Shea. And strange things *kept* happening—like the "Shoe-Polish Ball Caper," in which Hodges argued that his batter, Cleon Jones, had been hit with a pitch, and proved it by showing the umpire a shoe-polish scuff on the ball.

Although the Orioles had jumped to a 3–0 lead, Koosman was pitching well and the noise of the fans was pumping us up. The score stood at 3–3 in the last of the eighth when Cleon and Swoboda both doubled and Powell made an error, giving us a 5–3 lead.

Now we were three outs away. I paced in the dugout, watching Jerry work. He walked Frank Robinson to open the ninth, but Powell bounced out to Weis and we got a force at second. One down. Brooks flied to Swoboda for the second out. Then up came Dave Johnson, who seventeen years later would manage the Mets to their second World Championship. He flied out tamely to Jones in left, and the place went wild.

I don't think I've ever had another thrill as great.

Many honors and accolades followed for the team and for myself. I won the Cy Young Award for my 25–7 year, and narrowly missed the MVP award (it went to Willie McCovey) in one of those controversies over whether a pitcher can be considered more valuable than an everyday player. (Obviously, I vote for the pitcher.) "The Ed Sullivan Show," a ticker-tape parade down Broadway—all the things you only dream about—were now coming true.

But beyond the honors, the jubilation, the celebration, I came to understand something during those wonderful championship days that affected my entire career. One of my fondest memories of 1969 is a photograph of Gary Gentry and me standing on the mound in an empty Shea, the field torn to shreds by the rabid Met fans. As we stood there in a moment of postcelebratory quiet, I realized for the first time that the ultimate joy is not in the clubhouse, spraying champagne, as I had thought growing up as a boy watching earlier World Series victories. No, the biggest thrill is on the field, in joining with one's teammates in the competition, in the application of all your training, coaching, education, and teamwork to achieve one common goal.

That day I understood that the process in itself is the reward. It was a lesson in maturity, a moment of personal growth. That is why as long as I live, whatever I accomplish, I will always be a '69 Met.

39

Here Comes Henry

He swung the bat with such ease in hitting two of the most significant home runs in baseball history within a matter of days that it is startling to recall the pressures that Henry Aaron faced as he approached Babe Ruth's record. In the end, his ability to perform so gracefully under pressure was as big a story as the crumbling of Ruth's legendary record of 714 home runs in 1974.

For most of the years following Babe Ruth's retirement in 1935, his 714 homers represented a barrier that "would never fall." Even thirty years later, after two more generations of sluggers had come and gone, Ruth was nearly two hundred home runs ahead of Jimmie Foxx (534), Ted Williams (521), and Mel Ott (511). Among active players after 1964, there were Mickey Mantle (454), Willie Mays (453), Eddie Mathews (445), Ernie Banks (376), and Aaron (366), all in their middle or early thirties.

Although Stan Musial had recently retired at forty-two and Ted Williams at forty-one, we tended to think that players lasted only to thirty-seven or thirty-eight. Conditioning wasn't what it was today, and there were signs that some of these power players of the 1950s had already peaked. If any discussions were being held concerning Ruth's record, they were not about its imminent fall.

Even Aaron, the youngest active power player at thirty-one, was

348 homers away in 1965, and if he played to age forty—nine more years—he would have to average thirty-nine a season.

Ironically, people didn't even consider Aaron a home-run hitter when he first came up. He had been purchased in 1952 by the Boston Braves from the Indianapolis Clowns of the Negro American League, as it breathed its last gasps before finally disbanding, integration having sent most of the good Negro League players into Organized Baseball. (A year later, Ernie Banks would go from the Kansas City Monarchs to the Chicago Cubs.)

Aaron never played for Boston. By the time he had served his 224-game minor-league apprenticeship, the Braves were in Milwaukee, and Aaron joined them there in their first season. He was a converted infielder, and built like one, at six-foot-one, 170 pounds. He had more power than your ordinary middle infielder, which seemed to come from his wrists more than from upper-body strength. But even when people later spoke of the strong "wrist hitters" in the game, they tended to speak of Banks instead. Ernie had belted home run totals of forty-three, forty-seven, forty-five, and forty-one between 1957 and 1960.

Moved into the Milwaukee outfield as a rookie after making thirty-six errors at second base at Jacksonville in 1953, Aaron hit .280 with thirteen homers in 122 games. But Wally Moon of the Cardinals was elected Rookie of the Year.

Aaron became a "star" in 1955 and 1956, hitting .314 and then a league-high .328 while slugging twenty-seven and twenty-six home runs. In 1957 and 1958, he helped take the Braves to the World Series, and his home-run totals of forty-four and thirty gave him a five-year tally of 140, or twenty-eight per year on average. Having won the 1957 MVP award, and having become a regular starter in the National League All-Star outfield with Willie Mays and Roberto Clemente, Aaron seemed to be at the top of his game. So people thought of him as "great," and capable of leading the league in homers, as he did with the forty-four in 1957, but not as a fifty-a-year man who might break Ruth's record of sixty in a season.

By the time the Braves moved to Atlanta after the 1965 season, Aaron had hammered 398 homers in twelve years, building his average up to thirty-three a year. If they were looking into such things, mathematicians knew that to hit seven hundred, one would have to average thirty-five a year for twenty years. To reach that average,

Hank would have to lift his yearly total to about thirty-eight a season for the next eight years.

What suddenly made it all possible was Atlanta Stadium. The new ballpark proved to be a hitter's park and very much to Aaron's liking. He led the league with forty-four in his first season there, winning over the fans and seeming to enjoy the irony of hitting his uniform number. (He was to do it four times in his career.) He led the league again with thirty-nine in 1967, my rookie season, for a total of 481. He now seemed certain to enter the five-hundred club with Mays, Mantle, and his teammate, Mathews.

Facing Aaron as a rookie was some kind of a thrill for me. As I was growing up in Fresno, he was my favorite player, along with Sandy Koufax. For some reason, I had taken a real liking to the Milwaukee Braves, a power-hitting, successful team. I liked their uniforms, I liked their style, and I loved their power. Not only did I like Aaron and Mathews, but guys like Bill Bruton did it for me too.

Facing him for the first time was like standing on the mound and facing my image of him from TV. I was so in awe of this man that I turned my back as he went through his customary preparations to hit. I knew all his actions—how he would approach the plate, rest his bat against his upper right leg, put on his helmet, pick up the bat, and step in.

I actually got him to hit a sinker into the ground for a double play the very first time I pitched to him, but the next time up he put a three-run home run into the blue seats of Atlanta Stadium and taught me a little something about being overconfident.

Hank Aaron also taught me something very few people understand about the personal side of a star athlete's life.

He coauthored a book in 1967, and I sheepishly asked him for a copy when the New York Mets played the Braves in Atlanta after my introduction to number 44 on our previous trip there. I also asked Hank if he would autograph it for me and bring it to New York on his next road trip—thinking he would certainly forget. On the day the Braves pulled into Shea Stadium for their series with us, I thought not of my opponents and how I might pitch to them, but rather of Henry Aaron and my request. I parked my car in the bullpen lot, walked the dark, musty hall to the clubhouse . . . and there on the stool in front of my locker was a copy of *Aaron R. F.* On that day, Henry Aaron became more than an idol, more than just a symbol of consistent excellence.

Because my uniform number was 41, I found myself in the locker adjoining Aaron's at the '67 All-Star Game in Anaheim. It was one of those indelible moments from my rookie season in which I had to pinch myself to prove it was all really happening to me.

Mantle and Mathews retired in 1968, Banks in 1971, and Mays in 1973, Willie having finished with 660 homers. But by the end of the '73 season, Aaron was still going strong. He was now closer to two hundred pounds, and his swing had become a home-run swing of the all-or-nothing kind. He had hit 275 homers in his first seven years in Atlanta and had 673 through 1972, second only to Ruth, and only 41 behind him. Barring any serious injury (and he played his career remarkably injury-free), he could now actually make it. He entered the 1973 season at the age of forty and hit exactly that many home runs, to give him 713 at year's end.

But let's backtrack a bit. All during the 1973 season, outside pressures were mounting as the inevitability of his accomplishment became clearer. These were the same "ghosts" Roger Maris had dealt with in 1961 when he went after the single-season record. Some diehards pulled out pocket calculators to prove that "Aaron was no Ruth," that Babe had a much higher home-run-per-at-bat frequency, that he'd hit a great percentage of all home runs smashed in his era, that he'd topped 50 four times and Aaron had never done it. What did these people want Aaron to do, retire? For his part, Aaron issued all due comments lauding Ruth, especially when the Babe's widow spoke up in defense of her husband's record. Privately, Aaron must have thought this was an unnecessary exercise in diplomacy.

Unlike with the Maris accomplishment, however, the ugly side of this attempt at Ruth's record was the racial issue. There was still a part of American society that couldn't accept a black man's breaking a sacred "white" record. Aaron got a lot of anonymous hate mail in 1973, which only showed that twenty-six years after Jackie Robinson's debut, America still had deep-seated racial problems that might never be eliminated.

It was obvious that Ruth's record would be tied and broken early in 1974. When the Braves' officials announced that Aaron would not play in the opening series in Cincinnati so that he could hit his big homers at home in Atlanta (and they could pack the ballpark), commissioner Bowie Kuhn ordered him to play. With Vice President Gerald Ford in the stands, and Kuhn as well, Aaron came up to face the Reds'

Hank Aaron connects for home run number 715 off the Dodgers' Al Downing. (Atlanta Braves)

Jack Billingham, and on his very first swing of the season belted number 714, the magical Babe Ruth figure that had stood in the books for thirty-nine years. Aaron's swing was now so classic, so home-run grooved, it was as though he couldn't help but connect for the distance when he swung the bat.

He left the game and played no more in Cincinnati. Kuhn was satisfied, but decided not to follow Aaron's quest of 715. It was not intended as a slight; suppose it took two weeks? The commissioner had other matters to attend to. Aaron was offended by the decision, even though Kuhn had been in Cincinnati. So now there was the added "insult" to deal with.

Four days later, April 8, 1974, with NBC cameras covering the first "Monday Night Baseball" game, Al Downing, wearing number 44 on his Dodger uniform, walked The Hammer in the first inning, to the boos of the biggest crowd in Atlanta history, 53,775. In the fourth Aaron faced Downing again and, on a 1–0 pitch, pulled his bat back to take his second swing of the season. Everyone knew instantly what had happened as the ball soared to the Braves' bullpen, where Atlanta relief pitcher Tom House caught it. A long delay followed, with ceremonies on the field and a little "Thank God it's over" from Aaron, and then the game resumed. But many of the crowd filed out, having seen what they'd come to see. The Braves won 7–4, with only a handful of fans left at the end.

As it happened, 1973 was Aaron's last truly productive year. He hit twenty homers for the Braves in 1974, and then was traded to the Milwaukee Brewers for two final seasons as a designated hitter, belting only twenty-two homers over those two years before his old Wisconsin fans. He retired with 755 homers, and we are left now to assume that that record will last forever, for it will take 40 a year for nineteen years to reach it, and we don't see even the Cansecos, the Strawberrys, the McGwires, the Mitchells, or the Fielders doing anything like that.

Anybody who picks up this tome in a dusty old used-book shop sometime in the twenty-first century is welcome to have a laugh on me if someone has already passed Aaron. You see, we didn't think the home-run record would fall, either.

40

The Midnight Ride
of Carlton Fisk

Back in the 1970s, when Thurman Munson and Carlton Fisk were the American League's premier catchers, their rivalry was enhanced by the fact that their teams, the Yankees and Red Sox, respectively, had the longest-standing and most bitter rivalry in baseball. Munson, outspoken when the occasion called for it, never hesitated to put Fisk down, saying, "He gets all the glory and he's hurt all the time."

With Fisk still active into the 1990s—a rare four-decade catcher—and Munson the untimely victim of a 1979 plane crash, the words sound hollow. This durable symbol of fitness "hurt all the time"?

Ironically, Munson was on target at the time. Fisk did suffer a number of injuries in the 1970s. In both 1974 and 1975 he spent considerable time on the disabled list, missing more than half of each season, and again in 1979 he was sidelined for a long stretch. In '75 he didn't play at all until June 23 because of a fractured right forearm that was hit by a pitch in spring training. But from that point on, he batted .331 with fifty-two RBIs in only seventy-one starts.

That year, Fisk was a key ingredient in Boston's success, which found it winning the Eastern Division by four and a half games over defending division champion Baltimore, and then stopping World Champion Oakland's streak of three straight pennants with a three-game sweep in the League Championship Series (he hit .417 in the

LCS). It isn't easy to repeat a title, as we have seen since the advent of free agency, but it is no small feat to beat two defending champions, the Orioles and Athletics.

Fisk was in many ways the heart of the Red Sox. He had the New England ethic so admired by Red Sox fans: the dedication to excellence through hard work. He was also one of them, coming as he did from Vermont.

The Red Sox were underdogs for the 1975 World Series, against a mature "Big Red Machine" of Cincinnati Reds. Here were two historic, charter ball clubs, Cincinnati the first professional team, and Boston an original member of the American League. They had been playing baseball forever, these two proud franchises from working-class cities, but they had never before met in a World Series.

The Reds had been there in 1970 and 1972 under Sparky Anderson, with many of their 1975 players, including Johnny Bench, the National League's best catcher, Pete Rose, Tony Perez, Joe Morgan, and Davi Concepcion. In 1975 George Foster and Ken Griffey joined the regular lineup, Foster having been a reserve in the '72 Series. This was some team! In retrospect, it is hard to believe that it did not win the pennant in every year of the decade. But as history tells us, the Dodgers had superior enough pitching to overcome the Big Red Machine and win in 1974, 1977, and 1978.

Although Oakland was also a colorful and exciting band of ballplayers during its winning seasons in the early 1970s, the public was feeling somewhat apathetic toward baseball. It may have had something to do with the bitter feelings that divided the nation during the Vietnam War. Anything steeped in the aura of "establishment," such as the national pastime, was out of favor with young people, who questioned many values the nation had taken for granted. Baseball was not attracting their attention. Attendance was stagnant, and the game wasn't being marketed with much imagination.

The war officially ended for Americans in 1973, after which the nation's wounds began to heal. Maybe the timing was right for the 1975 World Series. Maybe the nation was prepared to accept and enjoy baseball. And maybe Fisk was just the right guy at the right time to win their hearts.

To set the scene, after five hard-played games, the Reds held a 3–2 lead and were one win away from their first World Championship in thirty-five years. The Red Sox, needing two, had not won since 1918.

You know the story: Before the 1920 season they sold Babe Ruth to the Yankees and have forever lived under the "curse" of that infamous transaction. Here were two hungry teams! If you think that sort of pressure isn't felt by players untainted by a franchise's previous failures, you're wrong. For most players, loyalty to an organization comes with winning. When a team is hot and he starts to read about the great stars and seasons from the franchise's past, a player gets caught up with what has come before him. For a Red player to know that a thirty-five-year drought might soon end, and for a Bostonian to know that it had been fifty-seven years since everyone went home happy, added another dimension to the drama.

Game Six at Fenway Park was scheduled for the night of October 21, after five days off due to travel and rain. This was only the fifth year in which World Series games were played at night, and while many fans and players grumbled about the break with tradition, it did create huge television audiences. There was a certain old-fashioned "charm" to the thought of America coming to a halt to watch daytime World Series games, but alas, the times called for a change. (A sad corollary has been the fact that schoolchildren are usually not able to watch these night games to their conclusions, since they run well past bedtime.)

So in the ballpark of the famous "wall," the Red Sox had their backs to it, needing two wins to stop the Reds. But, of course, they had to play them "one at a time," and started Luis Tiant in Game Six against Gary Nolan. Tiant was made for the Red Sox fans. He would take his pregame warmups in the bullpen beyond right field and then stride majestically to the dugout as the roar of the crowd grew louder with each step. He was a matador entering the ring. So theatrical, but so natural!

The Red Sox gave him three runs in the first on a homer by Fred Lynn, who was both Rookie of the Year and MVP that season. But the Reds tied it with three in the fifth, Lynn collapsing as he hit the outfield wall while chasing down a triple by Griffey.

The Reds got two in the seventh on a double by Foster, and one more in the eighth on a homer by Cesar Geronimo to take a 6–3 lead. Cincinnati was only six outs away from victory.

But in the last of the eighth, Bernie Carbo, a former Red, shook up the night with his second pinch homer of the Series, tying the game. In the ninth, in the tenth, and in the eleventh, no one scored. In the eleventh, Morgan belted what appeared to be a home run, but Dwight Evans made a spectacular catch in front of the right-field stands, and then fired to first for a double play. Talk about your money players!

The clock moved past midnight. It was now October 22, the same date on which Game Seven would be played—if there was to be a Game Seven.

As Pete Rose came to bat late in the game, he looked back at Fisk and said, "This is the greatest game I've ever played in." He then got hit with a pitch.

In the twelfth inning, Rick Wise allowed two hits but got Geronimo on a called third strike to end the inning. The clock read 12:33 A.M. as Fisk came to bat in the last of the twelfth. Pat Darcy, the Reds' eighth pitcher, was in his third inning of work.

The first pitch was high for ball one. You really didn't want to work Fisk high in Fenway Park. Carlton took the second pitch deep to left. There was no question that it had the distance—it was only 315 down the line. And there was no question that it had the height to scale the thirty-seven-foot wall. But was it fair or foul?

Like a member of the pro bowlers' tour, Fisk gave it all he could with his body as he leaned a few feet up the line from home plate. With his arms he waved "fair, fair, fair," hoping to coax the ball into history. When left-field umpire Dick Stello made it official with the fair-ball signal, the fans at Fenway Park erupted. But they weren't alone. It seemed that all of America once more fell in love with baseball that night. Television replays of Fisk's body English, as captured by the outfield cameras, only heightened the drama of the moment.

That should have been the end of the Series. Unfortunately, another game later in the day was needed to settle it all. And the Reds won that in less heroic fashion, with Joe Morgan blooping a single to center off a pitcher named Jim Burton in the top of the ninth for a 4–3 win. I think everyone, with the exception of Red fans and players, wished it had ended with the magic moment of the Fisk homer.

Fisk, who seemed as though he'd be a franchise player forever, left the Red Sox after the 1980 season and moved on to the Chicago White Sox, courtesy of an arbitration ruling after a contract error by Boston management. He was my battery mate in Chicago when I played for the Sox and never uttered a single word of regret about leaving Boston.

Carlton Fisk coaxes his home run in game six of the 1975 World Series to stay fair.
(UPI/Bettmann Newsphotos)

In fact, he so enjoyed his tenure with the White Sox that he never opted to become a free agent and return to his original team.

He has also become a four-decade catcher, testimony to modern training methods and hard work. In his forties he was still the best catcher in the league. We all call him Pudge, but few have better-conditioned bodies than Carlton Fisk.

There are individuals who, for one reason or another, will be forever identified with one special team. For example, I played in the major leagues for twenty years for four different teams, but my association with the New York Mets will certainly dominate the history of my career, even though I played for them for just over half of those twenty years.

And so it is for Pudge Fisk. He played for the Chicago White Sox longer than he caught for Boston, but he remains deep in the hearts of the Red Sox faithful. And that one moment, the dramatic display of emotion for one of the most memorable home runs in baseball history—willing the ball into fair territory over the green monster at Fenway Park—will dominate Fisk's brilliant career. It was shared by millions of Americans who, that night, rediscovered baseball as the national pastime.

The Age of Free Agency

Something happened to baseball between 1967 and 1975 that changed the course of the game.

In 1967, Charles O. Finley, owner of the Athletics, had a feud with first baseman Ken "Hawk" Harrelson and promptly released him in mid-season. The Hawk was no Hall of Famer, but he was one of the better offensive players for a few seasons, and he put people in the seats.

So Harrelson was a free agent in the middle of one of the toughest pennant races in American League history. And the Red Sox wound up signing him, and went to the World Series with him. They even gave him a bonus, $75,000.

Now it's eight years later. Again it's Finley, this time missing a payment to Catfish Hunter. Granted, Hunter was a better player than Harrelson, but this time, the free-agent bidding established Hunter's worth in the millions. And when everyone saw what a player's worth had become on the open market, it was inevitable that a new era would cross the moat and enter the castle. It took the decision of an arbitrator to make it happen, but it was destined to come about one way or another.

So what happened in those eight years? The game had grown up. Owners were willing to pay more to buy teams, and then pay more to obtain players. Conservatives in baseball, defending the reserve system and the "status quo," argued long and hard that free movement would destroy competitive balance, that the rich teams would win all the time, just as the Yankees used to do.

And in the early years of free agency, the Yankees did win a lot. They won in 1976, 1977, and 1978, but then it suddenly became more difficult for teams to repeat. Instead of an imbalance, the pennant races were thrown wide open, and franchise values soared as never before. In 1943, the Philadelphia Phillies were sold for $80,000. In 1973, the Yankees were sold for $10 million. Both figures are bargains today, laughable almost. A recent business publication valued the Yankee franchise at $225 million. A new order in baseball had forced the existing owners to find buyers who could play by the new rules. The new owners did not buy blindly. They knew the price of admission and paid it. The players now dictated movement, which was not terribly · different from the days when the owners did. Don't forget, they traded off plenty of star players when left to their own devices.

Because fans follow their teams with love and affection on a daily basis, they will embrace a new star within days, with no formal introduction necessary.

The events following free agency were seen by more people than the game's founders could have imagined. A prime-time World Series home run by a Kirk Gibson became the stuff of legend overnight. The "Golden Age of Sports" may have meant the 1920s to observers of the scene back then, but today's accomplishments, by athletes conditioned to play longer, are every bit as thrilling. Free agency has gone through its infancy, and the Republic has survived.

41

Four for Mike Schmidt

Mike Schmidt broke a lot of rules on the way to Cooperstown. Not the rules of the rule book, but the "rules" we have come to accept in the post-free-agent era.

For one thing, he spent his entire eighteen-year career with one club, the Philadelphia Phillies. The era in which this was customarily done, of course, is passé. There was once a time when, as a matter of pride, a "franchise" player like Mantle, Williams, Musial, or Banks would want to have his career records show the continuity of one club, line after line. But it didn't happen for Mays, or Aaron or Rose or Jackson, or even the guy the newspapers called "The Franchise" at Shea Stadium. The game just doesn't work like that anymore.

For another thing, Schmidt won eight home-run titles and hit 548 career "dingers." It's hard to imagine those feats being duplicated soon. There are no players in the current generation of sluggers anywhere close to the five-hundred mark. The most likely to get there someday—José Canseco, Mark McGwire, Darryl Strawberry—have so far to go and play in an era when they'll be making more money than they can ever spend by the time they get up in the three hundreds. The drive to keep playing, to keep punishing their bodies with the travel and conditioning now demanded of athletes is bound to diminish by that time. It is hard to imagine a modern player, with earnings of perhaps $50 million in a dozen seasons, who will want to play another six or seven years just to land on a listing in a record book. Some may drive themselves to excel, but most will falter along the way.

Schmidt's eight home-run titles are the most ever won by a National Leaguer. (His American League counterpart, Babe Ruth, had twelve titles.) The eight surpassed the numbers of such sluggers as Aaron, Mays, Mathews, Banks, Ott, and McCovey, the other National Leaguers with more than five hundred homers, and actually broke the record of Ralph Kiner, who won seven in a row (including three ties) but wound up with only 369.

Schmidt's unbroken, eighteen-year career in Philadelphia was also remarkably injury-free. From 1974 to 1987, he never played fewer than 145 games, and four times played 160 or more. The exception was the strike-shortened season of 1981, when he played 102 games, but that season was so productive for Mike that even a reduction of two months seemed to hardly have an impact on his yearly stats. He hit thirty-one homers and drove in ninety-one runs that year, both league-leading totals. As a matter of fact, playing 148 games in 1982, his RBI total actually dropped to eighty-seven.

The ability to remain so injury-free contributed to his handsome line of eighteen straight "Philadelphia, NLs" in the record book. He was a quick healer, not missing many games even after a dislocated shoulder in 1973 and a fractured rib in 1982. Ultimately it was the dreaded torn right rotator-cuff injury in 1988 that made a comeback at age thirty-nine very tough.

Incidentally, one innovation gained by modern collective bargaining is the rehabilitation visit a player makes to the minor leagues to work himself off the disabled list. This free trip, which does not count as an option, has resulted in minor-league performances being tucked into the lines of some great modern players, with no shame or stigma attached. Ron Guidry, Jim Palmer, Doc Gooden, Keith Hernandez, José Canseco, Rickey Henderson, and Tommy John are a few examples of first-rate players who have interrupted their major league careers with brief trips to the minors on rehab. Not so with Mike.

He won three Most Valuable Player awards, a total no one has ever topped, and he did it not only on the strength of his slugging but also for his fielding and base-running abilities.

When he first came up to the majors, no one thought of Mike as a brilliant fielder. He had been, in fact, a man without a position in the minors, spending time at all four infield spots. But he worked hard at

Mike Schmidt won his third consecutive home run title in 1976, and on one day in Wrigley Field hit four of his thirty-eight. (© 1976, Chicago Tribune Company, all rights reserved, used with permission)

third base and wound up winning ten Gold Glove awards, the most ever at that position in the National League.

He was also deceptively fast, and while his stolen base total for his final seven seasons was only nineteen, he did have twenty-nine in 1975. Combined with thirty-eight homers that year, he just missed joining the "thirty-thirty" club, which in those days had a very limited membership—Willie Mays (twice), Bobby Bonds (three times), plus Hank Aaron, Tommy Harper, and the first, Ken Williams of the 1922 St. Louis Browns.

Mike was twenty-three when he came up from Eugene, Oregon, at the end of the 1972 season. He had hit twenty-six home runs there, but it was considered a fairly easy home-run park, and he had, after all, hit only eight at Reading in 1971.

He joined a Philadelphia team that had hit bottom. In 1971, struggling through one of their worst eras, the Phillies had won only sixty-seven games in the new Veterans Stadium, finishing last but only four and a half games out of fifth. In 1972, they sunk to a 59–97 record, eleven games out of fifth.

Schmidt's late-season arrival that year to play in thirteen games (with one homer) was hardly noticed. The only thing Philly fans were talking about in 1972 was the debut season of Steve Carlton, who had been obtained from St. Louis in a trade for Rick Wise after Cardinal owner Gussie Busch had tired of Carlton's salary demands. Carlton, angry over being traded without consultation (there were still four years to go before free agency), showed the Cardinals what they had lost by winning twenty-seven games in a year the Phillies only won fifty-nine, total. Lefty hurled eight shutouts, led the league with a 1.98 ERA, and threw thirty complete games. The runner-up on the staff, Darrell Brandon, won seven games.

Desperate for new faces in '73, the Phillies handed Schmidt the third-base job, sending Don Money to Milwaukee. Mike was not ready for prime time. He was an easy strikeout, going down 136 times in 367 at-bats while batting only .196. But his eighteen homers, one for every twenty at-bats, indicated that with maturity and bat discipline, he might make it.

The strikeout problem never completely went away. The year Bobby Bonds was traded to the American League, Mike came to me in spring training and said, "Tom, if they can get me out of the league, too, you'll lose half your strikeouts."

I recall something else about the early seventies when the Phillies were struggling so badly. The rest of the teams in the National League were aware of what was "down on the farm" for the Phils. Word got around concerning a couple of right-handed hitters with unbelievable power—two guys named Schmidt and Luzinski who were tearing the Pacific Coast League apart and would change the face of the Phils.

When they were called to the big-league club, they would turn your head with their power. I looked at them both and saw a lot of strikeouts by two young, undisciplined hitters, but in the back of my mind, I thought, "If these guys ever learn to lay off the high fastball, cut down their strikeouts, and make more contact—watch out!" Guess what? After three strikeout "crowns" in his first four seasons, Mike never again led the league.

In 1974 Schmidt's talents came together, and he was clearly a major leaguer. His second season produced a league-leading thirty-six home runs. He drove in 116 and raised his batting average from .196 to .282. Carlton, unfortunately, became a twenty-game loser, and the Phillies remained in last place. But with Bob Boone, Greg Luzinski, and Larry Bowa maturing along with Schmidt, they were building toward a better future.

In 1975, Mike had his first of three consecutive thirty-eight-homer seasons. Then, in 1976, he had his greatest day as a big leaguer. It could only have happened on a windswept afternoon in Wrigley Field.

The season was only a week old. It was Saturday, April 17, and Carlton faced Rick Reuschel, the portly but effective Cub right-hander. Batting only .167 (3-for-18, with nine strikeouts and one homer) through the season's early going, Mike was dropped to sixth in the lineup from his normal number 3 spot. Wrigley Field was not his favorite park; he had hit only five homers there in the previous three years, despite its cozy confines.

Carlton was shelled by the Cubs, and Chicago took a 12–1 lead after three innings. All Mike had to show for it was a fly to center in the second inning. Then he singled in the fourth as the Phillies scored a run to make it 12–2. It did not figure to be a memorable day at all.

But Mike touched Reuschel for a homer over the left-field screen in the fifth with a man on, and then belted a solo homer in the seventh to help narrow the score to 13–7. This is the point at which announcers start saying things like, "Don't go away, fans. Anything can happen on a windy day in Wrigley Field."

Darold Knowles was on the mound in the eighth when Mike sent a three-run homer to center to make the score 13–12. The Phillies were on the verge of overcoming an eleven-run deficit and tying the National League record for the biggest comeback in history.

In the ninth, the Phillies got three to take the lead by 15–13, but the Cubs scored two in the last of the ninth to tie it up and send the game into overtime.

In the tenth, Mike faced Rick Reuschel's brother Paul, the fourth Cub pitcher (the Phillies used eight), and quickly converted a fastball into a two-run homer to center. Michael Jack Schmidt had belted his fourth home run of the game, as the Phillies hung on to win 18–16!

The four-homers-in-a-game club has a very limited enrollment. Only three American Leaguers have ever done it—Lou Gehrig in 1932, Pat Seerey of the White Sox in 1948, and Rocky Colavito with Cleveland in 1959. So it has been over a quarter century since it happened in the American League.

A fellow named Bobby Lowe was the first to do it in the senior circuit, in 1894. Ed Delahanty, a future Hall of Famer, did it in 1896 for the Phillies. In this century, it happened four times before Mike: Chuck Klein of Philadelphia in 1936; Gil Hodges of Brooklyn in 1950; Joe Adcock of Milwaukee in 1954; and Willie Mays of San Francisco in 1961. Since Schmidt, only one other player can boast of the accomplishment, Bob Horner of the Braves in 1986.

To put these feats in even greater perspective, the list of eleven is shorter than the list for perfect games (fourteen) and just three longer than the one for unassisted triple plays (eight).

Just when we thought it was safe to say that Brooks Robinson had surpassed Pie Traynor as the best all-around third baseman ever, Mike Schmidt came along and complicated the argument. But that's what makes baseball so much fun.

42

When the Straw Stirred the Drink

Although the New York Yankees won the 1976 pennant by ten and a half games, their four-game World Series loss to the Cincinnati Reds convinced owner George Steinbrenner that changes were needed. This was no surprise to Yankee fans, who knew that change and George Steinbrenner went together easily.

By happy circumstance, the loss coincided with the first year of free agency, giving him the opportunity to sample the wares made available by this new system, a system largely rushed into place by his own signing of Catfish Hunter two years earlier.

Hunter had been declared a free agent because Oakland A's owner Charley Finley had failed to make a contract payment on time. The huge bidding for his services made it loud and clear to all just how huge the dollar value of players would be on the free market. Hence, the Messersmith-McNally decision to cancel the reserve clause of player contracts was made in 1976, and at season's end, the process of the first free-agent draft was in place. The sacred perpetual option that clubs had always claimed on players had ended. The arbitrator, Peter Seitz, now recognized only a one-year reserve on a player contract.

The big fish in that first draft was clearly Reginald Martinez Jackson. So sure was Finley that he could never re-sign Reggie under the coming system that he traded him to Baltimore for the '76 season. And when it ended, Reggie found himself among twenty-two pioneer players who had gone through that season unsigned, prepared to enter new territory.

Jackson was preeminent not only for his ability to grab headlines but for his ability on the field. Only thirty years old, he was at the peak of his game. His forty-seven home runs in 1969 had propelled him into headlines, and his stardom on five consecutive Oakland A's division champions between 1971 and 1975, including an MVP award in 1973 and a titanic All-Star Game home run in 1971, had made him nationally known, even though he toiled in the small city of Oakland. He had two home-run titles to his credit, and in 1976, despite missing nearly thirty games in a contract dispute, he drove in ninety-one runs and stole twenty-eight bases. Up to that time, he had never batted .300, and he struck out more than anyone else in history, but no one ever left his seat when Reggie came up swinging.

By today's ever-rising standards, the Yankees got a bargain in signing Reggie to a $2.6 million contract, spread over five seasons. His annual salary was $700,000, and in those days, it left people in awe, much as a Jackson home run did. Others, it was said, had offered more money, but Reggie was on record as stating, "If I ever play in New York, they'd name a candy bar after me." He did, and they did.

When Reggie was signed, he brought with him the reputation of not getting along very well with his teammates. The Oakland A's had been a battling team, and Reggie, outspoken as usual, was often in the midst of the fracas. He was also a player who sought media attention. He courted the press; he invited reporters to talk after a game, learned their names and affiliations, understood the difference between a wire service and a local paper, between a network and a local station. This was never something that teammates were fond of. It separated a player from his club. It annoyed players, particularly after a losing game, to see one of their own conducting a press conference, evaluating the game. On the Mets, Ron Swoboda was a good guy, but he had the same habit, and a lot of his teammates resented it. Although many individual writers are just fine people doing their jobs, there has always been a clubhouse mentality that they are "outsiders" of sorts, peering into corners and seeing things they can't understand. So Reggie's courting of these people, largely to enhance his own popularity, was not appreciated.

Even as likable a fellow as Catfish Hunter had warned his Yankee teammates about Reggie, using such expressions as, "Not enough mustard to cover that hot dog." Still, he *could* swing the bat, and most Yankees decided to take a wait-and-see attitude with their new teammate as spring training approached.

No sooner did Reggie arrive on the scene, however, than he consented to do an interview with *Sport* magazine about his new ball club. And he proceeded to tell the writer that on the Yankees, "I'm the straw that stirs the drink." Referring to the Yankees' team captain and the 1976 American League Most Valuable Player, Reggie opined, "Thurman Munson can only stir it bad."

So much for wait-and-see.

Add to this mix the view held by his fiery new manager, Billy Martin, who considered Jackson to be "George's boy"—with whatever racial implications Reggie saw in that (Billy had been "Casey's boy" as a player). It was bound to be a difficult season. In mid-June in Boston, with tensions already high, Reggie loafed on a ball hit to right, and when he came into the dugout he was confronted by Martin, leading to a shouting match that nearly resulted in a punch-out on national television. Anyone who missed it was sure to catch it over and over on newscasts and highlight programs. With hardly a friend on the team, Jackson had to be having a very lonely summer in New York.

But he played well and justified his salary. He had thirty-two homers and 110 runs batted in, and the Yankees won their second straight pennant. Still, there was no love lost between Reggie and his manager, his teammates had little respect for him, and the fans were with him when he was hot, against him when he wasn't.

It's odd, when you think back, how the owners of baseball predicted that free agency would doom the game, how it would destroy the industry financially. What really happened was that people began to wonder how a ballplayer like Reggie Jackson could be worth a million dollars, and then flooded the attendance gates to find out. Certainly other factors existed, but arguably free agency was the beginning of the ten-to-twenty-fold increase in the value of the owners' franchises.

In the League Championship Series against Kansas City, Reggie was almost a nonperson. He was only 1-for-15 in the first four games, and Martin embarrassed him by sitting him down in the final contest. The Yankees won it, helped by a pinch hit from Reggie in the eighth inning, and it was on to the World Series against the Los Angeles Dodgers.

A Yankee-Dodger Series has that special, classic sound to it. The teams had met six times when the Dodgers were in Brooklyn and once more with the Dodgers in L.A. This eighth meeting was the first with all the hoopla of prime-time games, double-knit uniforms, instant-replay scoreboards, and Reggie Jackson.

Martin almost failed to write Jackson into his lineup for Game One, and Reggie responded in kind, getting one bloop single in the first two games, covering nine at-bats. He came alive in the middle three games in Los Angeles, homering in the fourth game, then homering again on his last at-bat in Game Five.

The Series returned to New York on October 18, with the Yankees up three games to two. Mike Torrez would work for the Yankees, and Burt Hooton for the Dodgers. Reggie was in his customary cleanup slot in the batting order.

Steve Garvey tripled home two runs in the first to put the Dodgers up 2–0. In the second, Reggie walked and scored on Chris Chambliss's home run, which tied the score. In the fourth, the Dodgers led 3–2 as Jackson came up with Munson on first. He belted Hooton's first pitch into the right-field seats and the Yankees were on top 4–3. The scoreboard said "REG-GIE, REG-GIE" to lead the fans in the cheering, as the Yankees' first World Championship in fifteen years now edged closer.

In the fifth, with Elias Sosa on the mound, Jackson stepped in again, took Sosa's first pitch, and sent another two-run homer to right, even deeper than the first one. Now it was 7–3, with Torrez pitching well, and the game seemed a lock. Reggie was the whole show now. This was his fourth home run of the Series, a feat previously performed only by Babe Ruth, Lou Gehrig, Duke Snider (twice), Hank Bauer, and Gene Tenace, Reggie's old Oakland teammate.

When Reggie came up in the last of the eighth, Yankee Stadium was all his. Even the Dodgers, three outs from defeat, knew they had a chance to see history made. Knuckleball pitcher Charlie Hough was on the mound. The fans were all standing, hoping for the impossible. Hough had fanned Reggie in Game Three on a knuckler. He would be tough.

Reggie put all he had into his first swing—and there it went, deep into center field, deeper than the first two. It was his third home run of the game, his fifth of the Series, and his fourth in four times at bat.

Reggie Jackson acknowledges the fans following his fifth home run of the 1977 World Series. Even Thurman Munson (catcher's gear) and Billy Martin (at the right) can smile. (New York Daily News)

Magnificent! Said losing Dodger manager Tommy Lasorda, "It was the greatest single performance I've ever seen."

The films of the moment show such happiness on Reggie's Teddy Roosevelt-look-alike face, such a burden lifted after his intense first season in New York. And you could see Billy Martin and even Thurman Munson grinning broadly, in spite of themselves. Everyone who ever thought ill of Reggie was in love with him at that moment, undoubtedly the highest point of his career.

Reggie was a career .262 hitter who batted .357 in twenty-seven World Series games. They said he loved to play in the spotlight, especially if that light helped to focus a network television camera. On that chilly New York night in 1977, when he became Mr. October forever, all the world adored him—even, perhaps, his teammates, who thought it was okay for Reggie Jackson to hold a press conference that evening.

43

Carrying On the Legacy

If it is true that the great ones rise to the occasion, one need look no further than the city of Pittsburgh for proof.

In the last quarter century, two Pirates stand out above all others— Roberto Clemente and Willie Stargell. Both had brilliant careers, were team leaders, and spent their entire careers with one team. Neither had many opportunities to play in a World Series, but when they did (two each), both made the most of it, selecting the October spotlight to demonstrate their leadership and talent for all the world to see. They did it with a grace and style that put them into Series history, although they'd already secured their places in baseball history long before and would make the Hall of Fame soon after.

Clemente, the greatest Latin American star to date, joined the Pirates in 1955 after the Brooklyn Dodgers failed to protect him from the minor-league draft. Only twenty years old when he reached the majors, he joined a Pirate team that was struggling to escape the depths of the National League standings. After a year of adjustment, Roberto hit .311 as a sophomore, his first of thirteen .300 seasons.

Writers called him Bob Clemente back then, because Latins were new to the game, particularly in Pittsburgh, and it was considered only natural to "Americanize" him. Of course, as a Puerto Rican, Roberto already was an American, and with a quiet dignity he saw to it that fans all over the United States came to know him as Roberto, not Bob. It is rare now that Latin players are given "American" nicknames, and Clemente was one of the main reasons.

Roberto was not beyond speaking out when he felt justified. He would on occasion call attention to the greater accolades being paid to Willie Mays and Hank Aaron, his outfield superstar contemporaries, but he would do so for what he considered a just cause—the effort to earn respect not only for himself, but for his countrymen.

Years later, in 1967, I had been in the major leagues for twelve weeks when I found myself standing on the pitching mound in Anaheim Stadium, wearing my gray Met road uniform, ready to pitch in my first All-Star Game. A year before I had been at Jacksonville, Florida. Two years before, I had been at USC.

As I rubbed up the baseball to work the fifteenth inning of the longest All-Star Game in history, I turned to the outfield. There stood Aaron in left, Mays in center, and Clemente in right. Had I died and gone to heaven or what? This wasn't Strat-O-Matic baseball, folks. This was the real thing. The major leagues were great, but I'd been looking at an outfield of Larry Stahl, Al Luplow, and Don Bosch back in New York. (I'm stretching the truth a little here.) I was no fool: Two of the three outs I got were fly balls to Mays and Aaron. I had a save and the National League had a 2–1 win.

As for the Pirates, they continued to improve under Danny Murtaugh's managing, and in 1960 they won their first pennant in thirty-three years. While Dick Groat was the league MVP and Bill Mazeroski the World Series hero, Roberto had a .314 regular season with ninety-four RBIs, and a .310 World Series. He was ready to emerge as a superstar.

The following season he belted a .351 with twenty-three homers, after having hit only forty-two over his previous six years. He had developed great wrist strength, and not only could he jerk one out of the park even when swinging late, but he could also drive an inside pitch to the opposite field. Take it from me: He was almost impossible to pitch to.

The .351 season was his first batting championship. He would win four in all, and four times he topped .350. In 1966, an "off year" with no batting title and "only" a .317 average, Clemente won the league's MVP award with 29 homers and 119 RBIs, both career highs.

In 1971, the Pirates returned to the World Series to face the Baltimore Orioles. Mazeroski and Clemente were the only players left

Roberto Clemente faces Jim Palmer in the 1971 World Series in Baltimore. Elrod Hendricks is the catcher.

from the 1960 team, and Maz was just a part-timer in his final season. Clemente, at thirty-seven, was an elder statesman but still at the top of his game. He had batted .341 in the regular season, and was still playing right field with the brilliance that had brought him twelve Gold Glove Awards.

The '71 Series proved historic, because it was the first in which night games were played. Baseball decided to give up the pastoral beauty of fall weekdays for the sheer number of fans who could watch the game in prime time on network television. Many hated the change, but it did win over millions of new converts who had previously only "heard" about the day's game.

And oh, how Clemente chose to make the show all his! He hit safely in all seven games, compiling a .414 average to lead both teams. He had twelve hits, just one short of a record. Five of the hits were for extra bases. He made breathtaking throws from right field and waved his bat like a wand. In the deciding seventh game, he came up in the fourth inning of a scoreless tie and belted his second home run of the Series to give the Pirates a 1–0 lead, a lead they would never relinquish. Steve Blass hung on for a complete-game 2–1 victory and the Orioles were beaten. For Clemente, a World Series MVP award was well earned. It was his finest moment in the sun—or, shall we say, in the lights.

In 1972, I faced Roberto on the next-to-last day of the season. He had 2,999 hits. I held him to 0-for-3, thanks in part to expert defensive positioning by Rusty Staub, who caught a wicked shot down the line in right.

The next day, he hit a ringing double to left-center off Jon Matlack for number three thousand. And that was it. Three months later, Roberto Clemente was dead at the age of thirty-eight. He was flying to Nicaragua on a humanitarian mission, the country having been hit by an earthquake, when his plane crashed. They never found his body. It was one of the greatest tragedies I ever experienced in the game. The Hall of Fame waived the five-year waiting period for electing a player and voted him in immediately, making the '73 induction ceremony unusually moving.

After Clemente's death, his good friend Willie Stargell assumed team leadership of the Pirates. Willie, who came to be known as "Pops" as he grew older, was a bear of a man, with a simple warmth and kindness that made all players on his club look to him with respect.

While Clemente sometimes had to speak out to gain his proper place, respect accrued quite naturally to Stargell.

Willie could get emotional over the loss of Roberto and always defended his memory. I was talking to him one afternoon about Roberto and he said something I found quite interesting. I had mentioned the criticism that had been leveled at Clemente for not playing unless he felt 100 percent physically. Pops said Clemente was such a proud man—proud of his abilities and his ethnic background—that he never wanted to embarrass himself by playing below his standards. If it wasn't 100 percent, Roberto Clemente was too proud to take anything else on the field.

Stargell had come up at the end of the 1962 season. A natural slugger who hit the first home run ever at Shea Stadium, he was a hundred-RBI man by 1965 and a .300 hitter the following year. In 1971, when the Pirates won the pennant, Willie belted forty-eight homers and drove in 125 runs. That season established him as one of the league's premier players. When Roberto died a year later, Willie responded in 1973 with forty-four homers and 119 RBIs. Although they usually came home a bridesmaid in pennant races, the Pirates were the most successful team in the National League East during the seventies, winning six times in the decade. And Willie was their undisputed leader.

As the decade came to a close in '79, the Pirates returned to the World Series. Pops was a big reason. Although now thirty-eight years old, heavy and slow, he batted .281, hit thirty-two homers, drove in eighty-two runs, and made them count. In a year in which the Pirates embraced a "We Are Family" theme after a rock hit of the time, Willie was the father of the family. So effective was his leadership that he was a cowinner of the MVP award for the regular season, even though he lacked the numbers usually associated with that honor.

I was with Cincinnati when the Pirates faced the Reds in the League Championship Series that year. The scouting report on Stargell was basically, "Don't let him beat you; he can still do it." Before we had time to notice, it was over. The Pirates knocked us out in three straight, winning 5–2, 3–2, and 7–1. Pops led all hitters with a .455 average—5-for-11—and hit two home runs. The first was a three-run shot in the top of the eleventh to win Game One. He homered again in the deciding game and won the MVP award of the LCS.

In the World Series, Pittsburgh faced Baltimore, as in '71, and it was the Willie Stargell Show again. Fans all over the country were loving every minute of it: a great star, rising to the occasion one more time. Willie batted .400 against Oriole pitching, blasting three homers and driving in seven runs.

In the deciding seventh game, the Orioles held a 1–0 lead after five. Stargell came up in the sixth, facing left-hander Scott McGregor and already the hitting star of the Series. You can still hear the echoes of the daily scouting report: "Don't let the big guy beat you." With one out and a man on first, Stargell drove his third homer of the Series over the right-field fence, giving Pittsburgh the game and the Series.

MVP of the World Series? You bet. A clean sweep—the regular season, the League Championship Series, and the World Series. It may be a long time before that happens again.

44

The Best League
Championship Series

Divisional play, and with it League Championship Series action, began in 1969 with an awkward, less-than-capacity acceptance by fans. One finds a crowd of only thirty-two thousand attending the deciding game of the '69 American League Championship Series at Minnesota, for example.

But by 1980, the twelfth year of League Championship Series play, it had become as thrilling to baseball fans as the World Series. In fact, many players were heard to say that the pressure was in the League Championship Series, that without a win there, the 162-game chase almost seemed as if it had been for nothing. A World Series defeat became somehow easier to accept. You still got rings and you were still champions of your league, a much more meaningful accomplishment than being division champs. (Go ahead. Name all the LCS losers in the last five years.)

The 1980 National League Championship Series produced some of the most exciting postseason games baseball has played. It was certainly the most thrilling LCS when it was still a best-of-five series, and it went the distance, with four of the five games decided in extra innings, and plenty of heroes, second-guessing, and controversial calls.

It was the Philadelphia Phillies versus the Houston Astros, and both played like previously unranked heavyweight champions, refusing to hit the canvas, seeing glory over the next horizon. Call them both "Rocky."

The Phillies hadn't won a pennant since 1950, or a World Series since 1915, their only World Championship. They had tried three times in the 1970s to win an LCS, after being the league's doormat team for most of the fifties and sixties. But they had failed all three times, losing to the Reds in 1976 and to the Dodgers in both 1977 and 1978. What still hurt about the '78 defeat was a misplayed fly ball to center by their Gold Glove perennial Garry Maddox.

The Astros first saw the light as the Houston Colt 45s in 1962, the same year the Mets were born. But while Houston had enjoyed greater success than the Mets in its early years, the Mets' miracle pennant of 1969 had left Houston in the Texas dust. Now called the Astros and in their nineteenth season, they were winners of their very first division title and seeking their first World Series, eleven years after the Mets' World Championship.

The Phillies were powered by Mike Schmidt (in an MVP season) and Greg Luzinski, with pitchers like Steve Carlton and Tug McGraw, fielding heroes in Maddox, Bob Boone, and Larry Bowa, and a team leader in Pete Rose, who the year before had come over from Cincinnati as a free agent. The signing of Rose was intended to give the Phillies what they needed to put them over the top after three straight LCS defeats. It didn't happen in Year One, but it was happening in Year Two.

Houston had talented stars like Cesar Cedeño, José Cruz, and Rose's ex-teammate Joe Morgan, along with pitchers Nolan Ryan, Joe Niekro, and Joaquin Andujar. This was not a nationally known ball club—not surprising for a team that hadn't made too many appearances on the "Game of the Week"—but it was a well-managed cohesive team that had learned how to win. (At the last moment, the Astros had almost *forgotten* how. Their final series of the season, against second-place Los Angeles, found them losing three in a row and forcing a one-game playoff with the Dodgers on Monday, October 6. Houston finally won one, 7–1 to move on to the LCS the very next day.)

The Astros had prevailed despite the loss in mid-season of their big right-hander J. R. Richard, who started the All-Star Game with a 10–4 record but was then felled by a stroke just two weeks later. Richard, who seemed on the road to becoming the league's dominant righty, never pitched again.

In Game One of the LCS, at Philadelphia before 65,000 fans, Bob Forsch was to face Carlton, 24–9, who was about to win his third of four Cy Young awards that year. Lefty was one of the game's strongest men, deeply into exercise and conditioning. He was also well known to reporters for his silence. In 1980 I was working for NBC, and I stopped by his locker before a game. He raised a hand in mid-sentence and said, ''Are we talking as friends or in your capacity with NBC?'' He needed to know where we stood.

Lefty was not his sharpest. He went seven innings, allowed seven hits and three walks, and struck out only three batters. But he had enough heart to set down the Astros 3–1, with two shutout innings from my former teammate McGraw saving it. Luzinski's two-run homer in the sixth made the difference.

So the Astros had now lost four of five big games in five days, and most people were writing them off. But they fought back on Wednesday to even the series at 1–1 when they scored four runs in the tenth inning to break a 3–3 tie. The Phillies might have won it in the last of the ninth when Bake McBride and Schmidt both singled to put runners on first and second with one out. Then Lonnie Smith blooped a single to right, which seemed sufficient to score McBride. But Lee Elia, coaching at third, held up McBride after Bake got a bad jump. It was one of those calls a third-base coach gets second-guessed on for an entire career after having sent home hundreds of runners safely without anyone noticing him. McBride was left stranded on a great relief effort by Frank LaCorte. And in the tenth, Andujar got Schmidt—who had hit forty-eight homers that year—on a flyout with the tying runs on and two out to nail down a 7–4 win. The Astros could return home after taking a long and satisfying deep breath.

Next came the first postseason game ever played indoors. It was another great pitching duel, with Joe Niekro and Larry Christenson matching zeros on the scoreboard. Christenson left after six, but Dickie Noles and McGraw kept the Astros scoreless through ten innings. Niekro put up ten zeros before leaving for a pinch hitter, and Dave Smith relieved in the eleventh. Finally, Joe Morgan led off the bottom of the eleventh with a triple. Tug walked the next two hitters intentionally, but a sacrifice fly by Denny Walling gave the Astros a 1–0 victory and a 2–1 Series lead.

Steve Carlton, coming off a 24–9 season, won the opener of the 1980 NLCS, the only game in the series that didn't go into extra innings. (Philadelphia Phillies)

The fourth game pitted Carlton against Vern Ruhle. The highlight of this game was a twenty-minute argument over what looked like a possible triple play. In the fourth inning, McBride and Manny Trillo singled. Maddox then lined softly back to Ruhle, who either caught it on a fly or trapped it in his glove on a short hop. Home-plate umpire Doug Harvey had his view blocked by Maddox. Ruhle fired to first to double up Trillo, and as the argument took fire, first baseman Art Howe strolled over to second and touched the base to claim a triple play. As fans watched replay after replay, the umpires decided that the ball had been caught, not trapped, but that it was a double play, not a triple play, as time had been called once the argument began. Both sides protested the game.

The Astros were leading 2–0 after seven and were six outs away from a pennant, when the Phillies erupted for three in the eighth, with Trillo's sacrifice fly to right putting Philadelphia ahead. Another argument ensued over whether Jeffrey Leonard had trapped Trillo's ball.

In the ninth, the Astros tied the game at 3–3 on a single by Terry Puhl, and the two teams went into extra innings for the third straight game. A run for the Astros would mean a pennant, and they had the home-field advantage.

But in the top of the tenth, the Phillies scored twice off Joe Sambito. Rose, who had started so many clutch rallies over the years, singled to center with one out. Luzinski, pinch-hitting, doubled him home, with Rose knocking over catcher Bruce Bochy. It was reminiscent of the Ray Fosse knockdown in the 1970 All-Star Game. Trillo doubled home an insurance run, McGraw stopped Houston in the last of the tenth, and the stage was set for a deciding fifth game.

This one had Nolan Ryan against rookie Marty Bystrom. Two Astros were nailed at home plate as the game progressed, and after six, the score was tied 2–2. In the seventh, the Astros had their fans dancing in the aisles as they scored three runs off relievers Christenson and Ron Reed, and again, the Astros were six outs from a victory. It was a great moment for a great pitcher, but even for the wondrous Nolan Ryan, the body sometimes says, "No more." Ahead in a game with but six outs to go, he was feeling the toll of having pitched 234 innings during the long season. Ryan, who will be inducted into the Hall of Fame the first year he is eligible, is a perfect example of the fragile nature of even the greatest athletes. He couldn't retire anyone in the eighth. Three singles loaded the bases and Rose forced a walk to score a run and make it 5–3. Two outs later, Del Unser, a first-class pinch hitter, singled home the tying runs, and Trillo tripled to put the Phils up 7–5. The Astro fans sat down.

In the last of the eighth, Houston tied it again on four singles off McGraw. No one scored in the ninth, and for the fourth game in a row, it was extra innings. This time, it was also sudden death for a pennant.

Frank LaCorte was on the mound for the Astros in the tenth when Unser doubled to right and Maddox doubled to center for an 8–7 lead. Dick Ruthven set Houston down in the last of the tenth, and it was the Phillies who became champions as Maddox caught the final fly ball, vindicating himself for his 1978 error.

The Phillies went on to beat the Kansas City Royals in the World Series for their first World Championship since 1915. The Astros, more than a decade later, are still waiting for their first pennant, after twice coming within six outs of it.

The five-game series to decide a pennant was last played in 1984. The following year the League Championship Series became a best-of-seven series. But in the sixteen years that the series ran best-of-five, the Phillies-Astros battle was clearly the best.

45

Almost There in Chicago

When I left the Mets for the second time after the 1983 season, it was because I'd been drafted by the Chicago White Sox as compensation for a lost free agent. I wasn't especially happy about it, and was more than just a little apprehensive about starting over in a new league at the age of thirty-nine. But I look back now at my seasons with the White Sox with a special kind of fondness—happy that I could find success in a new league at an ''old'' age, and delighted that I could experience the South Side of Chicago and all that made it special.

Chicago is one great baseball town! If only all teams could find a way to bottle the baseball formula from the Windy City, the game would go on to even greater prosperity. Each year Major League Baseball produces four division winners, one champion—and twenty-five losers. Somehow, perennially being among those twenty-five has never detracted from the enjoyment of the game for Chicago fans.

As this is written, the Cubs' last pennant was in 1945 and their last World Championship in 1908, the Fred Merkle season. The White Sox last won a pennant in 1959 and a World Championship in 1917, two years before they lost on purpose in the Black Sox Scandal. Some feel that for this franchise, at least, it's been a long period of payback, just as Boston fans feel they are still paying for the sin of trading Babe Ruth to the Yankees. (I had the opportunity to pitch for both of these ''jinxed'' teams.) The Cubs have no particular divine moment to ponder; they have just fallen short. Or maybe Warren Brown spoiled it for them. In 1946 he wrote the first history of the franchise, *The Chicago Cubs*, and he dedicated it "To P. K. Wrigley and the world's championship yet to come." The book is getting very dusty.

Pessimism is the common thread that seems to run between Chicago and Boston. From the sportswriter to the fan paying the price of admission to Fenway, Comiskey Park, or Wrigley Field, it's the train of thought that says, "What will it be this year? We will be teased but in the end, the final step—the championship of a World Series—will escape us." The histories of the organizations dictate this frustration.

Nevertheless, in compiling great moments from baseball for this book, I felt it appropriate to bring in some recent good seasons by the Chicago teams, even though their pennant hopes ultimately fell short. For when these teams are in a race, there is such happiness among the faithful Chicago fans—pessimism notwithstanding—that for the summer months, the city is truly a Garden of Eden.

The fans hate each other's teams, and never wish the other one success, but they do share the link of Bill Veeck, whose father was once president of the Cubs. In fact, the ivy-covered outfield walls in Wrigley Field were planted in part by young Bill.

In 1959 Veeck bought the White Sox, and they won their first pennant in forty years with the joyous "Go Go Sox" of Luis Aparicio and Nellie Fox. He put in the exploding scoreboard, sewed names on the uniforms, and had his franchise humming.

Three years later he was gone, off to write books and run racetracks, but in 1976, scraping together money from more backers than any team had ever assembled, he bought the Sox again, this time putting them in old-time uniforms and, on a few occasions, in short pants. He once forfeited a game on Disco Demolition Night when the fans hurled records onto the playing field, and all in all, made Chicago the fun-filled place to be in 1977. By 1980, the new salary structure of the game forced him out again, and he spent the rest of his years basking shirtless in the Wrigley Field bleachers, sipping a beer, and singing along with Harry Caray. Veeck was the one thing White Sox and Cubs fans could agree on: They both loved him.

After Veeck left the White Sox for the first time, in 1961, they were competitive for a few years, finishing second in 1963, 1964, and 1965 under Al Lopez. Their closest shot came in 1964, when the Yankees edged them out by a game in what became the final year of the Yankee dynasty. That was, ironically, their first season without Nellie Fox, but they had great pitching from Gary Peters, Juan Pizarro, Joel Horlen, and Hoyt Wilhelm, and they gave it a run.

In 1967, now led by Eddie Stanky, the Sox found themselves in a thrilling four-way race that was ultimately won by the "Impossible Dream" Boston Red Sox, with the White Sox finishing fourth, but only three games from the top.

Ten years later, with Veeck back, the White Sox had Bob Lemon, one of his old Cleveland Indian stars, as manager. Veeck's strategy was to obtain potential free agents who would be playing out their options and headed for greener pastures once the season ended. This short-term solution was no way to build a franchise, but it was a way to grab instant success. Signing men he couldn't re-sign for 1978, he put together a team that clubbed 192 home runs, including thirty by Richie Zisk, thirty-one by Oscar Gamble, and twenty-five by Eric Soderholm. This was a franchise whose all-time home run-leader going into that season was Bill Melton with 154, and whose single-season record was Dick Allen's 37. The fans loved the long ball. They began singing "Na na na na, hey, hey, good-bye" to opponents and seemed to care not at all that the team ultimately finished twelve games out and lost Zisk and Gamble to free agency. Comiskey Park was the "in place" in 1977.

In some ways, the season was even more fun than 1983, when the White Sox, of all teams, won the Western Division so easily that they set a record by finishing twenty games on top. That was the year Tony LaRussa, the manager, established his credentials before going on to further success in Oakland. The pitching staff was led by LaMarr Hoyt, Rich Dotson, and Floyd Bannister, along with my old partner Jerry Koosman. Again, it was long ball in Comiskey, with Ron Kittle hitting thirty-five, Greg Luzinski thirty-two, Carlton Fisk twenty-six, and Harold Baines twenty. This division title came so easily that it was hard to believe it had been twenty-four years since the Sox had won anything at all. Still, they were set down rather easily by the Orioles in the LCS, winning only the first game, and failing to homer even once.

Meanwhile, the team on the north side of town was having its own ups and downs. The Cubs' tradition goes back to 1876, the National League's first season, and to names like Cap Anson and Albert Spalding. Phil Wrigley, of chewing gum fame, bought the team in 1934 and held on until 1977. He was famous for being the first to sign up his roster each year, for refusing to put lights on Wrigley Field, and for cherishing the aesthetics of his beautiful single-deck ballpark, which dates back to the Federal League in 1914. Few players ever met Wrigley, but he paid well by the standards of the time, despite winning only two pennants in his long tenure, in 1938 and 1945. In 1977, he sold the team to the Tribune Company, which was better able to compete in the free-agent era.

After having spent most of the 1950s and 1960s near the bottom of the league, the Cubs began to put together a strong lineup by the late sixties. Under manager Leo Durocher, it all seemed to come together in 1969. Durocher, who had made his managerial debut in 1939 at Brooklyn, was a Chicago kind of guy: dapper, brash, and a night owl—perfect for day baseball.

In 1969, he not only had Cub legend Ernie Banks at first, he had future Hall of Famers Billy Williams in the outfield and Ferguson Jenkins on the mound. His infield included Ron Santo, Don Kessinger, and Glenn Beckert, his catcher was Randy Hundley, and Ken Holtzman, Bill Hands, Phil Regan, and Dick Selma joined Jenkins on the pitching staff. Man for man, this was the best team in the National League in 1969. The Cubs' day had come. The only problem was, they ran into a team of destiny, the Amazin' Mets, my club, and we wound up finishing eight games ahead of them in what should have been a magical summer for Cub fans. This was one that got away from the Cubs through divine providence, I guess. The '69 Cubs are as remembered in Chicago as the '69 Mets are in New York.

The Cubs contended again in 1970 but fell short, and then fortunes turned and Chicago retreated for another long stretch. The next time the fans could go crazy was in 1984.

This was the year that Ryne Sandberg came into his own as the league's premier second baseman. Although teams don't always look for offense from middle infielders, Ryne gave the Cubs plenty of it in only his second year as the regular second baseman. He hit .314, scored 114 runs, stole thirty-two bases, and had nineteen triples and nineteen homers. He won the MVP award while anchoring a lineup that also featured Leon Durham, Larry Bowa, Ron Cey, Keith Moreland, Gary Matthews, and Jody Davis. Rick Sutcliffe, obtained in mid-season from Cleveland, was 16–1, and Lee Smith saved thirty-three games. This looked like a team ready to win a pennant—until it lost to San Diego in five games in the LCS, dropping the closer 6–3 when the

LaMarr Hoyt won 24 games to lead the White Sox to a 20-game edge in the A.L. West in 1983. (Chicago White Sox)

Ryne Sandberg batted .368 in the 1984 NLCS and .400 in the 1989 NLCS, but the Cubs fell short both times. Here he celebrates the clinching of the 1984 N.L. East title with Rick Sutcliffe. (© 1984, Chicago Tribune Comapny, all rights reserved, used with permission)

Padres got four in the seventh. To be a Cub fan is to have your heart break.

Again in 1989, this time under Don Zimmer, the Cubs came oh-so-close. Sandberg hit thirty homers, Shawon Dunston came into his own at shortstop, and Andre Dawson, one of the great sluggers of his era, provided inspirational as well as offensive leadership. The Cubs finished six games ahead of the Mets but lost the LCS to the Giants in five games, never really getting on track. The Cubs thus finished the eighties as they had the fifties, sixties, and seventies—pennantless.

It never seems to matter to Chicago fans. Oh, attendance rises when the teams play well, but those are not the true fans turning out. Those Johnny-come-latelies are, in fact, looked upon with a measure of scorn by the regular patrons, who sit there day after day watching No-Neck Williams in Comiskey or Ed Bouchee in Wrigley. They may be baseball's best fans, and it was a kick for me to play in front of them for two years and understand what baseball in Chicago is all about.

46

The Joy That Was
Pete Rose

There is a Pete Rose story, one of hundreds, in which he is standing
with his buddy Tommy Helms around the cage during batting practice.
For the amusement of the surrounding sportswriters, Pete leans over
and says, "Tommy, you know what the difference is between you and
me? I can pick up the paper any day of the week and see what I'm
hitting. You have to wait till Sunday."

Yes, Pete usually was in the league leaders. And no, he never
seemed to lack for self-confidence or bravado, and the little needle into
Helms was typical Rose humor, designed to loosen up his pal while
entertaining onlookers.

Although there may have been two sides to "Pete Rose: Human
Being," as events would unfold, there was only one "Pete Rose:
Ballplayer." I don't think we ever saw an insecure Rose, one filled
even briefly with self-doubt. And maybe the bravado was so genuine
that it took him toward trouble, gave him a belief in himself so strong
that he felt surely nothing bad could ever happen to him.

I feel terrible for the misfortune that befell him after his playing
days—the lifetime suspension from baseball for gambling and the
prison term for tax evasion. He was my friend, and my teammate. He
paid a big price for his indulgences and his belief in his own infal-
libility.

But I choose here to dwell on the joy of Pete Rose on a baseball field. There was no one else like him in the years I played: a guy who couldn't run, couldn't throw, had no real position, had no power, and you couldn't win without him. He was a throwback, a fellow who could have played on the same field with Wee Willie Keeler and John McGraw, with Ty Cobb and Honus Wagner. He gave fans a chance to imagine what the game was like in baseball's dead-ball era, and he gave kids of average ability the message that with hustle and hard work, you could make it in the modern era.

When I first came into the league in 1967, Rose was in his fifth season and already talking about the goal of being "the first singles hitter to make a hundred thousand dollars." He got his one thousandth hit in my second year, when he singled off my teammate Dick Selma in Cincinnati. By then he was headed for his third 200-hit season and his first of three batting titles. Most fans talked about the way he would run to first on walks. And while he called himself a singles hitter, in those Crosley Field days he was good for as many as fifteen or sixteen home runs a year.

By the time the Reds moved to Riverfront Stadium, they were a powerhouse, and Rose was part of a cast that came to be known as the "Big Red Machine." With Johnny Bench, Joe Morgan, Tony Perez, George Foster, Lee May, Ken Griffey, and company, Rose was still either the first or second player to be mentioned when you rolled out the names of the Reds' hitters. He had hustled his way into the hearts of fans all over the country.

In New York he turned the fans against him when he went after Buddy Harrelson during the 1973 League Championship Series at Shea Stadium. Oh, how I remember that day. It was not unlike the 1934 World Series, when the commissioner of baseball had to remove Joe Medwick of the Cardinals from the game for his own protection after Tiger fans pelted him with garbage. At Shea, the fans threw so many objects at Rose in left field that a small contingent of Met players, myself included, walked out there and asked them to stop, lest we forfeit the game. Did I mention that Pete reminded us all of old-time baseball?

The Mets beat the Reds in the '73 League Championship Series, the only time the Big Red Machine was stopped in five LCS appearances during the 1970s. But Pete hit .381 in the series, with two homers in five games.

He always made an impact. You knew he was working his hardest, striving with every ounce to be the best he could be. And there is no perfect illustration of this point than what took place once in Cincinnati when we were teammates with the Reds.

Pete had gone 0-for-8 or 0-for-9 in a Sunday doubleheader, obviously a rarity for a man who would collect 4,256 hits in his career. I was showered and dressed and headed out the tunnel under Riverfront Stadium to meet my family when I heard the crack of a bat—somebody taking batting practice on the field. I made a small detour, and there was Pete back on the field, a batting cage surrounding home plate, and Russ Nixon throwing him batting practice. He swatted line drive after line drive as he tried to figure out why he had possibly gone hitless in a doubleheader. Considering there are not many evenings during a season for a player to enjoy a barbecue or simply relax with his family, it is a telling story of Pete's dedication to his profession.

I guess people began talking about his chances to break Cobb's hit record around the time of his three thousandth hit, which came in 1978. He was thirty-seven at the time, still at the top of his game, but those who discussed it felt it was unlikely. He was 1,191 hits behind Cobb's record of 4,191 and at two hundred a year he would still have to play regularly past age forty-two to come close enough to try and go for it. And no one thought he could keep up a pace like that.

He left the Reds as a free agent and joined the Phillies in 1979. At Veterans Stadium, they would put messages up on the scoreboard like "Phillies All-Time Hit Leaders," with such names as Richie Ashburn, Ed Delahanty, Del Ennis, Chuck Klein, and Sherry Magee. Pete would read the names aloud and say, "You call those names? You guys wanna see names up there? Watch these." And moments later, up would go something like "All-Time Hit Leaders: Ty Cobb, Hank Aaron, Stan Musial, Tris Speaker, Honus Wagner, Eddie Collins, Willie Mays, Napoleon Lajoie, Pete Rose." Pete would smile. He had brought civilization to Philadelphia.

He got his 3,500th hit in 1980, helping the Phillies to their first pennant in thirty years. In 1981, when baseball lost a third of its season to a strike, Pete passed Stan Musial with his 3,631st hit on August 10. Musial was there in Philadelphia to congratulate him, but Pete's mind was focused on Cobb, retired for fifty-three years, dead for twenty. Pete was going after 4,192. Everyone knew it.

He passed Aaron for second place on June 22, 1982, leaving only

Pete Rose breaks Ty Cobb's career hit record with number 4,192 off San Diego's Eric Show. (The Sporting News)

Cobb ahead of him. His wife had a baby boy and named him Ty. Pete was now a driven man.

Barry Halper, the sports memorabilia collector, loaned Pete a bat actually used by Cobb. Pete said he would use it to break the record. Instead, he broke the bat in batting practice.

In 1984 the Phillies let him go to Montreal as a free agent, and it was there that he became only the second man in history to reach 4,000 hits, getting a double off my old buddy Jerry Koosman of the Phillies on April 13, 1984. He was now forty-three years old, 192 hits shy, and no longer a dangerous hitter. (The previous year his hit total had dropped to 121 and his average to .245.)

He didn't play regularly at Montreal, and it looked as though the quest was over. Then, on August 16, Marge Schott brought him back to Cincinnati, the city of his birth, to play and manage for the Reds. He could now control his own destiny and resume his quest for 4,192, while accepting the new challenge of being a player-manager.

He finished the 1984 season with 4,097 hits, just 95 short. There seemed little doubt that he would play himself into the record books, no matter what it took.

Fans now waited out the inevitable, which came on Wednesday, September 11, 1985. Pete had already tied Cobb's record of 4,191 in Chicago with two hits off Reggie Patterson, a right-hander. Back in Cincinnati, before a hometown crowd of 47,237, many of whom had driven up Pete Rose Way to reach Riverfront Stadium, Pete came up in the first inning to face San Diego's Eric Show. The count went 2-and-1; and then Pete swung at a slider, down and in, and lined a single to left-center. It was a typical Pete Rose hit. He made the turn at first, clapped his hands, flattened his helmet, and returned to the base.

His teammates surrounded him while Show sat on the mound and watched the festivities. Prominent in the group was Pete's son, Pete Jr, wearing a ROSE 14 uniform. They hugged, and there were tears in Pete's eyes. He was not usually an emotional man; it was the first time I'd ever seen any tears. It must have been a tremendous moment of glory, but also the end of a huge burden, and maybe the realization that his career was truly nearing its end.

Pete continued to play, even into the 1986 season, finishing with 4,256 hits. He never could bring himself to retire. His last at-bat, which many had thought would have some grand drama to it, was a strikeout against Goose Gossage on August 17. As manager, he never put himself into a game after that, and never announced his retirement. He was released as a player on November 11 and finally, as all the world knows, he was banned for life and removed as manager by commissioner Bart Giamatti in 1989 for his association with gamblers and what Giamatti considered the likelihood that he'd even bet on baseball games.

Perhaps the greatest tragedy of that sorry ending will be that in future years, instead of Pete Rose's name bringing a smile to faces, it will bring a sigh and a head shake, as though to say, "Ah, Pete, you had so much going for you. What happened?"

47

Onward to Twenty-Seven Strikeouts!

Like pole-vault notches, the record for strikeouts in one game has inched up over the years. Tracking it piques my interest because I'm there on the list, at one time a co-record holder. It's now up to twenty, and someday, it could get to twenty-five or more. If the game survives long enough, you could even see a twenty-eight, provided the catcher cooperates and drops a third strike along the way. I wonder if Nolan Ryan will still be pitching when that mark is achieved?

Actually, professional baseball has had a twenty-seven-strikeout performance. As with most records, this one was set in the minor leagues. On May 13, 1952, nineteen-year-old Ron Necciai of the Bristol Twins of the Appalachian League pitched a no-hitter against Welch, West Virginia, and fanned twenty-seven batters. When his catcher dropped a third strike, that passed-ball rule did in fact require him to retire twenty-eight batters. He struck out twenty-four in his next start, had 109 in forty-three innings, and then 172 in 126 innings for the Durham Bulls. But arm trouble kept him from developing into a major league star, and a 1–6 record for the Pirates was his entire big-league mark.

Nolan Ryan's best one-game performance was nineteen, but it came in an eleven-inning game in 1974 when he was with California, and those extra-inning efforts are recorded separately. The extra-inning record, in fact, is twenty-one, held by a pitcher named Tom Cheney of the Washington Senators, who set down twenty-one Baltimore Orioles in a sixteen-inning game on September 12, 1962. Twenty-one seemed so out of reach at the time, but now the nine-inning record is almost there.

The first twentieth-century "standard" for the record was established in 1908, when future Hall of Famer Rube Waddell of the St. Louis Browns struck out sixteen of his old Philadelphia Athletic teammates on July 29. This was the Rube's first year with St. Louis, and one can easily imagine the joy he must have felt that afternoon. He had won nineteen for the A's the year before, but let the team down in a tight pennant race with Detroit, blowing a big lead in a key September game. Connie Mack decided he had borne all he could tolerate from the rogue, and sent him off to the Browns.

On May 19, 1908, Waddell made his first appearance in Philadelphia in an enemy uniform, and an overflow crowd of twenty-eight thousand turned out to see him whip the A's 5–2. The rematch, in St. Louis, found Waddell bragging that he would set a new strikeout record, and set it he did. He struck out Topsy Hartsel and Rube Oldring three times each, and the tough Eddie Collins twice. Still, it took a three-run, ninth-inning rally by the Browns to pull out a 5–4 win for Rube.

It wasn't until 1933 that the seventeen level was reached, and it took another zany left-hander to do it—Dizzy Dean, in his second season in the majors, hurling for the Cardinals. Dean was fun-loving, but not as irresponsible as Waddell. Still, it seemed natural that their names would become linked.

Dean's performance took place on July 30 against the Cubs in the first game of a doubleheader. Although he was only a second-year player, all of America knew and loved Dizzy Dean, who seemed to typify the free-spirited youth who made up the baseball profession. This was Depression America, and Diz was the kind of guy who made baseball a pastime to ease your troubles away.

Three years later, a farm boy with a more serious nature tied Dean's major league record while breaking Waddell's American League mark. Bob Feller, just seventeen years old, struck out seventeen Athletics on September 13, 1936, less than two months after his major league debut. His opponent that day was another teenager, Randy Gumpert. Feller, who never played in the minors, was pitching in the big leagues during his summer vacation, having just finished his junior year at Van Meter (Iowa) High School. He pitched only fourteen games that year, compiling a 5–3 record, but his great performance against the A's that September afternoon helped him to record seventy-six strikeouts in only sixty-two innings, making him an instant legend.

Two years later, on October 2, 1938, in his final appearance of a 17–11 season, Feller struck out eighteen Detroit Tigers for a new major league record, but lost the game 4–1. It was a thrilling afternoon in Cleveland, for more reasons than one. The Tigers' Hank Greenberg, with fifty-eight homers, had a doubleheader to try and tie Babe Ruth's record of sixty. The fans did not see a new home-run record, but they did witness a new strikeout record. In the ninth, Feller struck out Pete Fox for number seventeen to tie the mark, and then faced Greenberg. A new strikeout record, or homer fifty-nine? Greenberg flied out. Up came Chet Laabs, and down he went for the fifth time, accounting for five of the eighteen strikeouts all by himself. Feller was still only nineteen years old.

The next time we heard about the strikeout mark was in 1959, when Sandy Koufax fanned eighteen Giants on August 31 in a night game. This pitching achievement broke Dean's twenty-six-year-old National League record and put Koufax in the spotlight for the first time. Sandy was not yet his Hall of Fame version. The feat occurred during the Dodgers' second year in Los Angeles—a pennant year—but Sandy was still a bit player, compiling an 8–6 record and a 4.06 ERA. Still, if the Dodgers had any thought of giving up on him, the eighteen-strikeout performance changed their minds and a Dodger he remained.

I was present the first time the nineteen-strikeout plateau was reached, sitting in the Mets' dugout watching our rookie Gary Gentry oppose Steve Carlton on September 15, 1969. This awesome performance took place during the the final days of our "Miracle Mets" season, when miraculous things were indeed happening to us and everyone was expecting the unexpected every day. We were as hot as any ball club could be. It was a rainy afternoon in the new Busch Memorial Stadium, and the Cardinals, defending National League champions, were facing elimination.

Carlton, not yet Hall of Fame material either, fanned nineteen Mets that day. He served 152 pitches, and 150 of them stayed in the ballpark. Twice he made mistakes on Ron Swoboda, our right fielder, and each time the result was a two-run homer. Carlton set a new record, but lost the game 4–3. And we moved another game closer to a pennant.

The following year, on April 22, 1970, I took the mound in Shea Stadium to face the San Diego Padres in their second season. I had great control that afternoon and felt sharp, walking only two batters. We took a 2–1 lead after three, and there the score rested. I struck out the last batter in the sixth inning for my tenth K of the game.

In the seventh, I struck out Nate Colbert, Dave Campbell, and Jerry Morales consecutively. In the eighth, I caught Bob Barton looking and Ramon Webster swinging. That was six in a row and fifteen in all, to tie Nolan Ryan's team record. Then I struck out Ivan Murrell for number sixteen.

In the ninth I fanned Van Kelly for number seventeen and the eighth in a row, which tied a record held by four pitchers. One of them, Johnny Podres, was sitting in the stands that day.

The second out of the ninth was Cito Gaston, later the Toronto manager. That was nine straight, a new record. The final batter was Al Ferrara, and I got him for ten straight and a total of nineteen. The ten straight is a record of which I'm very proud. It's lasted nearly a quarter century.

It was in 1986 that the twenty mark was finally achieved. The hero was Roger Clemens of Boston, and the date was April 29, his fourth start of the year. This was the Rocket's third season, and like Koufax and Carlton before him, he was already on the road to establishing Hall of Fame credentials, although fans were not yet talking about it. He was a respectable 9–4 in 1984 and 7–5 in 1985. But this would be the game that made the nation sit up and notice Roger.

The scene was Fenway Park and the opponents were the Seattle Mariners. Adding to Roger's accomplishment was the fact that he didn't walk a single batter that day, winning 3–1. What a box score line he had: nine innings, three hits, one run, (a homer by Gorman Thomas) no walks, twenty strikeouts (eight of them consecutive).

Roger got at least one strikeout in every inning, and retired the side on strikeouts three times. Phil Bradley, a pretty tough hitter, went down four times, including number twenty in the ninth inning. Since Bradley was only the second out, Clemens could have reached 21 on Ken Phelps, but Phelps didn't cooperate, grounding to short.

By coincidence, I became Roger's teammate just two months later when I was traded to Boston from the White Sox on June 29. And I

Roger Clemens in triumph after his twenty-strikeout performance. (Peter Travers)

watched him put together a brilliant 24–4 season, a Cy Young Award, an MVP award, 238 strikeouts, and a pennant for the Red Sox. It was a privilege to see.

Roger is an intense competitor, as all the great talents are. He achieved notoriety during the 1990 American League Championship Series against Oakland by hurling profanity at home-plate umpire Terry Cooney and being ejected from the game. That will forever be a blemish on his reputation, but Roger will, I'm sure, overcome it and let the numbers speak for themselves. In his intensity lies his greatness.

Will the record advance, maybe to twenty-five? Many say no, but with expansion and the dilution of talent, and the likes of superb power pitchers such as Clemens, David Cone, and Doc Gooden, it could happen. One day it could all come together—everything will work: every slider will be on the black, every fastball will flash past the batter—and maybe, just maybe, we'll have a new record.

48

Second Miracle at Shea

I was there for the second miracle at Shea Stadium, which occurred in the 1986 World Series. But I wasn't in a Met uniform and I played no part in the game. I was in a Boston uniform, in the Red Sox's third-base dugout, having finished my season a number of weeks earlier with torn cartilage in my right knee. I couldn't pitch in the League Championship Series or the World Series because of my injury, and Boston gave the roster spot to Steve Crawford. So I was in no-man's-land, except for pulling for my teammates and watching in amazement as the gods of baseball once again looked over their shoulders at Shea Stadium to see that all was well in Metsville.

The big difference between 1969 and 1986 was that in '69 we weren't expected to win a thing, and each success brought new respect and wonder. In 1986, the Mets were supposed to be the best in baseball. But they barely got through the League Championship Series, and all but lost the World Series—in six games, no less—before the miracle saved them. At least I had a front-row seat to watch it from.

Like the Met champions of 1969 and 1973, the '86 Mets had good chemistry. They had a very strong pitching staff, a lot of leaders in the lineup, and some genuinely good guys to have on the club, players like Mookie Wilson and Ray Knight. It's a formula you usually find on pennant winners, although exceptions slip through, like the old battlin' A's of the 1970s who feuded with each other all the time. (It's also a formula that is sometimes first observed in hindsight, tailored to fit the moment.)

No telling of the 1986 World Series would be complete without first recounting the League Championship Series, which once again saw a valiant effort by the Houston Astros fall short, as had been the case in 1980 and 1981. The heavily favored Mets were stymied by the pitching of ex-teammate Mike Scott, and the LCS went on to be one for the ages. In fact, the deciding sixth game—the longest postseason match ever played—was itself the subject of an entire book by Jerry Izenberg, *The Greatest Game Ever Played*. Perhaps.

The LCS was tied 2–2, with Game Five scheduled for Tuesday, October 14, in Shea. It was Nolan Ryan vs. Dwight Gooden, two of the hardest throwers in the game's history and two of the most dominant pitchers of their time. Ryan went nine innings, struck out twelve, walked one, and left with the score 1–1. Gooden went ten, and it was still 1–1 when he finished. In the twelfth inning Gary Carter, 1-for-21 in the series to that point, stroked a single through the middle to drive home Wally Backman, ending the game. The Mets had a 2–1 victory, and a 3–2 lead in the series. They could win it all in Houston the next day, a game that was considered vital if they wanted to avoid facing Mike Scott again in Game Seven.

One beautiful thing about Game Six. It was an afternoon contest, like the not-so-distant old days of the World Series, when people found television sets or radios in offices and wouldn't leave for home until the game was decided. Crowds actually stopped along Main Streets across America to stare at TVs in the windows of electronics stores. For one afternoon in 1986, it was 1956 all over again.

Since both clubs saw Game Six as a "must-win," tensions were high from the start. Davey Johnson of the Mets started Bob Ojeda, while Hal Lanier had Bob Knepper on the mound. The Astros struck quickly with three in the first, runs that held up throughout the afternoon as Knepper performed artistry on the mound against the tough Met lineup. By the ninth, it was still 3–0, with Rick Aguilera hurling three shutout innings in relief of Ojeda.

Knepper opened the ninth with a 1-2 count on pinch hitter Lenny Dykstra, then hung a slider and yielded a triple to center. Mookie Wilson singled to break up the shutout. Kevin Mitchell, who would later become a major home-run star with the Giants, grounded out, but Keith Hernandez doubled home Wilson to make it 3–2. That was all for the plucky Knepper, who left thinking primarily about the mistake he'd made on Dykstra.

Dave Smith, who had worked in the heartbreaking 1980 LCS, came in and walked Carter and Darryl Strawberry. Ray Knight then flied to right, scoring Hernandez with the tying run. Roger McDowell came in to pitch the last of the ninth, and by the time his work was done, it was still 3–3 after thirteen innings.

The Mets scored in the fourteenth on a big single by Wally Backman, but in the last of the fourteenth, with Jesse Orosco on the mound, Billy Hatcher hit one of baseball's all-time clutch homers, to tie it again at 4–4 and keep the Astros alive. (Billy would later star in the 1990 World Series with Cincinnati.)

Finally, in the sixteenth inning, the Mets exploded for three runs off Aurelio Lopez and Jeff Calhoun. Hatcher misplayed a fly by Strawberry and it went for a double. Knight singled home Strawberry. There was a walk, a sacrifice, a wild pitch, a single, and a three-run lead. It looked like a Met pennant.

But the Astros did not quit. Davey Lopes, the old Dodger star, walked. Singles by Bill Doran and Hatcher made it 7–5. Glenn Davis singled to make it 7–6. Were the Astros coming back one more time? Kevin Bass, facing Orosco, went as far as you could go, to a 3–2 count, and struck out. The Mets were in the World Series! The Astros were left still waiting.

The Mets' pitching was supposed to dominate the World Series, but after five games Boston led 3–2 and needed one win in the final two games at Shea to wrap up its first World Championship since trading Babe Ruth to the Yankees. It bears repeating again: Many Red Sox fans feel a curse has followed the franchise all these years, ever since Harry Frazee sold Ruth to New York to cover his debts. Not only have the Red Sox never won it all since, but they have had more heartbreaks than any franchise should have to endure, including the last-of-the-ninth loss to the Reds in the great 1975 World Series and the shocking Bucky Dent playoff homer to cost them the 1978 Eastern Division title.

But now, on October 26, 1986, they stood on the threshold at last, especially since they were ahead in games, 3–2; they had their young ace, Roger Clemens, on the mound for Game Six; and they'd taken a quick 2–0 lead after four innings. The Mets had Ojeda, who'd pitched for the Red Sox in '85 in the Big Assignment again.

The Mets tied it in the fifth, helped in part by an error by the usually flawless Dwight Evans in right. Some sloppy play in the field led to a 3–2 Boston lead in the seventh, but the Sox pinch-hit for Clemens in the eighth, and New York tied it up in its half of the inning off ex-teammate Calvin Schiraldi, with old-time Met favorite Lee Mazzilli scoring the tying run on a sacrifice fly by Carter.

The Met fans were having a grand time in Shea all evening, filled with the spirit of exciting baseball being played at its best. As is always the case when Boston plays New York in anything, there are plenty of fans from the visiting side in attendance, and plenty of rivalries on and off the field. Shea was jumping.

The score remained 3–3 after nine. The Mets' big slugger, Darryl Strawberry, had left the game for defensive reasons in the ninth, as Mazzilli went to right and Aguilera came in to pitch.

Dave Henderson, who would perform more Series heroics later with Oakland, led off the top of the tenth with a home run. Shea fell silent, save for the Boston fans. This was what baseball history needed—an extra-inning, World Championship, game-winning homer to end a sixty-eight-year Boston drought. The Red Sox added another run on a double by Wade Boggs and a single by Marty Barrett, and took a 5–3 lead. Yes, it looked like it was finally going to be Boston's year, except . . . there was still a last of the tenth to be played.

So resigned to defeat were the Mets, after Backman and Hernandez flied out to open the inning, that the electricians working the Mets' scoreboard accidentally flashed a CONGRATULATIONS TO THE RED SOX sign on the board, visible for less than a second, but seen by many.

Schiraldi faced Carter for the final out, but Gary lined a 2–1 pitch to left for a single. Hopes were alive, though barely; one more out and it would be over. Mitchell batted for Aguilera and lined an 0–1 pitch to center, sending Carter to second. What was going on here? A buzz arose from the stands, and it sounded like "Things can still happen."

Ray Knight up. 0–2 count. Again, one strike to go. Base hit, center field. Carter scores and it's 5–4. In comes Bob Stanley, as the fans yell "Cal-vinnn, Cal-vinnn" to the departing Schiraldi, echoing the cries of Fenway fans who had showered Strawberry with "Darrr-yl, Darrr-yl" earlier in the week.

Mookie Wilson up, tying run on third. Wild pitch! Here comes

Mookie Wilson (center) celebrates the second miracle at Shea Stadium, after his grounder to first went past Bill Buckner in game six of the 1986 World Series. At top left is Kevin Mitchell, at lower left, Lenny Dykstra. (UPI/Bettmann Newsphotos)

Mitchell, and it's 5–5! To borrow a word from the '69 Mets, it's "Amazin'." To borrow from '73, "Ya Gotta Believe!"

The count goes to 3–2 on Mookie, and he hits a grounder to first. It's routine. It's going to be out number three, and on we'll go to the eleventh. But Bill Buckner, playing with bad ankles in special high-top shoes, watches the ball go between his legs as Knight races home with the game winner.

All season long, Boston manager John McNamara, for whom I had played in Cincinnati, had replaced Buckner on defense in the late innings. Had his not taking him out this time been a blunder? Probably not, because this play had nothing to do with Buckner's bad ankles or lack of mobility. It was simply human error. It could have happened to anyone, even someone with as fine a career as Bill Buckner's. Bill had over twenty-seven hundred hits in his career and was a one-time National League batting champion. That he should be remembered for this play is not so much unfair as it is a microcosm of life itself; baseball can be cruel, just as life can be.

The task of coming back the next day was so psychologically difficult for the Red Sox, it was amazing to see them jump to a 3–0 lead in Game Seven. But Sid Fernandez stopped them in relief of Ron Darling in the middle of the game, giving the Mets time to tie it in the sixth, go ahead in the seventh, and wrap it up in the eighth, 8–5, in a hard-played but anticlimactic game. As in the 1975 Series—also lost by Boston—Game Six was the one for the ages, Game Seven almost an inevitability.

On paper, the Mets were baseball's best team for the second half of the 1980s, but the '86 season marked their only World Series appearance of the decade. It was clearly one of the most exciting Series ever played, and certainly another "Miracle at Shea."

Since I was there in a Boston uniform, I've been asked time and again who I was pulling for in the Series, obviously because of my ten and a half years with the Met organization. To me the question has always seemed nonsensical.

This is a distinct case of not understanding what makes the professional athlete tick: You are on the field to top your opponent. The name across the front of your uniform represents the efforts of all your teammates, those individuals with whom you have ridden the buses and airplanes and worked seven days a week. The professional ballplayer pulls for the team he is on, not the team he once represented— no matter how full of miracles that team may be.

49

"The Natural" Comes to Life

The Los Angeles Dodgers were not expected to compete for the 1988 pennant. But Tom Lasorda is more than just ambassador extraordinaire for baseball. He's also an outstanding manager, and he may have demonstrated that most clearly in 1988, when his fortunes were aided by the "Big Dodger in the Sky," who seemed to look down on his club and decree miraculous performances by it during the stretch.

The '87 Dodgers had been a team in decline, sixteen games under .500, seventeen games out of first, and winners of just eight more games than the last-place Padres. The big news for '88 was the signing of free agent Kirk Gibson, a bold move for a club not famed for going after free agents. But Fred Claire, the new general manager, had risen from public relations director amid suspicions about his ability to hold such a high post, and was under fire to produce.

The Gibson move turned out to be brilliant, as Kirk played 150 games, batting .290 with twenty-five homers and thirty-one stolen bases. The former Detroit slugger, who had performed heroics with the 1984 World Champion Tigers, won the league's Most Valuable Player award, a rare honor for a first-year man in a new league.

Meanwhile, Orel Hershiser emerged as the ace of a pitching staff that had seen Bob Welch (15–9 in '87) depart for Oakland and

307

Fernando Valenzuela, the Dodgers' best pitcher for most of the decade, slip to 5–8.

Hershiser, a well-scrubbed, deeply religious twenty-nine-year-old, came through late in the season with an achievement that would have made any of the all-time greats proud. He accomplished something never recorded by Cy Young, Christy Mathewson, Walter Johnson, Grover Cleveland Alexander, Carl Hubbell, Bob Feller, Warren Spahn, or Sandy Koufax: Beginning on August 30, Orel hurled six consecutive shutouts, totaling fifty-nine consecutive scoreless innings.

Not only was this feat unprecedented, it came in an era when a complete game, let alone a shutout, is becoming extinct. In the National League that season, only five men hurled ten or more complete games. There was a time when each staff had someone with more than twenty, and several with more than ten. Today, the complete game is a dying art, and it often takes a shutout to accomplish it. For that matter, managers no longer feel sentimental about staying with a pitcher who's working on a shutout when a win is at stake. More and more "combined shutouts" are entering the books each year, and seldom does a starter pop off about being taken out. It's just part of the evolution of the use of pitching staffs.

No one working in relief understood that better than Dennis Eckersley of the Oakland A's. Eckersley had begun his career as a starting pitcher with the Cleveland Indians in 1975, and after three years went to Boston, where he and Luis Tiant were the mainstay Red Sox starters for many years. He was 20–8 in 1978, and always had a great strikeout-to-walk ratio. The fact that his control was so good made him a strong candidate to pitch relief, but so long as he continued to be successful in the starting rotation, there he remained. Later he spent three seasons with the Cubs, and was part of their division championship team of 1984. But in 1983, he had the highest earned-run average in the majors, 5.61. Then, just before Opening Day of 1987, he was dealt to Oakland.

At Oakland, Dennis discovered a mastery of the strike zone only hinted at previously. In his first four years with the A's, he walked only thirty-five batters. His strikeout-to-walk figures in those years were—incredibly—113–17, 70–11, 55–3, and 73–4. He saved 141 games in those four years, three of which were pennant seasons for the A's. Although the A's had a tremendous lineup in José Canseco, Mark McGwire, Carney Lansford, and Dave Henderson, and great starting pitching in Welch and Dave Stewart, Eck was clearly a vital force. Give the A's a lead after seven, hand the ball to Eck, and forget it. You knew he wasn't going to walk his way into trouble.

The Dodgers won the '88 National League West by seven games, thanks in part to Hershiser's September streak of zeros, and then surprised the Mets in the LCS by winning the pennant in seven games. The seventh game was yet another shutout by Hershiser, a 6–0 victory over the much-favored Mets. Furthermore, the Dodgers accomplished this win despite a .154 series from Kirk Gibson, who had a bruised left knee and a strained left hamstring. Although he got only four hits in the series, two were homers, including a thrilling twelfth inning game winner in Game Four to break a 1-for-16 slump. He hit another homer in the fifth game to put the Dodgers up three games to two, but by the seventh game, he could manage only a sacrifice fly before leaving the lineup, apparently too banged up even to be ready for the World Series.

Oakland, meanwhile, helped by four saves from Eckersley, won its LCS in a sweep over Boston.

The Series opened in Los Angeles on Saturday night, October 15. Dave Stewart, who was on a streak of four consecutive twenty-win seasons, started for the A's against Tim Belcher, Hershiser having just hurled the finale of the LCS.

Canseco got things rolling for the A's with a grand-slam home run off NBC's center-field camera in the second inning. He signed his name to the camera the next day, and as those devices go for about $100,000 each, the autographed camera could become the most expensive piece of memorabilia around.

Reserve outfielder Mickey Hatcher, who had been released in '87 by Minnesota, was playing left for the ailing Gibson, and he belted a two-run homer for the Dodgers. But going into the last of the ninth, Oakland led 4–3. As Tony LaRussa called for Eckersley to pitch the ninth, things looked grim for Los Angeles. Eck had forty-five saves in the regular season to go with his four in the LCS.

When Mike Scioscia popped to short and Jeff Hamilton struck out, it looked like a typical, and expected, Oakland victory. But then Eckersley did a strange thing: He walked pinch hitter Mike Davis.

What followed seemed to come straight out of fiction—specifically, *The Natural* by Bernard Malamud. The novel had just been made into a movie starring Robert Redford as Roy Hobbs, a worn-down old

Kirk Gibson connects for his Hollywood-like home run in the 1988 World Series.
(Jeff Carlick)

ballplayer who finds the magic in an aging body to produce a miracle, pennant-winning home run for the Knights, his fictional team. Pure fantasy. Good film.

In the Dodger clubhouse, balding Kirk Gibson, his legs wracked with pain, heard Vin Scully on television speak of the absence of Gibson on the bench, and thus the likelihood that he was simply unavailable to pinch-hit.

(Players do listen to broadcasters, even during games. The TV or radio broadcast is usually on in the clubhouse, and it is not unusual for players to pay a quick visit there during a ball game and hear a call-in-progress.)

Hearing Scully, Gibson had sent the Dodger batboy to the dugout to say, in effect, "If Davis gets on, I can take a swing." He knew it would hurt. He had practiced in his living room during the day. But he felt that if he could put everything he had into one poke—just maybe. . .

And so, into the dugout limped Gibson, whose last World Series at-bat, four years earlier, had sealed a Detroit victory over San Diego in the final game of the 1984 fall classic. His jubilant, arms-up run of the bases after that homer became the cover photo of the next spring's baseball magazines. Now here he was, four years later, four years older at thirty-one, swinging a bat as he emerged from the dugout.

The Dodger fans went wild. Here was their MVP. Here was the ultimate drama. Davis stole second, and the A's had the chance to walk Gibson, but Steve Sax was up next. With Gibson ailing so badly, the strategy would be to go after Kirk.

Eckersley ran the count full. Gibson fouled off one, two, three, four pitches. Each one hurt. If he had just one swing in him, he had seemingly used it up with those painful fouls.

Again Eckersley delivered. And now, like Roy Hobbs, Gibson connected. The right-center field bleachers awaited. Could it be? Yes! An incredible, game-winning, two-run homer off the invincible Eckersley by the courageous and triumphant Gibson! This was a homer for all time, a Hollywood ending, coming in, of course, Hollywood itself—or a few miles away, at Dodger Stadium.

The series was defined by that swing, but the next day Hershiser pitched another shutout, and even belted two doubles and a single. Returning to pitch Game Five in Oakland, Orel beat the A's 5–2 to finish off the upset World Series and give Tommy Lasorda his second and most satisfying World Championship.

Hershiser's season seemed too brilliant to be part of modern baseball. In his final 101⅔ innings, including postseason, he had allowed five runs; factored over a full season, that would have amounted to only a dozen! He had seven shutouts in that stretch, and became the first pitcher ever to hurl shutouts in both the LCS and the World Series in the same year.

His fifty-nine consecutive scoreless innings broke the record of former Dodger great Don Drysdale, who set his in 1968. Ironically, a year later, Drysdale had been forced to retire; Hershiser had another good year in 1989, but in 1990 went on the shelf for virtually the entire season, making his future questionable as well. When he came back in 1991, he returned strong, and pitched with traces of his preinjury brilliance. What the future holds and whether the surgery ended his position of prominence among National League pitchers remain to be seen.

If you want a lesson in pitching today, go see Orel when he's healthy. Maybe he doesn't have the stuff of a Nolan Ryan or a Roger Clemens, but if you can define pitching as using what you have to work with on that particular day, there is no better example of pitching—as opposed to throwing—than Orel Hershiser.

50

Only the Nolan

Before Nolan Ryan went to the California Angels, the best-known fact about him was that he developed blisters on his finger when he pitched and would soak it in pickle brine for relief. Those of us on the Mets thought it was pretty funny, but we also knew that Nolan was an extraordinary talent who just needed maturity and the opportunity to take his regular turn in the rotation to find his niche.

Of course, none of us ever expected, back there in the late sixties, that Nolan would still be performing sleight of hand in the 1990s, would become a three-hundred-game winner, would pitch more no-hitters than any other man in history, and would set just about every strikeout record known to man. But we knew the raw talent was there.

You will recall that in our magic season of 1969, Nolan was an important contributor with some key efforts down the stretch, including the pennant-clinching victory in relief against Atlanta and two and a third shutout innings against the Orioles in Game Three of the World Series to save a win for Gary Gentry. But Nolan could not get into a regular five-day rotation on our young pitching staff, and his top victory total was ten in 1971. After that season, desperate for third-base help, the Mets traded Nolan and three other players to California for the American League's All-Star third baseman, Jim Fregosi.

Few know that the trade was prompted by Jack Lang, then covering the Mets for the *Long Island Press*. At the winter meetings after the

'71 season, Lang chastised the Mets for not swinging a deal. M. Donald Grant, the team's chairman of the board, took the bait, and over the head of his baseball people, Gil Hodges included, made the Ryan-Fregosi trade.

It was not the Mets' finest hour, as Fregosi turned out to be a major disappointment, while Ryan achieved greatness for the rest of his career. Those things are going to happen in baseball. You have to do what seems right at the time. Most of us thought Ryan would go on to better things working in a regular rotation, but at the same time we supported the deal as being in the best interests of the team. I suppose that now it would be considered one of the worst trades ever made.

In his first year in the American League, Nollie had a 19–16 record for the Angels and struck out 329 batters in 284 innings. He was wild—he gave up 157 walks, one of seven times he would lead the league in that department—but the strikeout total was awe-inspiring. The three-hundred level just didn't happen very often. In 1903 and 1904, Connie Mack's zany hurler Rube Waddell had 302 and 349, the latter figure being somewhat in dispute due to questionable record keeping. This achievement became particularly interesting when Bob Feller got 348 in 1946, and either did or didn't break Waddell's record, depending on whose score book one trusted. By the 1970s, most people felt Feller's 348 was the American League record.

In the National League, three hundred was unheard of until Sandy Koufax got 306 in 1963 and then 382 in 1965 to break Feller's mark. He also had 317 in his final year, 1966, before retiring at the top of his game.

Along the way, Walter Johnson had 313 in 1910 and 303 in 1912; Sam McDowell 325 in 1965 and 304 in 1970; Mickey Lolich 308 in 1971; Vida Blue 301 the same year; and Steve Carlton 310 in 1972. The best I ever did was 289 in 1971.

Both Feller and Ryan suffered from wildness, and since both are or will be Hall of Famers, it is worth noting that the wildness did not stand in the way of their success. Only three times has a pitcher walked more than two-hundred men in a season: Feller walked 208 in 1938, and Nollie walked 202 in 1974 and 204 in 1977.

In his first season with the Angels, he twice had sixteen strikeouts in a game. He also had nine shutouts, a one-hitter, a pair of two-hitters, and a 1.07 ERA at home, holding opposing batters to a .143 average. And that was only the start.

The following season, 1973, was the breakthrough year for Nolan, the year that would set him on course for the Hall of Fame. He became a twenty-game winner for the first time, at age twenty-six. He became the fifth man in baseball history to hurl two no-hitters in one season, the first two of his career. By topping three-hundred strikeouts again, he joined Waddell and Koufax in recording consecutive three-hundred seasons. He got up to seventeen strikeouts in one game, and set records with thirty in two consecutive games and forty-one in three.

In his final start of the year, on September 28 against Minnesota, he needed to fan fifteen Twins to tie Koufax's season strikeout record of 382. It was a tall order, but sure enough, in by eighth, he fanned Steve Brye to tie Koufax. In getting Brye, however, Ryan tore a muscle in his right thigh.

The Angels' trainer and team physician worked on him between innings, but he had lost his fastball for the day. The legs provide the power behind the pitch, and it wasn't there for Ryan after the Brye strikeout. Still, he pressed onward, staying in the tie game, and in the eleventh found the strength to blow three in a row past Rich Reese for strikeout number 383 of the season, a new major league record.

What continues to amaze me today is that the record, which took seventy-three years of modern baseball to achieve, was set in the first season of the designated-hitter rule. That meant that Ryan's 383 were accomplished without his ever having faced a weak-hitting pitcher. Talk about tying one hand behind a man and then challenging him. He did something that had never been done before, and did it under extraordinary circumstances.

As mentioned, Nolan had two no-hitters that year. The first, on May 15 in Kansas City, was a 3–0 victory. The second, exactly two months later in Detroit, was a 6–0 gem with the seventeen-strikeout performance.

Nolan's third no-hitter tied Feller for the most ever pitched by one man. It came on September 28, 1974, in a 4–0 shutout of Minnesota. He then broke Feller's mark with his fourth no-hitter on June 1, 1975, beating Baltimore 1–0. From that point on, most players felt that Nolan was capable of a no-hitter every time he took the mound. It made him one of the most exciting performers the game has ever known.

Meanwhile, the strikeouts continued to mount. Between 1972 and 1977 he topped 300 five times, and in the following two seasons, he

Nolan Ryan is mobbed by his California Angel teammates following one of his remarkable seven no-hitters. (The Sporting News)

added two more strikeout crowns, for seven in eight years with the Angels.

At that point, Nolan moved back to the National League, signing with Houston as a free agent to be closer to his home in Alvin, Texas. He became the first $1 million-a-season player when he joined the Astros. He and Steve Carlton were on a pace to topple Walter Johnson's career strikeout total of 3,509, which had held up since The Big Train's last strikeout back in 1927. Baseball's modern era had produced a number of hard throwers who mounted bona fide challenges to the record, however, and among those who have passed Johnson are Don Sutton, Bert Blyleven, Gaylord Perry, myself, plus Carlton and Ryan. Phil Niekro, Ferguson Jenkins, and Bob Gibson have also passed three thousand. Gotta love those big-swinging home-run hitters of the modern era!

The question of who would overtake Johnson first kept the fans interested for a few years, and it was Ryan. Then Nolan went on; he passed not only Johnson's 3,509—but also 4,000 and 5,000, putting the record out of reach for at least the next few decades, if not forever.

Nolan never won twenty for Houston, but he did help the team to division titles in 1980 and 1986, and in 1981 he pitched his fifth no-hitter, a 5–0 win over Los Angeles. It appeared that would be his last one as he got older, reached forty and then some, and wasn't coming particularly close. Nonetheless, in his last two years with the Astros, he won two more strikeout titles and led the league in ERA with 2.76 in 1987.

Again opting for free agency, but remaining in his home state, Nolan returned to the American League with the Texas Rangers in 1989. Although he was now forty-two, there was really no sign of Nollie slowing down. He stayed in remarkable physical condition and threw as hard as he ever did. He was not the "crafty veteran," hanging on through finesse; he was still blowing the ball by people.

It was his first year with Texas, 1989, that he passed five thousand strikeouts by once again reaching three hundred, the first time he'd topped that level in twelve years.

Then, in 1990, he not only led the league in strikeouts again (his eleventh title) and won his three hundredth game, but on June 11 set down the World Champion Oakland A's 5–0 for his sixth no-hitter. And on May 2, 1991, he added another. (As he accomplished the feat a seventh time, at age forty-four, he knocked Rickey Henderson off the headlines, Henderson having broken Lou Brock's stolen-base record earlier in the day.)

The 3–0 win over Toronto, before a hometown crowd of 33,439 Texans, forced everyone to use the word "unbelievable," even though a no-hitter was what everyone by now always expects when he takes the mound. And he fanned sixteen batters in this one, the 209th time he has gotten more than ten, the 26th time he's struck out more than fifteen.

There has been only one "knock" on Nolan: He has been, when all is said and done, a .500 pitcher for most of his career. It's true he has won twenty games only twice. It's also true that his National League record was 135–132 and that 1969, with the Mets, marked his only World Series appearance. He's had seven sub-.500 seasons and has led the league in walks seven times. But somehow I suspect that there will be no problem filling up his plaque in Cooperstown five years after he retires. He has simply been one of the most remarkable American athletes ever, at the end of his career seemingly reaching immortal status, right there with Cy Young, Christy Mathewson, Walter Johnson, Lefty Grove, Bob Feller, Warren Spahn, and Sandy Koufax.

Nolan's success at his "advanced" age is a tribute to his personal conditioning as well as to his God-given talent. He has been fortunate to continue to work at a high level of achievement without suffering an "off year" late in his career, for once a pitcher passes age forty, there is little margin for error when rosters are prepared for the following season.

Nolan Ryan has been an achiever in four of the ten decades of this century, making him an appropriate subject for this final chapter. Players in the future would do well to follow his lifestyle, which blends modern training methods with the drive and desire to win we have found in the great ones since the earliest achievements on the baseball field.

51

Worst to First in a Year

We wrapped up the text of this book, knowing full well that there was
more history to come, that the game would perpetuate itself and
provide yet unborn fans with thrills for years to come. The reason?
Despite itself, despite all its labor woes, concentration on business,
and internal strife, the game on the field is still a dazzling event to
behold. When the players cross the foul lines onto the diamond and
revert to the timeless rules and symmetry of the game, it reminds you
of its inner beauty.

We did not know that the next great moment was right in front of us.
It was the 1991 World Series.

Had the Series been forgettable in terms of excitement, it would still
have been memorable in terms of its participants. The Minnesota
Twins, heir to the legacy of Walter Johnson and the long-suffering
Washington Senators, had risen from last place in the American
League West to the top in one season. While the rise was historic and
dramatic, so, too, had been their fall from grace. With many of the
same players, they had hit bottom only three years after winning a
World Championship, taking the St. Louis Cardinals in seven games in
1987.

That was the year they swept all four of their home games in the
Hubert H. Humphrey Metrodome. The decibel level of their fans had

the nation talking, and the crowds waving "homer hankies" seemed to inspire the Twins to victory in their enclosed, Hefty-Bag-like ballpark.

But now they had returned to the top, largely on the efforts of an unheralded pitching staff, pieced together in part when they traded their ace, Frank Viola, to the Mets in 1989 for several young pitching prospects. Two of them, starter Kevin Tapini and closer Rick Aguilera, became big stars in 1991. In addition, the Twins found a big winner in Scott Erickson and signed a fading veteran, Jack Morris, who went from being an eighteen-game loser for the '90 Tigers to being a nineteen-game winner with the '91 Twins.

Morris, in fact, reminded me a little of my old teammate Jerry Koosman, another native of Minnesota, who went to the Twins after his glory days with the Mets seemed to have passed and he responded with a twenty-win season in his first year, after a 3–15 record with the Mets the year before.

The Atlanta Braves had not tasted much success since they moved from Milwaukee in 1965. They had been our opponents in the 1969 League Championship Series, the first one ever, but had not returned to postseason play until 1982, when they were briefly "America's team," seen almost daily in cable households around the country on owner Ted Turner's Superstation. Those were years when Dale Murphy won back-to-back MVP awards, and it was a real shame that Dale wasn't around to make it into the World Series. By then he had been traded to Philadelphia, presumably to play out his final years.

The Braves were second in the West in both 1983 and 1984, but then fell to the bottom, languishing in either fifth or sixth place from 1985 through 1990, when they finished 65–97, dead last.

But the 1991 Braves not only overtook the Dodgers in the season's final days, but then stopped the Pirates in the playoffs when their young pitchers, Tom Glavine and Steve Avery, along with veterans John Smoltz and Charlie Leibrandt and late relief pickup Alejandro Peña, set down a talented Pittsburgh team. Aiding their effort was an enthusiastic bunch of fans who developed "the chop," using foam tomahawks, thereby offending many Native Americans but helping to inspire their team. Sitting with Turner and doing the chop was his then-fiancée, Jane Fonda, and former President Jimmy Carter, a native Georgian.

In the American League, the Twins stopped the Toronto Blue Jays, who simply seemed unable to get over the hump and into the World

Series, despite five near misses in seven years. The Jays' former manager, Bobby Cox, was now managing Atlanta, and another former manager, Jimy [sic] Williams, was his third base coach.

So the matchups were made in heaven: two former last-place teams in the World Series. Never before had a team gone form last to first in one year; now, two had done it together. (The 1914 Braves, of course, had gone from last to first in the *same* season. See chapter 7).

The Twins took the first two games behind their home-town fans, with Morris winning the first one behind a three-run homer from Greg Gagne, and Tapini the second. That one was a 3–2 win, the winning run scoring in the eighth on a homer by rookie Scott Leius, who with ex-Yankee Mike Pagliarulo, had replaced veteran Gary Gaetti at third for Minnesota. A controversial play in that game found the Braves' Ron Gant called out at first when Kent Hrbek seemingly lifted him off the base and tagged him. It stopped a scoring threat that might have been a game winner for Atlanta.

So the Braves were down two games to none, but when they won the third game 5–4 in twelve innings on an RBI single from little Mark Lemke, and the fourth game 3–2 with Lemke scoring in the last of the ninth (Twins catcher Brian Harper tagged him with his elbow, not with the ball), we had four straight home-team wins. Earlier in the game, Harper had hung tough on a tag play against Lonnie Smith at the plate. But fortunes change.

People were now recalling the 1987 Series, in which all seven games had been won by the home team, giving the Twins a 4–3 edge over the Cardinals. Could it happen again?

Game Five was the only blowout of the Series, a 14–5 Atlanta win, keeping the home-team streak alive and putting the Braves up 3–2 and needing only one win in Minnesota for the World Championship. It was in this game that Lonnie Smith homered for the third day in a row.

Smith was an interesting performer in this series. He was seeking a fourth World Championship ring, all the previous three coming with different teams: the 1980 Phillies, the 1982 Cardinals, and the 1985 Royals. He had been down and out with drug problems, but was now the full-time left fielder because the Braves' regular, speedster Otis Nixon, and been suspended for sixty days late in the season for failing a drug test. At the time, it was assumed that losing Nixon would knock the Braves out of the pennant race. It didn't happen.

The sixth game, back in Minnesota, was a 4–3 Minnesota win when

Kirby Puckett, the Twins' multitalented center fielder, belted a leadoff homer off Leibrandt in the last of the eleventh. It was Leibrandt's first relief appearance in over two years. It didn't work out. Leibrandt was so stunned, he bore the look of a man whose entire career had been placed at the crossroads after the blow. I had seen that look before. Some overcame it, some never did.

So the seventh game, the first since 1987, would decide the champion. The Twins turned to Morris working with three days' rest. While this was unusual for this day and age, Morris was just the sort who could go on short rest. He was a throwback, an old-line pitcher with a lot of heart, a man who had led the majors in victories during the 1980's, but he was still far from a household word. The Braves countered with Smoltz, who had faced Morris in Game Four but left after seven with a 2–2 tie.

You had a feeling this game would be special when Smith, leading off, reached back to shake hands with catcher Brian Harper, as if two boxers were about to square off. I'd never seen anything like that before.

Both pitchers excelled, and neither team converted scoring opportunities. For every runner on third with one out, there seemed a double play waiting to happen. Neither side could deliver the knockout punch, if a boxing match it was to be. A key play occured in the eighth, when Smith singled to right and Terry Pendleton, the league's batting champ and a key addition to the '91 Braves, doubled to left center. That could have been a World Championship blow, for with Smith's speed and the play in front of him, not behind him, he should have scored.

But Gagne, the Twins' veteran shortstop, and second baseman Chuck Knoblauch, the league's Rookie of the Year, manipulated what amounted to a Little League fake, pretending to be taking a relay from left field. Smith stopped, and by the time he realized his error, could only hustle on to third. If he was to be denied a fourth World Championship ring, he might have only himself to blame. With the infield in, Gant grounded to first, David Justice was intentionally walked to load the bases, and Sid Bream bounced into a double play, first to home to first, to end the inning.

Nine innings, 0–0. You sort of wished they could call it right there and give each team a trophy and each player a ring. But there has to be a winner in the Series, and there has to be a loser. On to the tenth.

Morris took the mound, and the graphic on the screen said he was

Jack Morris reacts to a double play which stopped the Braves in the eighth inning of the seventh game and kept a 0–0 tie intact, setting up Minnesota's tenth-inning victory (Wide World Photos)

the first pitcher to go ten since Tom Seaver in 1969. Could that really have been twenty-two years ago?

Manager Tom Kelly considered lifting Morris, but Jack was pumped and wouldn't hear of it. He told Kelly he wanted to keep going, and Kelly saw that there was a lot of fight left in him. Morris set down the Braves in the tenth.

In the last of the tenth, with Peña in for his second inning, Dan Gladden led off with a broken-bat double to left-center, aided by a high bounce from the artificial turf. Knoblauch sacrificed him to third. Both Puckett and Hrbek were intentionally walked.

Kelly called on Gene Larkin to pinch-hit, with the infield and the outfield drawn in. Larkin was a Columbia University grad who had broken several of Lou Gehrig's records while playing there. That had been the standard Larkin press note since he arrived in the majors with the '87 Twins. Now he was about to add another.

He hit Peña's first pitch over Brian Hunter's head in left. Gladden watched it land, raised his arms in triumph, and ran home. The Twins won the game 1–0 and had a World Championship once again. They were the only team to have two of those over the last thirteen years. And instead of running off the field to the confines of their clubhouse, many of the Twins stayed on the field to hug and congratulate their opponents. Like the handshake that opened the game, this was a new and touching moment.

Among the things that made the '91 Series truly amazing were the four games decided in the final at-bat, the five one-run games, the three extra-inning games, all home-team wins, the first extra-inning final since 1924, and the first 1–0 final since 1962.

Conclusion

BASEBALL HAS BECOME very much a game of stats and records and lists and top tens, and all of that has been great for the game. It has provided more fuel than fans have ever had before to keep conversations lively and well armed twelve months a year.

Being a former pitcher, I found the chapters in which we discussed the accomplishments of my predecessors and successors particularly interesting. The temptation to list the top ten pitchers of all time led me to number them this way:

1. Walter Johnson
2. Christy Mathewson
3. Sandy Koufax
4. Lefty Grove
5. Cy Young
6. Bob Feller
7. Steve Carlton
8. Bob Gibson
9. Warren Spahn
10. Nolan Ryan

I would have loved to see Johnson, Matty, Grove, and Young pitch, and I never saw Feller at his peak. But when I see their accomplishments, I feel comfortable placing them in a list with players I faced or witnessed on television. In fact, putting Johnson, Mathewson, Grove, and Feller in my top five is probably a reflection of the advantage of pitching so long ago that poor outings or bad seasons are long forgotten and only the legend remains. The more modern pitchers are more human to me. I saw them have slumps or weaknesses, and it is difficult to stand that against the mystique of the all-time greats.

Johnson is at the top of my list because, to my mind, he must certainly have possessed skills unlike any of his rivals'. We are told that he was basically a one-pitch pitcher, a man who relied on a fastball, and won time and again with little hitting support. Mathewson mastered a breaking pitch when such pitches were still in development, and how baffling that must have made him. Koufax makes my top five because although I saw him and he was of my time, he remains to me virtually flawless. When you win five consecutive ERA titles, you are in an extraordinary zone.

The monumental events described in this book brought me to the task of compiling another top ten, just for fun: the top ten baseball events of all time. I lead it with Babe Ruth's sixty home runs. True, sixty broke his own record by only one, and the season may not have been as pressure-packed as Roger Maris's later quest for the record. But the sixty took on a life of its own as the years passed. It became baseball's most famous record and, hence, its most famous number. Although it has been surpassed, it remains a number known by all fans. It became like the climbing of Mount Everest: It set the home run as the ultimate conquest, and left a standard for decades.

My list:

1. Ruth's sixty home runs in 1927
2. Robinson's integration of baseball
3. DiMaggio's fifty-six-game hitting streak
4. Johnson's 113 shutouts
5. Koufax's five straight ERA titles
6. Rose's breaking of Cobb's hit record
7. Aaron's eclipsing of Ruth's homer record
8. Gehrig's 2,130 consecutive games
9. Ryan's seven no-hitters
10. Maris's sixty-one home runs

They're just lists, just one man's opinion. Ask me next year, and without looking I might fill them out differently. But for now, it's something to get the conversation flowing. In baseball, more than in any other sport, that's half the fun.

Bibliography

Aaron, Hank, and Furman Bisher. *Aaron, R.F.* New York: Thomas Y. Crowell, 1974.

Alexander, Charles. *Ty Cobb*. New York: Oxford University Press, 1984.

Allen, Lee. *The Cincinnati Reds*. G. P. Putnam's Sons, 1948.

_____. *One Hundred Years of Baseball*. New York: Bartholomew House, 1950.

_____. *The World Series*. New York: G. P. Putnam's Sons, 1969.

Allen, Maury. *Jackie Robinson*. New York: Watts, 1987.

Appel, Martin, and Burt Goldblatt. *Baseball's Best: The Hall of Fame Gallery*. New York: McGraw Hill, 1977.

Barrow, Ed, and James Kahn. *My Fifty Years in Baseball*. New York: Coward McCann, 1951.

Benson, Michael. *Ballparks of North America*. Jefferson, N.C.: McFarland & Co., 1989.

Blake, Mike. *The Minor Leagues*. New York: Wynwood Press, 1991.

Broeg, Bob. *Super Stars of Baseball*. St. Louis: The Sporting News, 1971.

Brown, Warren. *The Chicago Cubs*. New York: G. P. Putnam's Sons, 1946.

_____. *The Chicago White Sox*. New York: G. P. Putnam's Sons, 1952.

Charlton, James. *The Baseball Chronology*. New York: Macmillan, 1991.

Cobb, Ty, and Al Stump. *My Life in Baseball*. New York: Doubleday, 1961.

Coberly, Rich. *The No-Hit Hall of Fame*. Newport Beach, Calif. Triple Play Publications, 1985.

Coletti, Ned. *You Gotta Have Heart*. South Bend, Ind.: Diamond Communications, 1985.

Cox, James. *The Lively Ball*. Alexandria, Va: Redefinition, 1989.

Danzig, Allison, and Joe Reichler. *The History of Baseball*. Englewood Cliffs, N.J.: Prentice-Hall, 1959.

Deutsch, Cohen, Johnson, and Neft. *Scrapbook History of Baseball*. New York: Bobbs Merrill, 1975.

Dittmar, Joseph. *Baseball's Benchmark Boxscores.* Jefferson, N.C.: McFarland & Co., 1990.

Feller, Bob, and Bill Gilbert. *Now Pitching, Bob Feller.* New York: Birch Lane Press, 1990.

Fleming, G. H. *The Dizziest Season.* New York: William Morrow, 1981.

————. *Murderers' Row.* New York: William Morrow, 1985.

————. *The Unforgettable Season.* New York: Holt Rinehart and Winston, 1981.

Gold, Eddie, and Art Ahrens. *The Golden Era Cubs.* Chicago: Bonus Books, 1985.

Graham, Frank. *The Brooklyn Dodgers.* New York: G. P. Putnam's Sons, 1945.

————. *The New York Giants.* New York: G. P. Putnam's Sons, 1952.

————. *The New York Yankees.* New York: G. P. Putnam's Sons, 1943.

Grimm, Charlie, and Ed Prell. *Jolly Cholly's Story.* New York: Henry Regnery, 1968.

Honig, Donald. *The All-Star Game.* St. Louis: The Sporting News, 1987.

————. *Baseball When the Grass Was Real.* New York: Coward McCann Geoghegan, 1975.

Hornsby, Rogers, and Bill Surface. *My War With Baseball.* New York: Coward McCann, 1962.

Izenberg, Jerry. *The Greatest Game Ever Played.* New York: Henry Holt, 1987.

Kennedy, MacLean. *The Great Teams of Baseball.* St. Louis: The Sporting News, 1929.

Lewis, Franklin. *The Cleveland Indians.* New York: G. P. Putnam's Sons, 1949.

Lieb, Fred. *The Baltimore Orioles.* New York: G. P. Putnam's Sons, 1955.

————. *The Baseball Story.* New York: G. P. Putnam's Sons, 1950.

————. *The Boston Red Sox.* New York: G. P. Putnam's Sons, 1947.

————. *Connie Mack Grand Old Man of Baseball.* New York: G. P. Putnam's Sons, 1945.

————. *The Detroit Tigers.* New York: G. P. Putnam's Sons, 1946.

————. *The Pittsburgh Pirates.* New York: G. P. Putnam's Sons, 1948.

————. *The St. Louis Cardinals.* New York: G. P. Putnam's Sons, 1944.

————, and Stan Baumgartner. *The Philadelphia Phillies.* New York: G. P. Putnam's Sons, 1953.

Logan, Bob. *Miracle on Thirty-Fifth Street.* South Bend, Ind.: Icarus Press, 1983.

Marichal, Juan, and Charles Einstein. *A Pitcher's Story.* New York: Doubleday, 1967.

Mathewson, Christy. *Pitching in a Pinch*. New York: Grosset & Dunlap, 1912.

Mays, Willie, and Lou Sahadi. *Say Hey*. New York: Simon & Schuster, 1988.

Neft, David, and Richard Cohen. *The Sports Encyclopedia: Baseball*. New York: St. Martin's Press, 1990.

————. *The World Series*. New York: St. Martin's Press, 1986.

Plimpton, George. *One for the Record*. New York: Bantam, 1974.

Povich, Shirley. *The Washington Senators*. New York: G. P. Putnam's Sons, 1954.

Reichler, Joe. *Baseball's Great Moments*. New York: Crown, 1979.

————, and Ben Olan. *Baseball's Unforgettable Games*. New York: Ronald Press, 1960.

Reidenbaugh, Lowell. *Baseball's Fifty Greatest Games*. St. Louis: The Sporting News, 1986.

————. *Baseball's Twenty-Five Greatest Pennant Races*. St. Louis: The Sporting News, 1987.

Ritter, Lawrence. *The Glory of Their Times*. New York: Macmillan, 1966.

Robinson, Ray. *The Home Run Heard Round the World*. New York: Harper Collins, 1991.

————. *Iron Horse*. New York: Horton, 1990.

Romig, Ralph. *Cy Young*. Philadelphia: Dorrance & Co., 1964.

Schoor, Gene. *History of the World Series*. New York: William Morrow, 1990.

Seaver, Tom and Marty Appel. *Tom Seaver's All-Time Baseball Greats*. New York: Wanderer, 1984.

Seymour, Harold. *Baseball: The Golden Age*. New York: Oxford University Press, 1971.

Shatzkin, Mike, ed. *The Ballplayers*. New York: Arbor House, 1990.

Smelser, Marshall. *The Life That Ruth Built*. New York: Quadrangle, 1975.

Sowell, Mike. *The Pitch That Killed*. New York: MacMillan, 1989.

Spalding. *Official Baseball Guide*. Annual. New York: American Sports Publications, 1900–1939.

Sporting News. *Official Baseball Guide*. Annual. St. Louis: The Sporting News, 1942–1991.

Spink, J. G. Taylor. *Judge Landis and Twenty-five Years of Baseball*. St. Louis: The Sporting News, 1974.

Stark, Benton. *The Year They Called Off the World Series*. Garden City Park, N.Y.: Avery, 1991.

Sullivan, Neil. *The Dodgers Move West*. New York: Oxford University Press, 1987.

Sugar, Bert. *Baseball's Fifty Greatest Games*. New York: Exeter, 1986.
Thorn, John and Peter Palmer. *Total Baseball*. New York: Warner, 1989.
Treat, Roger. *Walter Johnson*. New York: Julian Messner, 1948.
Tygiel, Jules. *Baseball's Great Experiment*. New York: Oxford University
   Press, 1983.
Vecsey, George, ed. *The Way It Was*. New York: McGraw-Hill, 1974.
Veeck, Bill, and Ed Linn. *Veeck as in Wreck*. New York: G. P. Putnam's
   Sons, 1962.
Voigt, David. *Baseball: An Illustrated History*. University Park, Pa.: Penn-
   sylvania State University Press, 1987.
Walker, Robert. *Cincinnati and the Big Red Machine*. Bloomington, Ind.:
   Indiana University Press, 1988.
Wheeler, Lonnie, and John Baskin. *The Cincinnati Game*. Wilmington,
   Ohio: Orange Frazier Press, 1988.
Wolff, Rick, ed. *Baseball Encyclopedia*, 8th ed. New York: Macmillan,
   1990.

Tom Seaver and Marty Appel. (Photo by Nancy Seaver)

Index

331